Haynes
Computer
Manual

U.C.B.
LIBRARY

© Haynes Publishing 2010

First published 2001
Revised 2nd edition 2002
Reprinted 2003
Revised 3rd edition 2004
Reprinted 2005 and 2006
Revised 4th edition 2007
Revised 5th edition 2010

Published by: Haynes Publishing
Sparkford, Yeovil, Somerset BA22 7JJ
Tel: 01963 442030 Fax: 01963 440001
Int. tel: +44 1963 442030 Fax: +44 1963 440001
E-mail: sales@haynes.co.uk
Website: www.haynes.co.uk

British Library Cataloguing in Publication Data:
A catalogue record for this book is available from the British Library

ISBN 978 1 84425 928 1

Printed in the USA.

Haynes

Computer
Manual

The step-by-step guide to upgrading, repairing and maintaining a PC

Haynes Publishing

Contents

Introduction

Let's begin by asking two questions. Do you consider your home desktop computer system to be a fabulously powerful, immensely flexible, wholly essential and user-friendly tool? Or do you regard it as an overly complex, befuddling contraption, riddled with conflicting standards, prone to break down in any number of bizarre ways, instantly obsolete and bedevilled with an incomprehensible jargon developed by, and for, fully-fledged geeks?

Your answer to both questions is probably 'yes'. That's where we come in.

If you enjoy using your computer and want to make the most of your hardware (and your money) without becoming a dyed-in-the-wool techie in the process, this is the book for you. We'll show you in a series of clear step-by-step guides just how to upgrade, improve and enhance your system. We'll also consider how best to trouble-shoot problems and keep it all running smoothly. Above all, we'll endeavour to make everything easy.

Do please remember one thing: a computer is not like this year's model of a particular make of car. It's simply not possible for us to predict with any degree of certainty what's sitting on your desktop. Quite the reverse, in fact. The very essence and, indeed, appeal of the personal computer is that one size resolutely does not suit all: you can make of your system just what you will. This inevitably means that there are limitations to what we can cover here, and so our approach throughout is to focus on the most likely and common configurations.

The alternative – and there is only one – is to try to cover all angles, all bases, all permutations, all possible problems. What you end up with then is a massively unwieldy tome that ties itself in knots with cross-references and tables and endless ifs and buts … and still doesn't succeed in its aims.

No, we've striven instead to cover the basics and to give you enough background knowledge to tackle your own computer setup with confidence.

To that end, we're making certain assumptions here.

First, about you:

You have a working (although not necessarily thorough) knowledge of Windows

You don't have an unlimited budget (or else you'd buy a brand new computer every six months and stay ahead of the game)

You're not scared to perform minor surgery on your computer (but you'd rather know what you're doing than fumble in the dark).

And secondly, about your computer:

It has an Intel Pentium/Celeron II, III or 4 processor or the AMD Athlon/Duron equivalent

It's running Windows 98, Millennium Edition, XP or Vista

It dates back no further than 1997–8 (any older and you really should be thinking about a replacement)

It's a PC, not a Mac!

Just a word on that last comment. Mac users are a sorely overlooked species in much computer literature. True, there aren't that many of them around, relatively speaking, despite the popular iMac and Power Mac ranges, but that's no excuse. The real point is that a Mac has quite a different architecture to a PC and a significantly different operating system, and it's simply impractical, unhelpful and ultimately unfair to stick in the odd 'oh, and if you have a Mac, you might want to try this…' section in a book that deals primarily with PCs. That is why we wrote a separate manual specifically for Mac users, entitled *The Haynes Mac Manual*. This, then, is the manual for the discerning but probably somewhat frustrated owner of an 'average' Windows-based Pentium-powered PC. We can't promise to turn it into a supercomputer overnight but we certainly hope to help you prolong its lifespan and/or make it significantly better. We keep the jargon to a minimum and practical guidance to the fore. After all, reading about computers is probably not high on your list of priorities and upgrading, repairing and maintaining your hardware is not, with the best will in the world, what you might call fun. But using your computer should be fun and that's the point of this manual: to help ensure that your PC serves you well both now and in the future, however your needs may change.

How to use this book

 Single click on the left mouse button

 Double click on the left mouse button

 Single click on the right mouse button

 Check or uncheck this option by clicking the left mouse button

 Type the following text on your keyboard

In the text, consecutive directions are sometimes expressed as e.g. Click Start > Programs > Accessories. The > symbol means 'followed by'. Wherever possible, we illustrate actions with screenshots and describe them in the text.

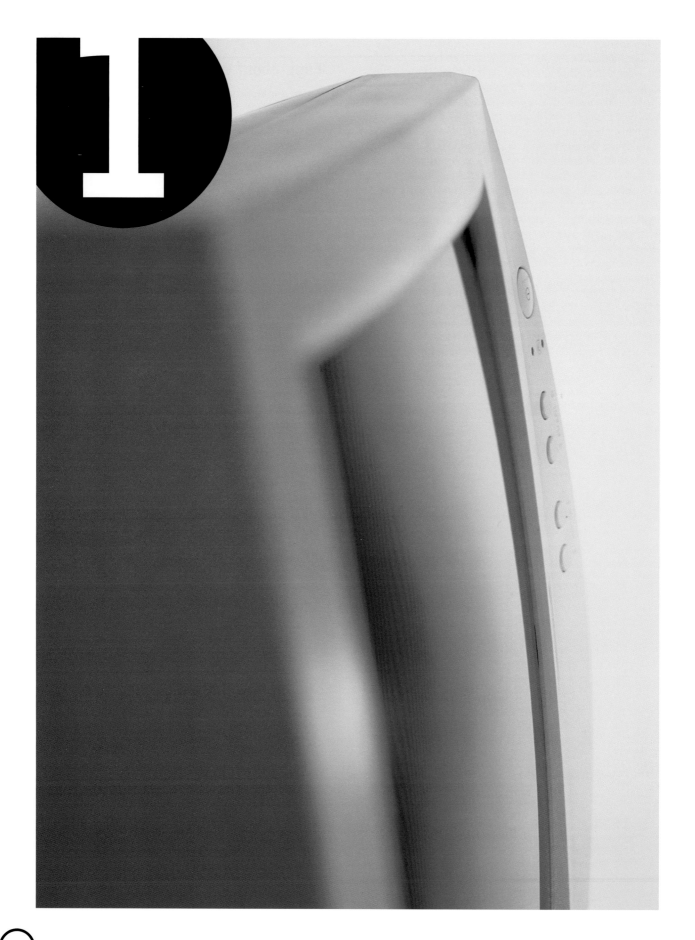

1

PART **1** Getting to know your PC

First things first. Before we start poking around under the hood, let's take stock of your current computer setup. We're not exactly doing rocket science here but the best place to start is undoubtedly with a little basic background knowledge.

PART

A brief history of personal computing

It has become something of a cliché to say that the Apollo moon missions were managed with less computing power than you'll find in today's typical car, electronic organiser, digital watch or musical greetings card… but it illustrates the pace of progress well. These days, everything from your kettle to your key ring carries a microchip and that bland, beige box perched on your desktop is capable of performing more calculations in a split second than any mere mortal could achieve in a hundred lifetimes.

But it's a mistake to allow yourself to be overawed by technology. Always remember that a computer is a tool – no more and no less. It may be faster but you're smarter. (No, honestly, you are.) The chances are that you'll never really understand how your computer works, but so what? What counts is understanding how all the various bits and pieces work together. Grasp that and you'll soon be stripping, upgrading and rebuilding your PC before breakfast.

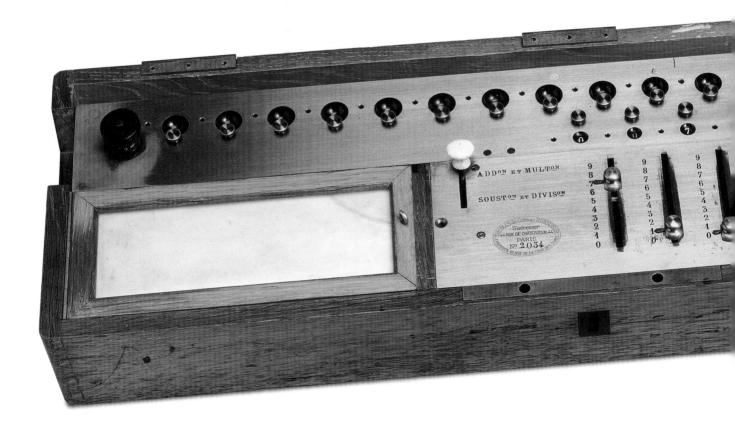

A functioning computer is essentially comprised of three parts

Hardware: *the motherboard, memory, processor, monitor, keyboard, modem, mouse and all the other nuts and bolts.*

Operating system: *the master program that makes the hardware and software work together in perfect harmony (usually).*

Application software: *programs that let you do useful things with your PC such as write letters, perform calculations, surf the internet and much, much more.*

If you can get the distinction between hardware, the operating system and application software clear in your mind from the outset, then you've overcome one major hurdle. Not that it's altogether straightforward, mind: Microsoft Windows infamously blurs the lines between software required to run a computer and extras that make life easier for the user and/or stifle commercial competition. Anyway, if for now you don't know Windows from Word, ROM from RAM or a chipset from a chipolata, don't panic. You will, we promise.

So just how did we get here? Well, ask any two specialists about what really matters in the story of computing and you'll likely get two very different answers. But the one thing that they – and we – will agree upon is this: despite the chequered, convoluted and complex evolution of the personal computer, these days just about anybody can get to grips with the technology. What was once the exclusive province of boffins is now familiar territory to millions.

And that's a good thing. All you need is a little patience, a dash of logic, the confidence to tinker – and, of course, this manual as your guide.

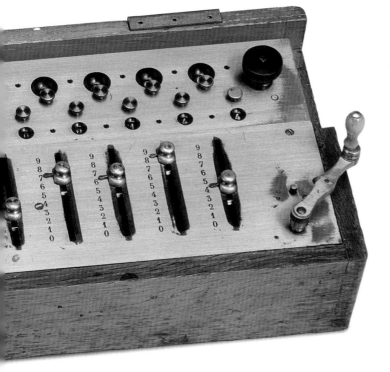

Charles X Thomas de Colmar invented his Arithmometer in 1820. It was the first commercially successful calculating machine and could be used for addition, subtraction, division and multiplication.

A controversial timeline

500BC   Ernie the Egyptian invents the abacus. Blame him

1642   Blaise Pascal invents an automatic adding machine of sorts

1674   Gottfried von Leibniz upgrades the Pascaline by adding multiplication

1822   Charles Babbage designs his Difference Engine, a mechanical calculator, but can't raise sufficient venture capital to build it

1833   Babbage upgrades his earlier invention to an Analytical Engine but doesn't build this one either

Right: A Chinese abacus, the Suan Pan is the oldest form of abacus still in use.

Below: Charles Babbage's Difference Engine was finished in 1822. It was a decimal digital machine.

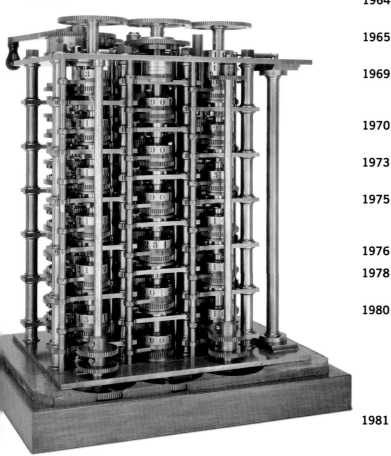

1890   Herman Hollerith comes up with a method for using punched cards to store data

1911   The Computing-Tabulating-Recording Company is founded in New York, and soon becomes IBM (International Business Machines)

1939   John Vincent Atanasoff and Clifford Berry invent the first true digital computer

1943   Alan Turing invents the *other* first true digital computer, Colossus, and uses it to crack the Germans' wartime Enigma code

1946   John Presper Eckert and John Mauchly develop ENIAC (Electronic Numerical Integrator And Computer), a fully-fledged computer replete with processor. It weighed in at 30 tonnes

1951   Eckert and Mauchly unveil UNIVAC (Universal Automatic Computer), the first computer to be sold commercially on the high street. It cost around $5m

1958   IBM develops a computer that uses transistors instead of valves

1964   The integrated circuit is used for the first time in computer design

1965   Digital Equipment Corporation launches the first minicomputer, the PDP-8

1969   The US Department of Defense sets up a computer network called ARPANet (Advanced Research Projects Agency) that will one day become the internet

1970   The UNIX operating system is developed. So is the 8-inch floppy disk

1973   The first hard disk arrives courtesy of IBM: a 30MB tiddler called Winchester

1975   The Altair 8800 – the first microcomputer, or PC – is sold to the public. It cost $400 and you had to build it yourself. Bill Gates and Paul Allen found Microsoft

1976   Steve Jobs and Steve Wozniak found Apple Computer

1978   The 5.25-inch floppy disk becomes the (temporary) standard medium for portable, removable storage

1980   British inventor Clive Sinclair launches the kit-form ZX-80 computer. Sales of soldering irons soar and a generation of geeks is born. It cost £79.95 plus £8.95 for the power supply. Ready-assembled model launched a month later at £99.95 to wicked and unsubstantiated rumours that they were customer-assembled models returned to Sinclair for repair

1981   The IBM PC hits the streets at £3,000 and Acorn releases the popular BBC Micro. The 3.5-inch floppy disk also makes its first appearance

The large disk is from an IBM system of 1984 and can hold 4MB, compared with the small hard disk from 1999 which can hold 6GB!

The Altair 8800b microcomputer of 1975.

'PalmPilot' palmtop computer of 1998. Manufactured by US Robotics.

1982   The PC wins *Time Magazine's* 'Man of the Year' and the Sinclair ZX Spectrum brings computer games to the mass market

1984   Apple introduces the Macintosh computer. It uses a mouse and clickable icons and menus

1985   The first commercial version of Windows is launched by Microsoft

1988   Apple sues Microsoft for copying the graphical look and feel of its operating system. Then again, Apple allegedly pinched the idea from Xerox

1991   Tim Berners-Lee invents the World Wide Web. Life is never quite the same again

1994   Jeff Bozos quits Wall Street and decides to start an internet bookstore, Amazon.com

1995   Microsoft introduces Windows 95, which looks suspiciously like the Apple Mac. People suddenly find PCs easy to use, sales skyrocket, and Bill Gates becomes rather rich

1996   Microsoft introduces Internet Explorer and sets off a browser war with Netscape, ultimately making web browsing software free

1999   Internet businesses become the hottest stocks around the world. Millionaires are created as fast as you can say IPO

2000   The great dotcom crash! Reality kicks in and web businesses go to the wall in droves

2001   In the wake of the crash, PC and peripheral prices fall, making computer hardware the best buy ever

2002   Processors are now well into the 2GHz-plus range, i.e. capable of performing over two billion calculations per second

2003   Worms and viruses hit the headlines and make computing temporarily miserable for all affected. The Recording Industry Association of America sues a bunch of file swappers. Weblogs make a mark

2004   Google floats and heralds the start of Dotcom Boom Madness Part 2, Microsoft patches the millionth hole in Windows, processor speeds top 3GHz and defy the laws of physics, PCs finally make it into the living room in the guise of home entertainment centres

2007   Windows Vista is launched and processors grow multiple cores

2010   Windows 7 replaces Vista (hurrah!) and we all start using Google Docs instead of office software. It's enough to make Ernie the Egyptian spin in his sarcophagus with the excitement of it all. Now let's get to work …

PART 1 Why upgrade?

Back in 1965, a rising young engineer called Gordon Moore who went on to co-found Intel noted that computers had a habit of doubling in power every 18 months or so. His observation came to be enshrined as 'Moore's Law' and, remarkably, still holds true today (although physical constraints on the complexity of processor circuits are beginning to threaten it). Ironically, we long ago passed the point where we actually need more computing power in our homes and offices, and yet still we rush lemming-like to upgrade or replace hardware that's barely out of warranty. Why?

Because I can? No, no, no… that's the answer of an inveterate geek. Now there's nothing wrong with being an inveterate geek – well, okay, there is, but we won't go into that here – but if you're the type to fix things that positively ain't broke, this ain't the book for you.

Because I want to? *Really?* You get kicks from tinkering with hardware? Really? There's certainly much satisfaction to be had from fixing or improving a PC but we'd draw the line at calling it fun.

Because I must? Absolutely. This is the only time when it makes true sense to upgrade your PC. There are, in fact, three distinct but related good reasons to upgrade.

Boosting, repairing and enhancing a PC are all good reasons for minor surgery.

Three good reasons to upgrade

To improve performance This is when your existing setup simply isn't up to the demands placed upon it, often as a result of changes in your own work or play habits. A system purchased to look after the accounts is unlikely to cut the mustard at 3-D gaming.

While performance-enhancing upgrades can significantly prolong the lifespan of your PC, it's important to make the right upgrades. As we go along, we'll consider which upgrades are practicable and worthwhile – and when it's better to admit defeat, throw the whole system in the skip and start afresh with a brand new computer!

To repair a broken component Unfortunately, unless you're a dab hand with a soldering iron, your chances of actually repairing anything are slim indeed. You could take a can opener to a stalled hard disk or hotwire a sound card… but we wouldn't recommend it. No, the fact is that when something breaks down, it almost always need replacing – and in such cases it's easy to make a virtue of necessity by installing something altogether better. Why replace an ancient, slow CD-ROM drive with like for like when you could just as easily fit a shiny new recordable DVD drive? True, if you want to make your own movies, you might need a memory upgrade as well, and perhaps even a faster processor – which takes us back to improving performance.

To add new features Need a backup device? Run out of hard disk space? Fancy a bigger, flatter, lighter monitor or a better printer? Want to edit images from your digital camera? How about adding a hub to hook up two or more PCs in a home network? These are examples of upgrading a system by adding things that are currently lacking – as indeed would be adding a recordable DVD drive to replace or complement a CD drive. Again, we'll look at all the main options.

But before we get carried away, let's consider two further questions

Do you really *need* to upgrade? Please understand that we're not trying to discourage you from upgrading your PC – quite the reverse – but there are times when a little sober reflection can pay dividends and save you money. For instance, is your software placing unnecessary demands on your hardware? Do you really need that full-blown, memory-hogging monolithic office suite just to balance the household budget? Would it be worthwhile buying a dedicated games console instead of converting your dusty old computer to a lean, mean fighting/driving/flying machine? Is your hard disk clogged with seldom-used programs that could easily be deleted to free up space? And would simply defragmenting your hard disk make a world of difference to your PC's performance?

If much of this sounds deeply mysterious right now, read on: we'll cover all the angles in detail soon enough. But if you're contemplating an upgrade simply because your once fleet-of-foot system is now limping lamely, jump straight to the Maintenance section in Part Seven. A little rudimentary housekeeping can work wonders – and save you a packet.

Can **you upgrade?** The ongoing trend in computer design is to integrate as many features as possible on the central circuit board, or motherboard, rather than relying on hardware expansion cards. A computer with an integrated graphics chip and audio chip is cheaper to make and sell than one kitted out with separate graphics and sound cards. It also means that PCs can become smaller, less power-hungry and consequently quieter. However, this trend has one unfortunate downside, which is that it becomes tricky to upgrade to more powerful graphics or sound cards later.

Similar thinking dictates that outmoded 'legacy' interfaces should be swept aside in favour of cheaper, more reliable machines that can be expanded indefinitely through USB and FireWire ports. Again, however, this can render older but still serviceable peripherals obsolete. Many a printer with a parallel port has found itself unemployed when the new PC arrives sans suitable interface. If your PC is relatively recent, you may find that your upgrade options are hampered by design. This will become evident when we lift the lid and look inside. The good news is that there are almost always workarounds, and we'll mention these as we go through.

One day, perhaps, PCs will be ten a penny and it'll be cheaper to buy a new one than fuss around with upgrades and repairs. One day, perhaps, PCs will be genuinely easy to use. And one day, just perhaps, the PC will cease to exist in anything like its current shape and form.

But not today, and probably not tomorrow. For now, millions of us own computer systems that are teetering on the edge of obsolescence but are not quite ready for the skip. This is the manual for people who can use a screwdriver but not a soldering iron; people who won't throw good money after bad but don't want to buy a new computer unless and until they absolutely have to; and people who are allergic to acronyms.

If you want to upgrade an older computer to use the new Windows Vista or Windows 7 operating system, you may need to upgrade the hardware first. We'll consider this in detail on pp166–171

PART **1** Outside explained

Optical drive *The term 'optical' relates to the fact that CD and DVD drives use lasers. Older computers often have two such drives: a CD-RW (Compact Disc Rewriteable) drive that plays audio CDs, reads data CDs (such as computer programs) and lets you make your own CDs from files on your computer, including music and video; and a DVD-RW drive that looks similar but uses discs with far higher capacity. DVD drives are now absolutely standard and, since all DVD drives can play, read and record to CD media, it is usual to find only a single drive that does pretty much everything.*

Spare drive bays *Most computers allow room for expansion by providing one or more spare drive bays. These are simply masked holes in the case into which you can install additional drives.*

Media card readers *Digital cameras, mobile phones, some music players and a host of other mobile devices use a form of portable storage called media cards. These small, slim cards can hold data in the same way as a CD or DVD. Computers often come with media card readers that let you pop the card into the PC in order to transfer files to the hard drive. For instance, you can copy photos from your digital camera by reading the media card. There are many different formats of media card so a well-equipped computer will have different slots to encompass all the main types.*

Handy sockets *Almost invariably, these sockets (if present) duplicate other sockets around the back of the PC. They are positioned here simply because it's more convenient to plug, say, an external hard drive into the front of the computer than around the rear. Here we see an array of (from left to right) video and audio sockets for connecting a digital camcorder or similar device; audio sockets for plugging in headphones, a microphone and anything you might wish to record from (such as a cassette player); three USB sockets; and a FireWire socket.*

On/off switch *Does just what you'd expect. This button can also be used to restart, or reset, the system. Not one to push in error.*

Power LED *This light lets you know that your computer is switched on, just in case the fan wasn't loud enough to clue you in.*

Drive activity LED *A light that flashes when the computer is busy reading or writing data from or to the hard disk. For information only.*

Case *The majority of PCs now come in tower format (tall and narrow) rather than desktop (flat and wide). There are various standards governing case design, related to the size and shape of the motherboard within. The current trend is to integrate as many features on the motherboard as possible, which makes it possible for PCs to be squeezed into ever-smaller cases. Many of the latest 'Media Center' models look more like DVD players than computers.*

Interface All this talk of ports and sockets and connectors may sound baffling – and, let's be honest, you couldn't contrive to concoct a more counter-intuitive, jargon-riddled language if you tried – but keep in mind that these are just different types of interface. An interface, of course, is just a way of connecting two bits of kit and getting them talking to each other. It would be easier if everything used the same interface, but then you wouldn't need this manual. See Appendix 2 for a close-up guide to common connectors.

Power switch If present (don't worry if it's not), this switch controls the internal power supply. As a rule, you would leave this switch at the on position and use the on/off switch on the front of the case to turn on the PC.

Power socket A three-pin power cable plugs in here to connect your computer to the mains electricity.

Parallel port A 25-pin female socket commonly used to connect a printer. Windows refers to this port as LPT1. Again, it's pretty much obsolete these days and not included in most new computers. This is potentially a pity if you have an old parallel port printer and you buy a new PC, for there will be nowhere to plug it in. The solution is a parallel-to-USB adapter.

Serial port A 9-pin male socket commonly used to connect external modems and older mice. Two such ports are the norm, known to Windows as COM1 and COM2. Virtually obsolete.

USB and FireWire ports USB (Universal Serial Bus) and FireWire are competing technologies that do essentially the same thing, which is allow you to connect external devices to your computer. Everything from cameras to external hard drives use USB or FireWire, and just about every PC provides both types of socket.

Audio connectors A PC will typically have one or two outlets for speakers and jacks for connecting a microphone and other audio equipment. This example features both built-in audio circuitry (top) and a separate sound card (bottom). This means that the computer can produce (and record) sounds through a chip on the motherboard, to which the upper sockets are connected, but it has also been equipped with a separate, and presumably more powerful, sound card. When both are present, the built-in circuitry is invariably disabled to allow the sound card to run the show.

PSU cooling fan The power supply unit runs very hot and carries its own fan to ensure adequate cooling. Be sure never to block this area of the case – always leave a good gap between the back of the PC and a wall.

PS/2-type ports 6-pin female sockets, one for the mouse and one for the keyboard. These are generally colour-coded green and purple respectively. The current trend is for both keyboard and mouse to use USB sockets instead, or to go cordless and 'talk' to the computer via radio waves.

Cooling Fan Air inlet for the internal fan. Without suitable cooling, a PC would soon get hot enough to fry an egg. And its own circuitry.

Ethernet connector If the PC is equipped to be connected to a network, there will be an 8-pin RJ-45 socket for connecting it to a hub or directly to another computer.

Monitor connector(s) This is where you plug in a monitor. It is now common to find two sockets: a blue VGA socket for connecting older analogue monitors, and a white DVI socket for connecting newer digital monitors. Here we also see an S-video TV-out port (black, round) for hooking up the PC to a television set. Some graphics cards also have TV-in ports to which you can attach a television aerial cable and watch or record TV programmes on the PC. Alternatively, a TV-in port can be supplied by a separate expansion card called a TV tuner.

Games port Useful for connecting an old-fashioned non-USB joystick, but not much else.

Modem connector If the PC has an internal modem, there will be a 6-pin RJ-11 socket to connect it to the telephone system via a cable.

PART

Inside explained

We don't suggest for a minute that you dive straight to the innards of your PC but we're going to be talking a lot about motherboards, components and expansion cards as we go on. Here's a sneak preview of what to expect under the hood.

Optical drive *The CD or DVD drive is housed within a drive bay inside the case.*

Memory *Random Access Memory, or RAM, comes in sticks called memory modules that sit in slots on the motherboard. RAM is a temporary working space in which the PC's business is conducted from moment to moment. The more you have, the more you things you can do simultaneously (a.k.a. multitasking).*

Processor *Usually thought of as the brains of a computer, the processor does number crunching on a grand scale. Chances are you'll have either an Intel or an AMD processor onboard, sitting either in a socket mounting (flat on the motherboard) or in a slot (on edge). You won't actually see a socketed processor because there will be a cooling unit bolted on top.*

Hard disk *The hard disk is a device that permanently stores data until such time as you decide to delete or modify it. Every time you hit the Save button in a word processor, for instance, the document you're working on is copied to the hard disk, so it's safe even if the power is suddenly switched off. The process of saving data is called* writing to the hard disk; *retrieving it is* reading from the hard disk.

Power supply *A metal-cased assembly that converts AC utility power into the special low current voltages required by your computer.*

Motherboard *A great big printed circuit board. You really can't miss it because everything else plugs into it one way or another. Think of it as your PC's nervous system – a series of channels and conduits transmitting information from any one part of the system to any other. Getting hold of the manual that came with your motherboard is going to save a lot of headaches and uncertainty later.*

Graphics *The graphics card is a printed circuit board responsible for producing the images that you see on your monitor screen. It's possible to build the circuitry right into the motherboard, as here (a cable provides the monitor socket on the outside of the case), or to use a separate expansion card (discussed on pp80–85).*

Free expansion slots *These are motherboard interfaces into which you plug circuit boards to add new features to your computer. A sound card is merely one example of many possibilities.*

PART  # Peripherals explained

The items on these pages are examples of what are commonly referred to as peripherals. You may be surprised to find the monitor comes under this heading – after all, you can't do much with a PC without one – but the hard disk is also, strictly speaking, a peripheral device. That is, a computer is still technically a computer without a storage device, a display unit or input devices. What it patently is not is useful! That's where peripherals come in: they let you do exciting, fun, useful stuff with your computer.

Speakers *These range from cheap, tinny and worthless to quite extraordinarily powerful. Speakers either plug directly into the sound card or, if you have a surround sound setup, into a separate amplifier or subwoofer. Here, the subwoofer is the big black square box.*

Mouse *Small plastic clickable rodent that lives on a mat. The premiere pointing device, the mouse allows you to issue commands and move objects without typing.*

Keyboard *A dumb typewriter renowned for accumulating crumbs and other debris. It translates the motion of your fingers pressing keys into digital codes that your computer interprets as numbers, letters and commands.*

Peripherals It's possible to add no end of peripheral devices to a computer. Indeed, it's this very expandability that makes the PC such a flexible tool. A webcam, for instance, lets you make face-to-face calls to family overseas via the internet; a graphics tablet turns a computer into a digital easel; and a MIDI keyboard opens up all manner of musical possibilities.

Webcam.

Graphics tablet.

MIDI keyboard.

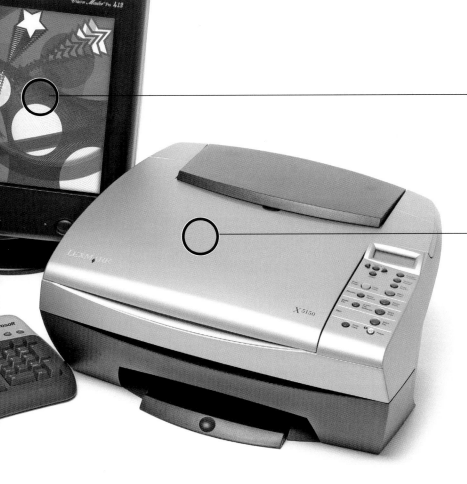

Monitor *A display screen housed within a big, deep, bulky box – or, if it's modern, a smaller, flatter, sleeker box.*

Scanner *Scanners take digital pictures of documents or printed photographs. You can then view, edit and print these images on the PC. Optional but rather useful. Here, the printer and scanner have been integrated in the same box, imaginatively known as a multi-function device (MFD).*

Printer *Despite the dream of a paperless office, hard copies of documents still have a place in most of our lives. The printer turns your computer's output into hard copy, nowadays with photo-realistic colour and near-professional quality levels.*

PART  Taking stock

If you've ever bought off-the-shelf software, you'll know that there's usually a panel on the box stating the 'minimum system requirements'. Something along the lines of:

- **Intel Pentium II 266MHz** or better
- **Windows 2000/XP/Vista**
- **64MB** of RAM (128MB recommended)
- **500MB** free hard disk space
- **CD-ROM** drive
- **Sound** card
- **Internet** connection

But what does it all mean? And does your PC come up to scratch? That's one issue; another crops up when you come to go shopping for upgrade components. You see, you can't just buy a bit more RAM without knowing what kind of RAM you need. And how much. And whether there's space for it on the motherboard.

The good news is if you start off with a thorough inventory of your current system, you really can't go far wrong. First of all, dig out the paperwork that came with your new PC. Here, you should find all the main specifications clearly laid out. However, that's only going to get you so far (and, of course, it's highly possible that you no longer have or simply can't find the original documentation). Thus we turn to Windows.

Check the minimum system requirements before you splash out on software.

Device advice
(Windows 98 and Millennium Edition)

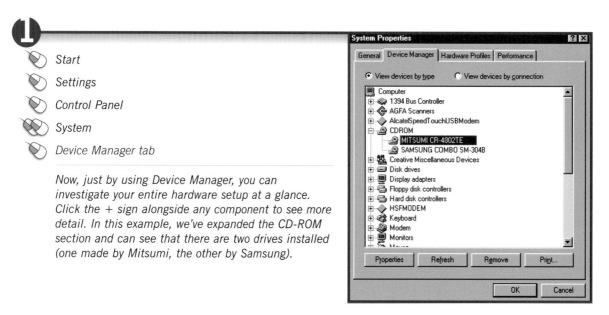

1

- *Start*
- *Settings*
- *Control Panel*
- *System*
- *Device Manager tab*

Now, just by using Device Manager, you can investigate your entire hardware setup at a glance. Click the + sign alongside any component to see more detail. In this example, we've expanded the CD-ROM section and can see that there are two drives installed (one made by Mitsumi, the other by Samsung).

General tab

Here you can see how much RAM is inside your PC – in this case, 256MB. We can also see that the processor is an AMD model.

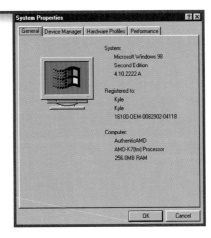

Device advice (Windows XP)

The two main system requirements you need to know about that aren't immediately obvious are processor type and speed and hard disk space. Getting this information is a breeze.

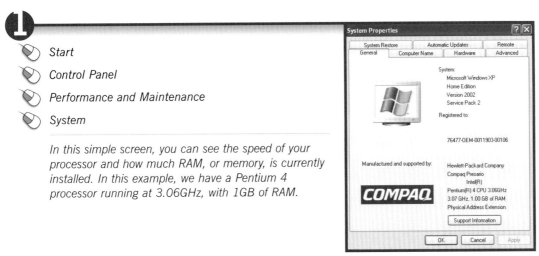

Start

Control Panel

Performance and Maintenance

System

In this simple screen, you can see the speed of your processor and how much RAM, or memory, is currently installed. In this example, we have a Pentium 4 processor running at 3.06GHz, with 1GB of RAM.

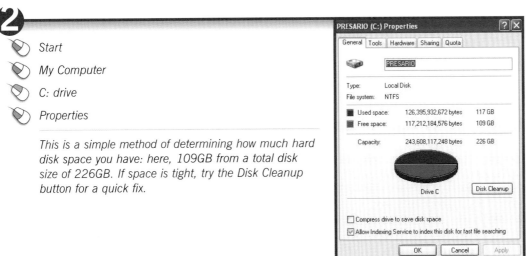

Start

My Computer

C: drive

Properties

This is a simple method of determining how much hard disk space you have: here, 109GB from a total disk size of 226GB. If space is tight, try the Disk Cleanup button for a quick fix.

Device advice (Windows Vista)

Windows Vista goes further with the introduction of the Experience Index. This is a tool that rates the speed of the processor, memory and hard drive, and also checks the graphics processor's capability. This information is then presented as a 'base score' of somewhere between 1 and 5. Software developed to run under Windows Vista will carry a minimum base score rating (sometimes, both a required and a recommended rating), so all you have to do is ensure that your computer's base score matches or exceeds the score specified by the software. If a software box says that a base score of 3 is recommended, you'll know to steer clear – or at least to expect poor performance – if your PC scores less than this.

1

Start

Control Panel

System and Maintenance

System

Windows Vista has a route to system information that is similar to XP. You can also check hard disk space in exactly the same way as on XP.

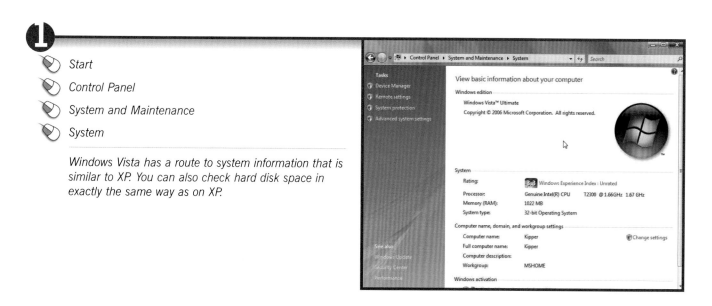

2

Start

Control Panel

System and Maintenance

Performance Information and Tools

Refresh Now or Update my score

Allow Windows Vista time to run the full hardware diagnostics. The result is an Experience Index base score that you can use as a reference when shopping for software. Our score of 3.2 is about average, certainly nothing spectacular.

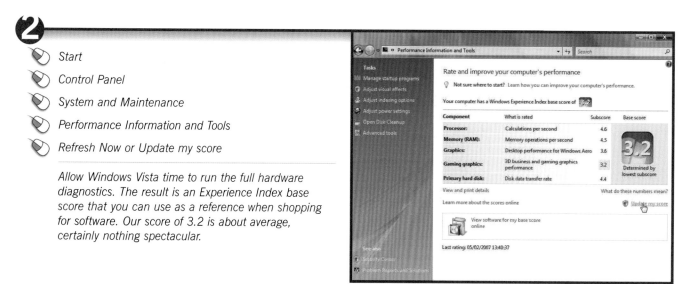

PART

Taking precautions

Before turning another page, and certainly before taking a screwdriver to your computer, ask yourself these questions:

● How would I cope if my PC refuses to restart?
● How would I cope if my files become corrupted?
● How would I cope if my PC is stolen?

Temporary inconvenience or a major catastrophe? If your computer went badly awry, perhaps after a virus infection or a coffee spill, would you lose a day's work, a week's work, or the sum total of your efforts over the past year?

Safe or sorry?

It's important to recognise the difference between a computer failure and the loss of data. In the case of a software problem, it's usually possible to reinstall Windows (and any of your programs that you need to) from scratch. Tedious, but possible, and with luck all your documents and files will survive. However, a better idea is to take precautionary measures now, and that means a backup routine. This way, you can always recover from disaster – even if you have to buy a new PC.

There's nothing like a computer failure to make you wish you had backed up your files and programs.

Backing up your files

How you make copies of your valuable files depends largely upon your system. A CD-writer drive lets you back up 700MB of data at a time, and quickly; whereas a DVD-writer drive offers even greater flexibility at a minimum of 4.7GB per disc. USB 'flash drives' are fantastic for copying a few hundred megabytes of data at a time; an external hard drive lets you back up the entire system. You can, of course, make multiple copies of files on the same computer as the originals but they're as much use as a chocolate teapot if the computer itself gets lost, stolen or irretrievably broken.

With USB flash drives now so cheap, it's crazy not to keep copies of at least your most important files.

An external hard drive connects to your computer via USB or FireWire and allows you to back up a copy of the computer's entire internal hard disk.

The ultimate safety routine

A disk image is an exact copy, or clone, of a hard disk. That is, it encompasses every last bit and byte of data, including Windows itself. But why is that important?

Well, with a normal backup you copy specific files and folders. In the event of disaster – the theft of your computer, say, or total hard disk failure – you can at least recover your work. So long as you still have your original Windows and program discs, you can also start afresh on a new PC. It's a drag, though: reinstalling Windows and all your software and then setting everything up the way you like it once more can take an age. However, with an image of your hard drive, you can reinstall everything at a stroke: Windows, software, settings, files, folders, the works.

You can save a disk image on recordable CDs (lots of them, probably) or recordable DVDs (fewer will be required) or on a separate external hard disk. So long as you keep the image somewhere physically separate from the PC, you should be OK come what may.

Unfortunately, Windows itself cannot perform disk imaging so this is one occasion where you'll need a third-party utility. One such is Acronis True Image, currently in version 10 and compatible with Windows Vista. You can download a fully functional demo version free of charge from **www.acronis.com**.

There are a few things to know about disk imaging before you start:

- **Full image:** This is where you make an exact copy of everything on the hard disk.
- **Selective image:** Alternatively, you can instruct your imaging software to back up only specific files and folders, such as your My Documents folder. Of course, you can do this easily yourself without the need for special software, as we shall see in a page or two.
- **Full or selective restore:** Let's say you lose a particular file on your computer. So long as the file was included in your last imaging procedure, whether as part of a full or a selective backup, you'll be able to locate and restore it simply by exploring the image. You don't need to restore anything else so a selective restoration like this takes only seconds – but how grateful you will be if that lost file happens to be your great unfinished novel! A full restore on the other hand, means replacing many or even all files in a single hit.

- **Incremental image:** This is where you start by making a full copy of the hard disk, but do so only once. The first incremental image simply copies the changes that have occurred since the full image was created, and subsequent incremental images copy changes since the previous incremental image. You end up with a chain of files that are all inter-dependent.
- **Differential image:** Here, you also start off with a full image. Thereafter, each differential image procedure produces a single file that encompasses all the changes that have occurred since the original image was made, rather than a chain of incremental changes.

Confused? There's no need to be. Our advice is to make a full disk image every time and not worry about incremental and differential routines until you're comfortable with the basics.

Here's a walkthrough with Acronis True Image. We strongly suggest that you invest in an external hard drive on which to save and store your images.

Backup

Install Acronis True Image and connect your external hard drive if that's what you're going to use as a backup location. You'll have the opportunity to select it in a moment. From True Image's opening screen, select Backup.

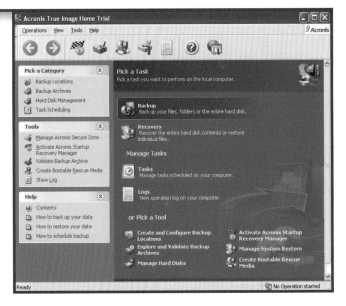

Next

My Computer

Next

When the wizard starts, tell True Image that you wish to back up your entire computer. You could opt for a selective backup here but let's go the whole hog.

○ *Hard drive*

 Next

You'll be asked to put a check mark against the drive that you wish to back up. This is invariably C: unless you have a fancy multi-drive setup (in which case take care which drive or partition you select).

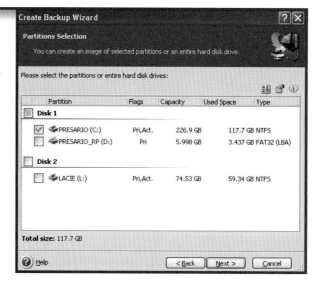

○ *Backup location*

Now tell True Image where to save the backup. This is a two-stage process. First, select the destination drive in the left-hand pane. In this case, we're pointing to an external hard drive called LACIE with drive letter L:, and we've selected a folder on that drive called My Backups. The 'path' (directions) to this location now appear in the Folder field below.

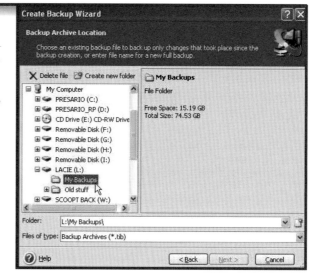

 File name

 Next

Now enter a descriptive file name for your disk image in the Folder field immediately after the slash in the path. Including the date in the file name is a sensible idea.

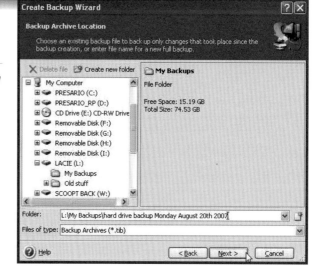

Create a new full backup archive

 Next

As discussed, we want to create a complete copy of everything on the hard disk. Next time you do this, you might want to choose an incremental or a differential backup.

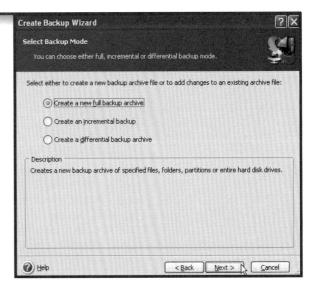

 Use default options

 Next

 Next

 Proceed

The subsequent screens allow you to modify the nature of the backup. You can, for instance, protect it with a password and select various levels of compression (which make the resulting disk image file smaller). Explore at your leisure but, for this first time, just accept the defaults. True Image will now copy the hard drive you selected in Step 3 onto the location you specified in Step 4. You are well advised to leave your computer completely alone for the duration, which may take upwards of an hour. When all is finished, store the backup drive somewhere safe, preferably in a different building.

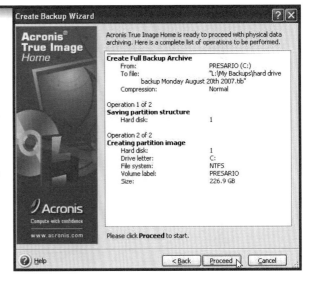

The True Image help files will talk you through a selective or a full restore but essentially you can restore one, some, many or all files from an image, up to and including your operating system, all installed software and every last file. Disk imaging is a powerful tool.

Quick backups

Windows XP supports CD burning and Windows Vista finally adds support for DVD burning. What this means is that you can pop a blank recordable or rewriteable CD or DVD into the drive and copy files and folders to it directly from within Windows.

In Windows XP, place a blank CD-R disc in the drive, open My Computer, and double-click the drive letter that corresponds to the drive – probably the D: or E: drive. This should open a new window where you see CD Writing Tasks on the left-hand side. Drag and drop the files you want to back up into this window, click Write these files to CD and follow instructions. It's as straightforward as it ought to be.

In Windows Vista, you can do just the same, with the advantage that you can also use blank DVD media.

Alternatively, or additionally, keep a USB flash drive handy and back up key files and folders as you go along. The beauty of a flash drive is that it 'just works' within Windows without any configuration. The drive appears in My Computer like any other drive and you can copy files to and from it immediately.

In Windows Vista, you can back up key files and folders directly to CD or DVD media.

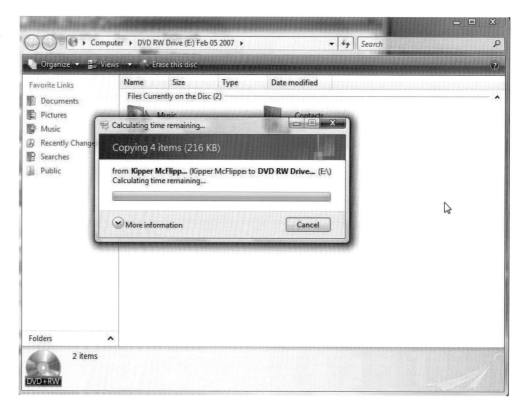

PART

The tools you'll need

As we remarked earlier, fiddling with computers isn't rocket science. Nor is it brain surgery. It's a whole lot easier than replacing a car's suspension, or even the brakes on a bicycle, and it requires neither skill nor experience. Short of spilling your coffee over the motherboard, you're very unlikely to actually break your computer. However, do give yourself plenty of space to work. For even the simplest internal task, it's worthwhile shifting the whole shebang from a cramped desktop to somewhere more suitable. At the very least, ensure that you have sufficient room to work comfortably with a tower PC lying on its side.

If you can change a fuse, you can upgrade a computer.

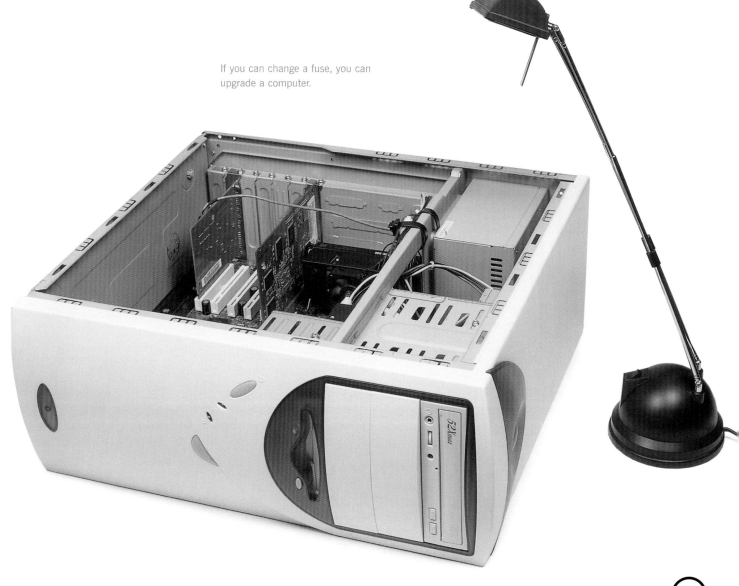

You'll need five tools to work on your PC's delicate innermost parts

A manual for your motherboard and, ideally, all the other manuals and paperwork that came with your PC and peripherals. Now visit the manufacturer's website and cross your fingers that there's a downloadable manual available.

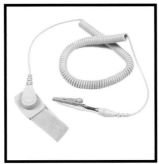

An antistatic wrist-strap. It won't save your life if you upgrade a running PC from the comfort of your bath but it will disperse any build-up of static electricity in your body and thus safeguard delicate circuitry from an unwelcome fry-up. Your computer will thank you for it – and so will your wallet. Wear one with pride.

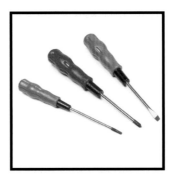

Screwdrivers. One small Phillips will probably suffice – that's the one with the cross shaped pointy end – but have a flathead screwdriver to hand just in case. If you can't resist, buy one of those handy 'PC upgrade' kits.

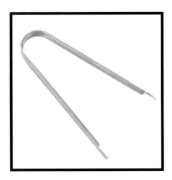

Tweezers or delicate long-nosed pliers. Essential for retrieving dropped screws.

A torch. Miniaturisation ensures a surfeit of nooks and crannies inside your computer, and they're all dark. A good adjustable desktop lamp will suffice at a pinch.

There's only one other must-have, and that's patience. Always a virtue, a measure of patience is truly essential when it comes upgrading a PC. The task at hand might not be successful at the first attempt. You might have trouble installing drivers or any of a million minor niggles may strike without warning. But don't rush it. Ever. Take your time, work through the manual that comes with any new device or component (even if it's written in Jargonese, as is the norm). Think and act logically. Don't replace a hard disk on a Monday morning or network the office on a Friday afternoon when you'd rather be elsewhere.

We also strongly suggest that you back up your important files (preferably the entire hard disk – see pp26–9).

There. Now are you ready to peek inside?

PART **1** Lifting the lid

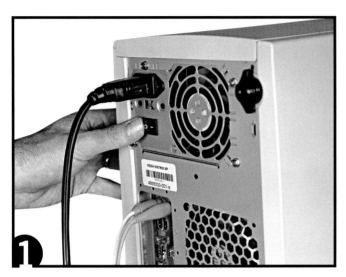

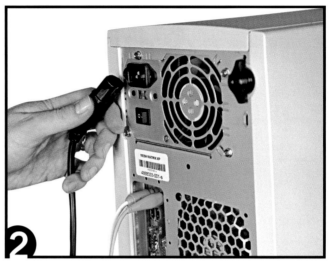

1 *Opinions vary on* whether it's safer to leave the PC's case connected to the mains while you work – with the power turned off at the wall, of course – or to unplug it completely. Leaving it connected provides a path to earth for static electricity and protects the computer's components. It is, however, still plugged in and that just gives us the jitters. We prefer to unplug the machine and use an antistatic wrist-strap. Begin by switching off the power supply (if indeed it has an on/off switch).

2 *Unplug all other cables* and connectors from the back of the machine. If it helps, make a note of where everything goes, perhaps using sticky labels or diagrams. In practice, thanks to the myriad different interfaces present on the back of your PC, the plug on the end of a peripheral's cable will typically fit only one socket. The awkward connections tend to be speaker and modem cables.

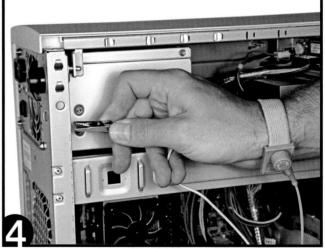

3 *Dig out the manual* that came with your computer and figure out what holds it together. Yes, we know that sounds rather vague but there are any number of ways to screw a case together, and few of them are obvious. We've even seen designs where to get at the retaining screws you have to forcibly prise off the front of the case. Talk about counterintuitive!

4 *Touch something metal* like a radiator to discharge any static electricity in your body. Before going near anything internally, put on your wrist-strap and connect it to a metal part of the case. Now peer inside. Does it look like a computer? Good. Now let's make it a better one.

2

PART  # Straight to the heart

You would think, would you not, that the quickest way to speed up an ailing PC would be to give it a brainpower boost? Surprisingly, this isn't always – indeed, not even usually – the case: less radical measures are generally more effective and *much* easier.

PART  Motherboard architecture

If you understand the importance and role of the motherboard, you can do just about anything with a PC. Every area of this manual touches upon the motherboard in one way or another because this is the central component in a PC to which everything else is attached. In fact, installing a new motherboard is tantamount to building a PC from scratch rather than effecting an upgrade, and we look at this in some detail in Appendix 3.

Mouse and *keyboard* sockets.

USB (Universal Serial Bus) Two USB interfaces for connecting external devices.

Parallel port One parallel interface, usually reserved for the printer. All new printers now use the USB interface instead.

Serial port Two serial interfaces for connecting external devices (hidden below parallel port). External modems, some mice and handheld computers used to use the serial port; now, again, USB takes care of everything.

Good reasons to replace your motherboard

You want a faster computer All motherboards support, or work with, a limited range of processors, and only those from within a given family (be this Intel's Pentium/Celeron or AMD's Athlon/Duron). The problem is that you can't simply pop a new, more powerful processor in an old motherboard and expect it to work. If you have the manual and it specifies support for a faster processor than the one you already have, then fine; but if not, a new motherboard with explicit support for the processor you want is a much safer option.

Your old motherboard has given up the ghost It's not a common failure, but it happens. If your PC is playing up, and you're sure it's down to the motherboard, the PC equivalent of open-heart surgery can save the day. Why not take the chance to upgrade to a better model at the same time?

You'd like to upgrade once and once only Many modern motherboards incorporate all the circuitry required for graphics and sound output, and often include a modem, networking and more. This makes for an economical, relatively fuss-free route to a full multimedia system.

Good reasons *not* to replace your motherboard

You may have to reformat your hard disk or at least reinstall (or, in the case of XP, reactivate) Windows. The shock of finding a whole new motherboard under the hood can induce an operating system identity crisis. Then again, a fresh software start is the perfect complement for a new motherboard.

Your old components may no longer fit Will that old ISA soundcard find a home on your swanky new motherboard? What will you do with your PCI graphics card if the new motherboard has an AGP or PCI Express slot? Chances are you'll have to replace your old memory modules to comply with new improved standards. If you discover that you have to buy new components throughout, it might be as cheap (and much easier) to start all over again with a new PC, perhaps hanging onto your old monitor, printer, keyboard and mouse. That said, a new motherboard with integrated multimedia neatly skirts such issues because you'll be able – in fact, forced – to ditch your old expansion cards.

The motherboard itself may not fit Motherboards and computer cases adhere to 'form factor' industry standards that govern size and shape so it's never safe to assume that a new motherboard will fit in an old case without first checking. By far the most popular form factor is ATX, in which a full-sized motherboard measures 305mm x 244mm and the case is designed to accommodate it. This is almost certainly what you have if your PC was made within the last seven or eight years, so finding a new ATX (or one of its smaller derivatives) shouldn't be a problem. See Appendix 3 where we install a Micro ATX motherboard in a full-sized ATX case.

Motherboard features

Let's have a detailed look at two motherboards from different generations. You'll see that they share many of the same characteristics. However, it is important to note the subtle differences between their slots and sockets. We'll highlight the key points of departure on the second motherboard model.

Slot 1 *This is the slot design for processors, where the processor sits vertically in a motherboard slot and has a fan or other cooling mechanism bolted onto one side. Slotted processors are no longer in production so this design is now obsolete (but still found in abundance in older PCs).*

Older motherboard

RAM (Random Access Memory) *RAM is installed in modules that plug into these slots. Expect to find two, four or, less commonly but as seen here, three slots.*

CMOS battery *A replaceable battery that keeps the CMOS alive when the power is switched off. Home to all your hardware settings (see p209).*

IDE/ATA controllers (Integrated Drive Electronics/Advanced Technology Attachment) *Two of these as standard. The hard disk plugs into the primary IDE/ATA channel (or controller or socket – pick your terminology!), usually labelled IDE 1, and the CD or DVD drives into the other. Two internal drives can share a controller by means of a cable with two plugs. IDE controllers carry a speed rating – something like 100MB/sec – which describes how quickly data can pass through the socket into the rest of the system. This has a bearing when you shop for a new hard drive, as you'll want to match the drive speed to the IDE speed in order to get the best performance.*

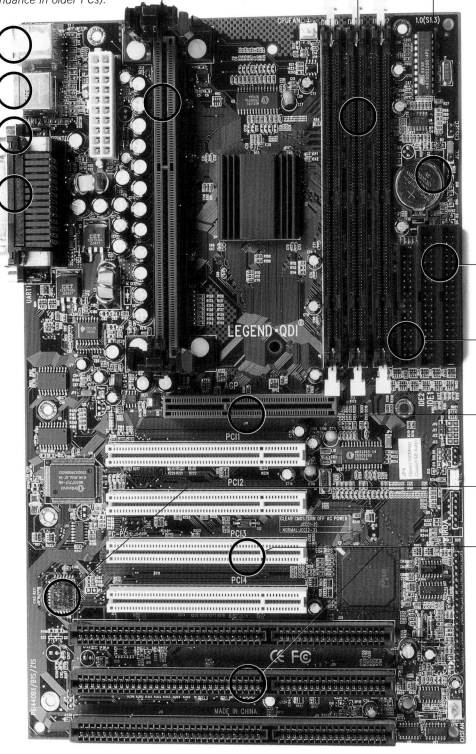

Floppy disk controller *The floppy disk drive, if present, plugs in here. Floppy disk drives are now virtually extinct.*

AGP slot (Accelerated Graphics Port) *An expansion slot reserved for a high-performance graphics card.*

BIOS *A memory chip that kick-starts a PC before Windows wakes up.*

Expansion slots *A wide variety of expansion cards can be installed in these slots to add to a PC's features. The shorter white slots are relatively fast PCI (Peripheral Component Interconnect) slots and the longer black slots are ISA (Industry Standard Architecture). The PCI standard replaces ISA so you'll only find ISA slots in older, very dusty computers.*

PCI Express *As well as two standard PCI slots (white), this motherboard has four PCI Express slots. Two of these are single-speed slots (1x) and two are sixteen-speed slots (16x). As with everything, faster means you can do more. In particular, a 16x PCI Express slot is designed for a very high performance graphics card, typically used for gaming.*

New motherboard

Integrated audio *Less obviously, but importantly, this model has a high-definition surround-sound audio chip built right into the motherboard. This means that you don't need a separate sound card to produce quality audio output. Some motherboards feature integrated graphics so you don't need a graphics card either.*

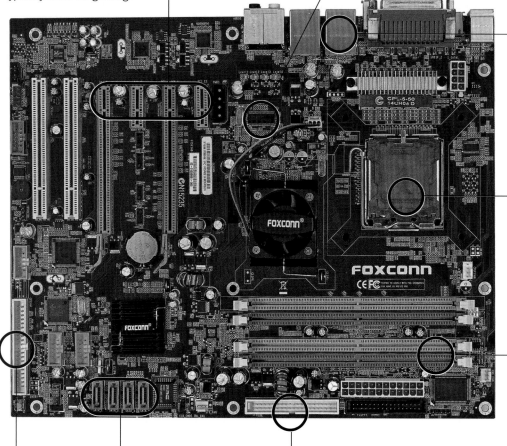

FireWire, Ethernet, USB2 *On this panel, you'll find FireWire alongside fast USB sockets, plus a pair of Ethernet sockets for connecting the computer to a network. The older model had only slower USB1.1 sockets, which are now obsolete.*

Socket 775 *All current processors now use a socket design where the processor is flat and square and installs horizontally into the motherboard via a socket. The cooling unit then sits on top of the processor.*

RAM *Although these memory slots are similar to the previous ones, they are designed to hold a very much more powerful kind of module. The upshot is that you can almost never reuse memory from an old PC in a new motherboard.*

SATA (Serial ATA) *This is the current standard for internal drives. SATA is an improvement to the old IDE specification; it basically allows drives to transfer data to and from the system more quickly than before. You can't share a SATA socket between two drives so a motherboard like this typically comes with several SATA interfaces. This model has four. Note that it also comes with two IDE sockets (circled) so you don't have to throw out old hard drives and optical drives.*

PART

Upgrading RAM

Without RAM (Random Access Memory), your PC would be an expensive paperweight. Every time you run a program, it's loaded into your PC's RAM and the bigger the program the more RAM it needs. Windows itself needs RAM, and over the years it has become increasingly hungry: while Windows 95 needed 8MB to get out of bed, 16MB to operate reasonably smoothly and 32MB to do anything useful, Windows 98 needed 64MB, Windows Millennium Edition needed 128MB, and Windows XP was pretty much useless with less than 256MB. The latest version of Windows, Vista, is even hungrier.

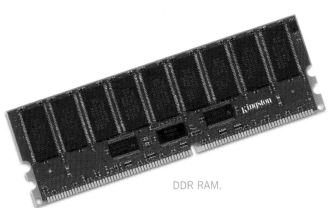

DDR RAM.

SD RAM.

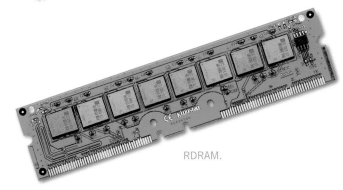

RDRAM.

Bill Gates probably regrets opening his mouth back in 1981, when he said 'nobody will ever need more than 640K of RAM'. That's just over half a megabyte; today, Windows Vista isn't happy on systems with less than half a gigabyte – 1,000 times more than Gates thought we'd ever need.

It's important to note that those figures are just for Windows itself; everything you do in Windows – every program you run, every file you open, every security program that scans your system – will add to the RAM requirements. It's a good idea to take the memory requirements and double them. While Windows XP is reasonably smooth on a system with 256MB, it's much happier with 512MB; and while Vista does work with 512MB of RAM, you'll find that 1GB makes for a much more enjoyable experience. If you need to do really demanding things such as video editing, you'll need even more.

What happens when you run out of RAM

When your PC's memory fills up, the first thing you'll notice is a major deterioration in performance. At that point your PC has four choices: it can give up and crash (which, thankfully, is less common than it used to be); it can freeze solid; it can refuse to do anything else until you free up memory by closing programs, or it can wave a magic wand and find extra RAM from nowhere. Amazingly, Windows PCs prefer the fourth option.

So how can your PC find extra RAM when your memory is full? It doesn't. Rather, it uses a bit of your hard disk as pretend RAM, called Virtual Memory or a 'swap file'. When your RAM puts up the No Vacancies sign Windows starts storing data in the swap file instead, which is good news and bad news: good, because it stops your PC from crashing – but bad, because hard disks are much, much slower than memory chips. If your hard disk is chuntering away more than usual with a cacophony of clicks and whirrs, it usually means that Windows is using the swap file. The hard disk noise is called 'thrashing' and, while it won't damage your system, it won't give you decent performance either.

If your PC's prone to thrashing, it's a safe bet that your system needs more RAM – and thankfully the days when memory chips cost more than cars are long gone. As we'll discover, it's very easy to find and fit additional memory, and the difference it makes can be dramatic.

Using memory cards as extra RAM

No more room for RAM? Then why not use your camera's cards?

Windows Vista has a clever trick up its sleeve: if you run out of RAM, you can use a memory card – such as the one from your digital camera – to improve your PC's performance. The feature's called ReadyBoost and it can use high-speed SD cards, CF cards or even USB thumb drives with capacities of up to 4GB.

ReadyBoost doesn't magically give you more RAM, but instead of using your hard disk it stores a swap file on your memory card or USB drive. Such devices use flash memory, which offers faster data access times than most hard disks, and the result is a noticeable improvement in performance when your system's

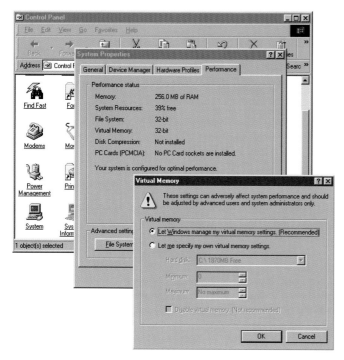

Windows uses the hard disk to make up for any RAM deficiency. A proper memory upgrade is much more efficient.

RAM modules sit in slots on the motherboard.

running out of real RAM. It's cheap, too: at the time of writing, upgrading our laptop's memory would cost between £60 and £120 – but a ReadyBoost-compatible 1GB memory card was just £11. And that included postage.

Before you reach for your wallet, though, it's important to note that ReadyBoost won't work on cards or USB drives that aren't fast enough – so check out the blog of ReadyBoost boss, Tom Archer, to see the system requirements: **http://blogs.msdn.com/ tomarcher/archive/2006/06/02/615199.aspx**

What you need to know

Inevitably, RAM comes in assorted flavours and you have to be sure to buy the right type for your particular PC. Here's a guide to the critical specifications.

Capacity RAM modules are measured in megabytes and are available in several sizes, including 64, 128, 256, 512 and 1,024MB (also known as 1GB).

Adding new RAM isn't just a matter of buying the biggest chips you can afford, though. Every motherboard has a limit to how much RAM you can install, so while our desktop's motherboard can handle up to 4GB of RAM – which is more than most people will ever need, at least until Windows Vista's replacement demands 4GB just to get out of bed – our laptop can only handle a maximum of 2GB. Older motherboards' limits may be even lower, so you might find that if your PC can't cope with intensive tasks such as editing digital video or working with ultra-high resolution images, a new, more expandable motherboard is a sensible purchase.

Type Like everything else in the PC world, RAM has evolved apace. Brand new systems might come with souped-up versions called RD RAM or DDR RAM (Rambus Dynamic and Double Data Rate memory respectively), but older systems will probably have SD (Synchronous Dynamic) RAM installed. The wrong kind of RAM won't work in a PC that doesn't support it, so check your motherboard manual, or dig out the order or delivery paperwork just to make sure.

Slot type RAM comes in modules loaded with storage cells that sit in slots on the motherboard. There are three main types – SIMM (Single Inline Memory Module); DIMM (Dual Inline Memory Module); and RIMM (Rambus Inline Memory Module) – and you simply can't mix and match. To install an extra RAM upgrade, you either use a free slot on the motherboard or, if necessary, replace an existing RAM module with a higher capacity version e.g. ditch a measly 16MB module to free up space for a 256MB module.

One complication, and an important one, is that SIMMs must be grouped together in pairs, or 'banks', where each module has the same capacity. The motherboard in a typical older Pentium PC would have four sockets (i.e. two banks), so possible configurations would include:

1st bank	2 x 16MB SIMMs
2nd bank	2 x 16MB SIMMs
Total RAM	64MB
or	
1st bank	2 x 16MB SIMMs
2nd bank	2 x 32MB SIMMs
Total RAM	96MB

What you can't do is pluck one 16MB SIMM from its home and replace it with a 32MB module unless you simultaneously do the same with its partner. However, the newer DIMM memory modules have no such restriction. We might also add that if your motherboard has SIMM-style slots, you really should be thinking about scrapping it in favour of a DIMM model.

Curiously, Rambus memory complicates matters again. RIMM modules must be installed in matching pairs just like the old SIMMs, and you have to fill any unused sockets with dummy modules called Continuity RIMMs.

Speed It may seem odd to think of memory in terms of speed, but RAM modules talk to the processor at different rates. This is important because it relates to the speed of the chipset on the motherboard, so again check the motherboard manual and be sure to buy memory modules that the motherboard supports.

Buying RAM

If you bought your PC from a shop or an online manufacturer such as Dell or Acer, finding the right RAM couldn't be easier: memory firms such as Crucial (**www.crucial.com**) and Orca (**www.orcalogic.co.uk**) have online 'memory finder' tools that enable you to enter the make and model of your computer and then see what will work.

If you don't know the make and model of your PC, the sites can still help: for example, Crucial's site also has a downloadable

Use the Belarc Advisor to reveal your motherboard's secrets

Computer Profile Summary

*Computer Name:*Tinman (in MSHOME)
*Profile Date:*26 May 2004 12:03:55
*Advisor Version:*6.1
*Windows Logon:*Kyle

Click here for Belarc's PC Management products, for large and small companies.

Operating System	System Model
Windows XP Home Edition Service Pack 1 (build 2600)	*No details available*

Processor [a]	Main Circuit Board [b]
2.40 gigahertz Intel Pentium 4 8 kilobyte primary memory cache 512 kilobyte secondary memory cache	Board: Gigabyte Technology Co., Ltd. 8PE667P 1.x Bus Clock: 133 megahertz BIOS: Award Software International, Inc. 6.00 PG 09/12/2002

Drives	Memory Modules [c,d] - Buy More
242.00 Gigabytes Usable Hard Drive Capacity 113.08 Gigabytes Hard Drive Free Space	1024 Megabytes Installed Memory Slot 'A0' has 512 MB Slot 'A1' has 512 MB

HL-DT-ST DVDRAM GSA-4040B [CD-ROM drive]
PLEXTOR CD-R PX-W4824A [CD-ROM drive]
3.5" format removeable media [Floppy drive]

HP psc 2210 USB Device [Hard drive] -- drive 5
Maxtor 6Y080P0 [Hard drive] (81.96 GB) -- drive 0, s/n Y2Q5P1FE, rev YAR41BW0, SMART Status: Healthy
OEI-USB CompactFlash USB Device [Hard drive] (90 MB) -- drive 3
OEI-USB SM/MS/SD USB Device [Hard drive] -- drive 4
ST380023A [Hard drive] (80.03 GB) -- drive 2, s/n 3KB0YG4S, rev 3.33, SMART Status: Healthy
ST380023A [Hard drive] (80.03 GB) -- drive 1, s/n 3KB0B3AH, rev 3.31, SMART Status: Healthy

Local Drive Volumes		
c: (on drive 2)	80.02 GB	53.29 GB free
f: (on drive 0)	81.96 GB	32.22 GB free
g: (on drive 1)	47.99 GB	26.95 GB free
h: (on drive 1)	32.04 GB	622 MB free

Network Drives

System Scanner that pokes around your PC to find out what kind of RAM you've got and what you can install.

If you made your PC yourself or you've upgraded its innards, have a look at the motherboard manual to check the specs – or use the excellent Belarc Advisor to jog your (own) memory.

Belarc Advisor (**www.belarc.com/free_download.html**) is a free downloadable utility that summarises system information in a handy, relatively clear format. In the screenshot on p41, for instance, we can see that the PC has a total of 1,024MB of RAM installed as two 512MB modules. The motherboard – or Main Circuit Board – is a Gigabyte 8PE667P. Armed with this information, we could turn to the Orca or Crucial memory configuration utilities and uncover our upgrade options (not that a PC with 1GB of RAM really needs an upgrade, you understand, but the principle holds true regardless).

This we did and found out that:

- The motherboard has three 184-pin DIMM slots (two of which we know from the Belarc Advisor are already filled)
- It supports a maximum of 2,048MB RAM (so our best upgrade option would presumably be a 1,024MB module – but read on)
- It supports two different speeds of memory (PC2100 and PC2700, to be precise). We could conceivably use an even faster flavour of RAM, such as, PC3200 but we wouldn't see any real-world benefit.

Having come this far, the next step is to pay the motherboard manufacturer's website a visit and look for further details on this particular motherboard. This is important mainly to establish whether there are any restrictions governing module support. If you check the Support section of the website, you might be lucky and find a downloadable manual for your particular motherboard.

We did – and a good job it was, too. Buying a 1GB (1,024MB) module for the vacant DIMM slot on this Gigabyte motherboard would have been a costly mistake. The trouble is that the motherboard supports only four banks of memory, which equates to two double-sided modules or one double-sided module plus one or two single-sided modules. It already has two double-sided modules *in situ* so a further upgrade is out of the question. In fact, the only possibility is replacing one of the existing modules with another of a higher capacity.

But the details in this example don't really matter. What does matter is the point that you have to check carefully before making a purchase.

These 184-pin DIMM modules are compatible with your system.

1GB — CT12864Z265	DDR PC2100	CL=2.5	Non-parity	US $249.99 (each)	Buy
1GB — CT12864Z335	DDR PC2700	CL=2.5	Non-parity	US $271.99 (each)	Buy
1GB — CT12864Z40B	DDR PC3200	CL=3	Non-parity	US $389.99 (each)	Buy
512MB — CT6464Z335	DDR PC2700	CL=2.5	Non-parity	US $99.99 (each)	Buy
Most Popular! 512MB — CT6464Z265	DDR PC2100	CL=2.5	Non-parity	US $100.99 (each)	Buy
512MB — CT6464Z40B	DDR PC3200	CL=3	Non-parity	US $105.99 (each)	Buy
256MB — CT3264Z265	DDR PC2100	CL=2.5	Non-parity	US $55.99 (each)	Buy
256MB — CT3264Z40B	DDR PC3200	CL=3	Non-parity	US $57.99 (each)	Buy
256MB — CT3264Z335	DDR PC2700	CL=2.5	Non-parity	US $57.99 (each)	Buy
128MB — CT1664Z265	DDR PC2100	CL=2.5	Non-parity	US $31.99 (each)	Buy
128MB — CT1664Z335	DDR PC2700	CL=2.5	Non-parity	US $31.99 (each)	Buy
128MB — CT1664Z40B	DDR PC3200	CL=3	Non-parity	US $31.99 (each)	Buy

The Crucial online memory configuration utility makes choosing memory simple.

Here we tracked down our motherboard model to the manufacturer's website. The Manual link on the left leads to a downloadable copy of the long-lost paper manual originally supplied with the system.

Oops. Our motherboard already has a full complement of double-sided memory modules and cannot be further upgraded without sacrificing one of the existing 512MB modules. Better to learn this now than later.

Step 2: Install memory modules

The motherboard has 3 dual inline memory module (DIMM) sockets, but it can only support a maximum of 4 banks of DDR memory. DDR sockets 1 uses 2 banks, DDR sockets 2&3 share the remaining 2 banks. Please refer to the following tables for possible memory configurations supported. The BIOS will automatically detects memory type and size. To install the memory module, just push it vertically into the DIMM socket. The DIMM can only fit in one direction due to the notch. Memory size can vary between sockets.

Support Unbuffered DDR DIMM Sizes type:

64 Mbit (2Mx8x4 banks)	64 Mbit (1Mx16x4 banks)	128 Mbit(4Mx8x4 banks)
128 Mbit(2Mx16x4 banks)	256 Mbit(8Mx8x4 banks)	256 Mbit(4Mx16x4 banks)
512 Mbit(16Mx8x4 banks)	512 Mbit(8Mx16x4 banks)	
Total System Memory (Max2GB)		

Notes: Double-sided x16 DDR memory devices are not support by Intel 845E/G /PE/GE chipset.

Install memory in any combination table:

DDR1	DDR2	DDR3
S	S	S
D	S	S
D		X
D	D	X
D	X	D
S	D	X
S	X	D

D:Double Sided DIMM S:Single Sided DIMM

DDR

PART 2

Step-by-step RAM upgrade

Installing a new RAM module is easy. Here we add a
second module alongside an existing one. With DIMMs, you
would normally install a second module in the slot labelled
DIMM 2 and a third in DIMM 3 but be sure to follow the
motherboard manual's directions and restrictions.

Before attempting *any internal work on your PC, re-read the
safety precautions on p33.*

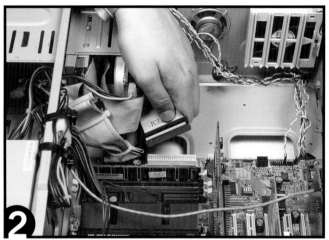

Ensure that *you have clear access to the RAM slots. This might
mean temporarily removing other components or unplugging
cables. Just be sure to put everything back the way you find it.
Making notes is a good idea.*

The DIMM socket *has a locking tab at either end. Press down
on these tabs to open them.*

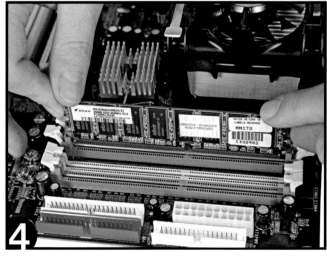

Carefully remove *your new module from its antistatic bag and,
holding it gently by the edges, align the notches on the lower
edge of the module with those in the slot.*

5

Press down firmly on the module until it sits level in the slot. Be sure to keep it vertical. As you push it home, the locking tabs should engage with the keyed ends of the module and snap shut. Give them a helping hand, or finger, if necessary.

6

When both tabs have locked into place, the module will be held securely in the slot and you can consider the installation complete. Now replace anything that you set asunder earlier in order to access the sockets.

```
AMIBIOS(C)2001 American Megatrends, Inc.
BIOS Date: 02/19/03 19:39:18  Ver: 08.00.02

Press DEL to run Setup
Checking NVRAM..

196MB OK

Auto-Detecting Pri Master..IDE Hard Disk
Auto-Detecting Pri Slave...Not Detected
Auto-Detecting Sec Master..CDROM
Auto-Detecting Sec Slave...
```

7

When you restart the computer, watch the screen carefully. When the system runs through its standard start-up procedure, check that the total RAM reported is now what you would expect e.g. if you just installed 128MB into a system with 64MB, the total should now be 196MB. And that's it: no fuss with drivers, no fiddly configuration, just a much improved PC. Enjoy.

TROUBLE-SHOOTER

If the RAM upgrade does not register when you start the system, check the details in the General tab of System Properties (see pp22–23). If this looks right, reboot and try again.

Still not registering? Repeat the installation process and ensure that the new module is properly locked in place. Also try running a Belarc Advisor report.

If this is a SIMM upgrade, check that you've followed the bank rules, i.e. installed two SIMMs of equal capacity in each bank.

As a final test, remove the new module and move one of the existing modules (DIMM only) into the now-vacant socket. Restart and ensure that the original quantity of RAM still registers. This way, you'll confirm that you're doing everything correctly; the socket itself is fine; and the new module must be faulty. Exchange it!

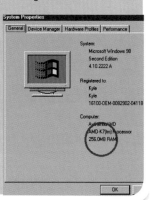

PART  # Understanding processors

Imagine this manual was double its current size. Now double it again. Now cram it full of hieroglyphic tables, small print, warnings, disclaimers and impenetrable jargon. You *still* wouldn't have enough information on hand to perform a processor upgrade in all possible circumstances. There are just too many angles, too many possibilities, too many permutations to cover all bases. This book is much too short to make such an attempt. So is life.

But surely, you protest, it's merely a matter of out with the old and in with the new? How hard can it be? Well, the physical procedure for changing the component is indeed straightforward, but getting to that point is fraught with difficulties. The first really seriously limiting factor is whether a new processor will even fit onto your existing motherboard.

The most common connectors

A processor installs in the motherboard either in a slot, much like a memory module, or flat in a socket. Slot designs have been ditched by both Intel and AMD, the two leading manufacturers of processors, in favour of sockets.

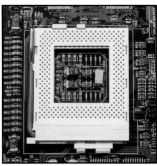

Socket 7 *A flat socket on the motherboard. Compatible processors include Pentium and Pentium MMX; AMD K6; Cyrix 6x86 MX and MII.*

Slot 1 *A groove in which the processor cartridge sits on edge. Compatible processors include Intel Celeron, Pentium II and Pentium III.*

Socket 370 *A newer style socket. Compatible processors include Intel Celeron and Pentium III (yes, these two ranges are available in both slot and socket designs).*

Slot A *Similar to Slot 1 but designed exclusively for AMD's Athlon and Duron ranges.*

Socket A *(also known as Socket 462) An alternative socket approach for AMD Athlon and Duron processors.*

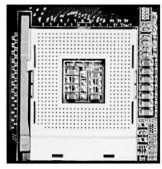

Socket 478 *The most popular of the lot these past few years. It plays host to Intel Pentium 4 and Celeron processors.*

Socket 775 *The replacement for Socket 478 is LGA775, also known as Socket 775 or Socket T.*

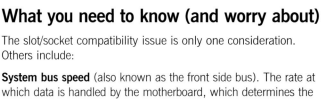

A motherboard bus.

Keeping cool is a critical consideration for processors, hence the need for bulky heatsinks.

So-called boxed processors are supplied with compatible heatsinks. This is the only safe way to buy one.

What you need to know (and worry about)

The slot/socket compatibility issue is only one consideration. Others include:

System bus speed (also known as the front side bus). The rate at which data is handled by the motherboard, which determines the true speed of a PC. A processor can work flat out for all it's worth but if the motherboard (or, more precisely, the chipset) can't process its results quickly enough, that equates to a lot of wasted effort. Most motherboards include a feature called a multiplier that enables them to accept faster processors than they were originally designed for, but there are constraints – see Techie Corner opposite.

Cooling All processors must be adequately cooled and the faster they run, the hotter they get. The standard cooling mechanism for a socket-based processor is a solid-state contraption called a heatsink that sits on top of the processor and dissipates heat through convection and with the help of a built-in fan. When buying a new processor, always insist on a 'boxed' or 'retail' (as opposed to an OEM, original equipment manufacturer) version. As the name suggests, it comes in a branded box but is also supplied with a compatible heatsink/fan unit. You can buy these units separately but you'd be ill-advised to do so unless you are absolutely confident that it offers sufficient cooling for your particular processor.

The BIOS chip If your computer was manufactured before the processor to which you now want to upgrade was developed, as is likely, the motherboard may not recognise or work with the new chip. Motherboards are usually designed with some built-in forward compatibility but only ever within certain limits. A subsequent significant change in processor architecture could make an easy upgrade impossible, even though a new processor physically fits the old socket.

One possible solution is a BIOS upgrade, which involves downloading a program from the motherboard manufacturer's website and 'flashing' the BIOS chip with a set of updated instructions. However, BIOS upgrades are not always available. Even when they are, they can't always ready an older motherboard for a newer processor. So, unless your motherboard already offers explicit support for the processor you wish to install, as confirmed by the manual or manufacturer's website, we'd strongly suggest going for a new motherboard at the same time as upgrading the processor. See Appendix 3 for details.

Voltages Does your motherboard support the required voltage of the processor? As a rule, modern processors run at lower voltages (i.e. cooler) than their predecessors, and a 3.3v model will soon blow up or burn out in a 5v socket. It's vital to check that your motherboard and processor upgrade are compatible. Again, may we suggest that a new motherboard makes sense?

Speed demon For all their power, processors deal exclusively in the 1s and 0s of binary code. That in itself sounds baffling until you consider that a 1 is merely a signal generated by an electric current ('on') and a 0 the lack of such a signal ('off'). The code 101, for instance, translates as power on–off–on again. The

BIOS (Basic Input/Output System) is a chip on the motherboard that controls the fundamental operations of a computer.

processor then runs these signals through its many, many microscopic transistors, interprets them according to certain logical rules, and outputs a binary response. Simple, huh? It's all controlled by an internal clock (of sorts) that beats at a certain rate. A 1GHz processor ticks one billion (yes, *billion*) times every single second, with each tick representing an opportunity for the processor to do something useful. Thus a 1GHz processor can do more work in a shorter time than a 500MHz (500 million ticks per second) model.

But it's not *all* about speed. A fast processor in an old system will run like a Ferrari in a car park, and you will virtually always see a much greater gain by slotting in an extra slice of RAM.

Here's a quick glance at how quickly Intel processors have evolved:

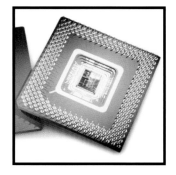
Pentium – 1993
60–200MHz

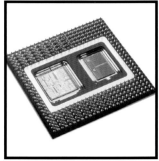
Pentium Pro – 1995
150–200MHz

Pentium MMX – 1997
166–233MHz

Pentium II – 1997
233–450MHz

Pentium III – 1999
450–1.13GHz

Pentium 4 – 2000
1.3–3.4 GHz…and rising

TECHIE CORNER

ZIF ZIF stands for Zero Insertion Force and describes the mechanism used to install processors in motherboard sockets. Rather than you having to forcibly pry a processor out of its socket with clumsy fingers or a screwdriver, a little lever unlocks the socket so you can lift the chip out cleanly. Older PCs often have a LIF socket (the L stands for Low), in which case there's no lever and you need a special tool called a (wait for it) chip remover to gently prise the processor free. But be careful when putting a processor into a LIF socket – the force required is not at all that low and perilously close to that required to crack the motherboard. Intel recommends against home replacements of LIF chips. This is sound advice that we happily endorse.

Core 2 Duo – 2006
1.6–2.93GHz…and rising

Dual-core Chips

Our old friend the Pentium Processor is no more; these days Intel-powered PCs are sold with Core 2 Duo or Core 2 Duo Extreme processors (or in the case of laptops, their mobile equivalents), while AMD has its own multi-core processors. So what on earth are they?

As we entered the 21st century, processor firms began to realise that they were picking a fight with the laws of physics – and the laws of physics were winning. Squeezing more speed out of existing chip designs was becoming increasingly difficult, not least because more speed meant more power consumption, which in turn meant even hotter processors. If manufacturers couldn't come up with an alternative, the next generation of

processors would use so much electricity you'd need a power station in your shed and they'd get so hot that within an hour of switching your PC on, it would have burned its way to the very centre of the Earth.

Initially processor firms decided that the answer was to put two or more processors into a PC, but that wasn't an ideal solution: twin-processor machines were extremely expensive and they weren't cheap to run either. So they went back to the drawing board and came up with dual-core technology.

A dual-core processor uses the latest manufacturing technologies to cram two processor cores – essentially the brains of the processor – onto a single chip. The result is considerably more efficient than a pair of individual processors. However, you won't get the full benefits of the technology if your software doesn't support it; so while on paper a 2.8GHz dual-core chip should be faster than a 3.6GHz Pentium, if you play Half-Life 2 you may well discover that it's less impressive on the dual-core than on the single-core machine. That's because at the time of writing many programs, Half-Life 2 included, don't take advantage of dual-core technology (although the developers of Half-Life 2 are working on it).

The good news is that Windows does support dual-core technology, and if you're running Windows XP or later then dual-core technology delivers real benefits – particularly in multitasking, when you're doing more than one thing at once. For example, if you're ripping CDs to Windows Media Player while downloading programs from the internet, running a virus scan and writing angry letters to the bank, a dual-core system will handle these multiple jobs more smoothly than a single-core system.

As if that weren't enough, quad-core processors are already here – albeit only in the most expensive systems – while Intel recently built a single chip containing a staggering 80 processor cores, each of which runs at 3.16GHz. It's not a one-off, either. Intel reckons 80-core chips may start appearing in PCs by 2011.

Intel or AMD? Quite frankly, who cares? The only thing duller than a debate about the relative merits of the Intel P4 versus the AMD Athlon is the equally interminable competition between devotees of the PC and the Apple Mac. Both camps thoroughly befuddle the consumer with incomprehensible numbering systems – Intel's currently rewriting the rules all over again – and making like-for-like comparisons is as tricky as it is fruitless. The truth is that a recent processor from either manufacturer will do you very nicely indeed, and you can certainly save a packet by opting for a version that's a few months old rather than the absolute latest model.

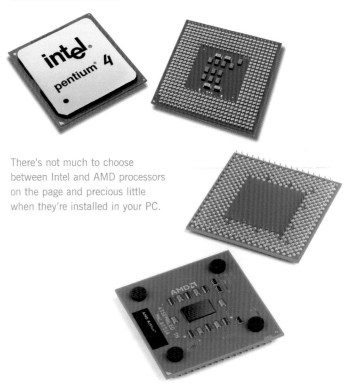

There's not much to choose between Intel and AMD processors on the page and precious little when they're installed in your PC.

Installing a new processor

When you buy a boxed or retail processor, full instructions are provided. There's really nothing to it. Here we look at the process for a Pentium 4. It's virtually identical for an AMD Athlon, although the processor socket and heatsink designs are slightly different.

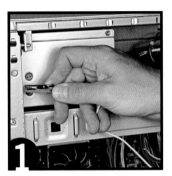

Before attempting any internal work on your PC, re-read the safety precautions on p33.

The existing heatsink is connected by a thin cable to a three-pin power socket on the motherboard. Locate this and unplug the cable. Now free the heatsink from its tether to the motherboard – it should have a fairly obvious release mechanism – and remove from the case.

Raise the ZIF lever that runs along the side of the socket and carefully remove the old processor. Examine the socket and you will see that the corner adjacent to the lever's hinge is missing two pin-holes. This is known as the Pin 1 position.

Holding the new processor by the edges only, check the pin array on its underside. One corner will also be missing two pins and marked with a gold triangle. This is Pin 1 position on the processor.

The trick is now to position the processor in the motherboard socket matching Pin 1 to Pin 1. No pressure should be required to complete this operation: simply drop the processor into place. When you are confident that the processor is seated securely in its socket with no gaps around the edges, lower the lever to lock it into place.

There has to be a thermal bond between the base of the heatsink and the top of the processor. This will be supplied as a glue-like substance in a syringe or tube, or as a self-adhesive pad, or, as here, pre-applied to the heatsink base.

Now install the heatsink according to the directions supplied. It will attach securely to a frame surrounding the socket (in the case of an Intel Pentium) or to the socket itself (in the case of an AMD Athlon). Finally, connect the heatsink power cable to the same motherboard power socket as the old heatsink. Job done.

PART **3**

COMPUTER MANUAL
Adding a new drive

Breathing new life into an ailing PC with major surgery is one thing, but there's more than one way to skin a cat (or mix a metaphor). Some of these upgrades will boost its performance, others will prolong its useful lifespan, but all will make your PC a more productive tool and a better toy.

PART  Why upgrade your hard disk?

Here's a funny thing: no matter why you first bought your PC, you're almost certainly using it for something entirely different now. As we become more proficient and confident, we explore new avenues and discover just what all this hardware and software can really do for us. Thus it's no surprise to find a book-keeping machine roped into editing digital video or a system purchased primarily for internet access functioning as a full-blown home entertainment centre. That's why upgrading a PC is so often a compelling, and frequently pressing, affair.

One of the key components that comes under pressure soonest is the hard disk. It's amazing just how quickly a seemingly cavernous disk can fill to capacity. A single megabyte might be sufficient storage space for the entire text of a novel, but that equates to a mere six seconds or so of uncompressed music. Throw in a few high-resolution images or video files and take into account the size of modern software applications, including the operating system itself, and it's little wonder that we run out of space sooner than we thought possible. This is when our thoughts turn to upgrading the hard disk.

When your hard disk falls behind the times, it's time to upgrade.

Short of disk space? An external hard drive provides hundreds of megabytes of extra capacity.

How to upgrade ...

There are essentially three upgrade options. First, you might install a secondary internal hard disk alongside your existing one. This is akin to building a warehouse in the car park, providing additional space without changing your current working environment. Alternatively, you might prefer to replace your existing hard disk. This has the virtue of neatness but the distinct disadvantages that you must also reinstall the operating system from scratch and somehow transfer all your existing files onto the new disk. Of course, if your original disk was to suddenly fail – a rare occurrence but always a possibility – this might be your only option (at which point, needless to say, the value of having a good, recent backup or, preferably, a disk image becomes all too apparent).

Finally, you might plump for an external hard disk. We look at the ups and downs of this approach in a moment.

... and how not to

If storage space is your only concern, do consider removable media before splashing out on a new disk. For instance, a DVD drive can help you permanently archive all your older files and thus lighten the load on the hard disk. A single DVD holds a minimum of 4.7GB so it's easy to salvage considerable space. An external drive is an even better bet, allowing you to move hundreds or even thousands of megabytes at a time.

As hard drives grow in capacity, you can store thousands or even millions of files on a single device.

What you need to know

The hard disk is a device used for storing data. For instance, when you save a letter in your word processor, it is recorded as data directly onto the magnetic surface of the hard disk. That file can then be retrieved, deleted, moved or simply re-saved at will. Crucially, the file doesn't disappear when the power is switched off. By contrast, if you don't save the letter, it is stored only in RAM, which is a kind of dynamic memory that changes all the time. If you lose power, files stored in RAM do get lost. It therefore pays to save your work to the hard disk frequently as you go along.

The hard disk drive is the mechanism that controls the disk, including the magnetic heads that do the hard work and the case in which it's all held. But since the disk and the drive are in practice inseparable, we'll just talk about disks.

So how do you go about choosing a new one?

Capacity Without question, size matters when it comes to hard disks. Modern disks comfortably top 300GB.

Speed #1 Not an obvious consideration, perhaps, but hard disks spin at different rates. You'll see rotational (or spindle) speeds of 5,400rpm, 7,200 rpm and 10,000rpm and it doesn't hurt to get the nimblest disk that you can afford. The faster the disk spins, the faster it can spit out data to your eagerly waiting computer.

Note, however, that it's never worth upgrading a hard disk for speed alone. We're talking about differences on the scale of milliseconds.

Speed #2 The speed that matters more involves something called direct memory access (DMA), a process whereby data moves from the hard disk into RAM without going through the processor. Look for ratings of 33, 66, 100 and even 133 megabytes per second. This is the measure of the drive's theoretical maximum data throughput. But even if the faster option is within budget, check the rating of the IDE/ATA interface on your motherboard. Installing a 100MB/sec disk on a 66MB/sec motherboard is a waste of time.

With SATA, the replacement for IDE, these speeds shoot up dramatically, starting at 150MB/sec.

Speed #3 Just to throw a spanner in the works, the truth is that DMA data throughput itself is rather misleading. What really matters is the *sustained* data transfer rate i.e. the speed at which the drive transfers data over a prolonged period of average activity, not just in frantic bursts. Naturally, you'll find this information hard to come by. Rather than relying upon manufacturers' data, look for independent tests and reviews in computer magazines and websites.

Drive size Internal hard disks are 3.5-inch drives. This is fine so long as you have a free 3.5-inch drive bay available – and you'll probably have to open up the case to find out – but otherwise you'll need a special mounting bracket to secure it in a 5.25-inch bay. Such a bracket may or may not come in the box, so check first.

Mounting brackets enable a 3.5 inch drive to use a 5.25 inch bay.

Check the specification carefully before buying a new hard disk.

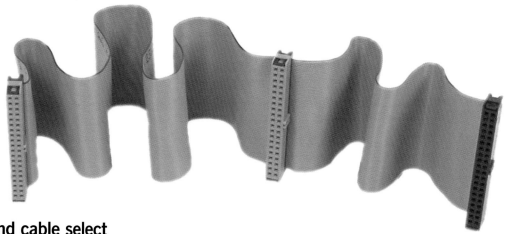

To install a second hard disk, you'll need a cable with three connectors.

Selecting cables ... and cable select

As we discuss in a moment, older hard disks connect to the motherboard by means of a flat ribbon IDE/ATA cable. Four important points here.

● Ribbon cables are not all the same, although you could be forgiven for thinking they would be. Certainly, any cable will fit any drive and motherboard. However, older cables have only 40 internal wires, or conductors, whereas newer cables have 80. For all new drives, an 80-wire cable is a must. The extra wires reduce signal interference.

● If you want to install a second hard disk alongside your existing disk, you'll need a cable with three connectors: one for the motherboard and one each for the drives. You may well find a suitable cable in the box when you buy a new drive but this isn't guaranteed.

● Note that the IDE/ATA ribbon cable is coloured pink or red along one edge. This corresponds to 'Pin 1' and is there to ensure that you connect the cable correctly. Always identify the Pin 1 position on both your drive and the motherboard socket before making a cable connection. It should be clearly marked but you may have to consult the manual.

● Where two drives share a socket (or channel, to be precise),

one must be designated the 'master' and one the 'slave'. This merely indicates the order in which Windows allocates drive letters to devices (for instance, C: to the master drive and D: to the slave). There are two ways to determine master or slave status. Hard drives have 'jumpers', little plastic sheaths that sit over an array of pins in a number of possible patterns. The pin arrangement tells the motherboard that a particular drive is the master or the slave on the channel. The trouble starts if you mistakenly configure both drives as the master or slave, in which case neither will work.

There is an easier way, however, and that's setting the jumpers to a third possible position called Cable Select. As the name suggest, the cable itself then decides which drive is which. It's a simple business: the drive connected to the far end of the cable – i.e. the opposite end to the motherboard – is automatically the master.

With SATA drives, you can ignore all of this. It's strictly one drive per channel and you don't need to worry about jumpers. Many hard drives come with both IDA and SATA sockets, giving you a choice. If your motherboard has SATA, that's the way to go.

From left to right we see: an older 40-wire IDE/ATA cable, an 80-wire version – essential for fast hard disks – and the new skinny Serial ATA cable.

RAID

RAID stands for Redundant Array of Independent Disks, which doesn't sound too promising. However, this is a method – or rather several methods – of combining multiple hard disks to best advantage.

At its simplest, when you install a new hard disk, be it internal or external, you gain some extra storage space. That's probably precisely what you wanted and you'll be happy to leave it at that. The new drive will show up in Windows with its own drive letter and you copy files to and from it with ease using Windows Explorer or any other file management program. You can also save files directly to the drive.

With RAID, though, you can go further. The two main techniques are called 'striping' and 'mirroring'. With striping, also called RAID level 0, you can treat two drives exactly as if they were a single device. For instance, if you have a 30GB hard disk and install a new 160GB upgrade, you can 'stripe' them to appear to Windows as a single 190GB drive. The sole advantage of this is faster performance, because data can be saved to and read from the separate disks simultaneously. This improves the overall sustained transfer rate (see Speed #3 on p54). The trouble is that if one disk fails, recovering data from the other may prove impossible. In other words, striping is high performance but high risk.

With mirroring, or RAID Level 1, all data saved to one drive is simultaneously copied to the second drive. This is thus a kind of instantaneous backup regime: if the primary disk should fail, you're guaranteed to have a copy of all lost files. On the other hand, the new drive won't offer any additional storage capacity.

It's possible to combine striping and mirroring for performance plus security, but this requires four drives. There are also several other RAID possibilities – Levels 2 through to 6 – that offer degrees of error correction and fault tolerance.

If any of this appeals, you'll need to buy a RAID adapter. This is an expansion card that provides additional hard disk interfaces (IDE/ATA or preferably SATA) and the hardware/software to run RAID successfully. Alternatively, many new motherboards come with RAID capability built in. Be sure to look for this at the time of purchase.

Interface face-off

When it comes to installing a new hard disk or, indeed, any other kind of drive, the first consideration is how to connect it to the rest of the computer system. What it needs is an interface of some description i.e. a gateway that enables the exchange of data between the drive and the rest of the PC through the motherboard; or a socket into which it can plug. There are, of course, several possibilities.

IDE/ATA (Integrated Drive Electronics/Advanced Technology Attachment) The most common interface for hard disk and CD drives, IDE/ATA hides under various nicknames (see Techie Corner opposite). Virtually all motherboards have one or two IDE/ATA interfaces (or host adapters) onboard, depending upon their age. In most cases, the hard disk is connected to one controller and the CD-ROM drive to the other, both by means of flat, wide ribbon-like cables. If you examine each ribbon, you may or may not find a spare connector somewhere along its length. This is because each IDE/ATA interface is a channel that can host two separate drives. This allows a total of four drives to be connected to the motherboard. If the ribbon in your PC does not have a spare connector, you'll need to replace it before installing an extra drive (see the Selecting cables section on p56).

The advantages of going down the IDE/ATA route are pretty compelling: your PC already has the requisite sockets in place, and the vast majority of drives come ready equipped to plug in and play with a minimum of fuss. However...

SCSI (Small Computer System Interface, but just call it 'scuzzy') SCSI is an alternative channel with one big benefit over IDE/ATA, namely that multiple devices can share a single adapter. So, instead of a maximum of four devices sharing two IDE/ATA channels, a SCSI-equipped PC can have 7 or 15 devices all daisy-chained together – or even more if it has a second SCSI adapter. What's more, SCSI drives can be considerably faster than their IDE/ATA counterparts.

But there are disadvantages. One is simply the cost: gigabyte for gigabyte, SCSI devices are more expensive to buy. The other is that motherboards do not generally come with a SCSI adapter onboard, which means that you have to fit one yourself before installing a SCSI device. This is as simple as fitting an expansion card, of which much more shortly, but it does use up a

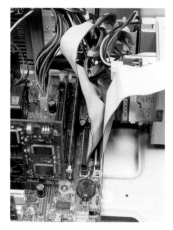

IDE adapters should be clearly marked on the motherboard. If not, they're easy enough to find.

If you already have four drives in your system – two hard disks, a CD and a DVD drive, say – you can add extra IDE/ATA interfaces with an expansion card.

A SCSI adapter expansion card adds a new dimension to your drive possibilities but it's far from essential in a domestic computer.

There is no channel sharing with Serial ATA: one drive per cable and socket.

This PCI expansion card has no less than four internal Serial ATA sockets.

free expansion slot and adds considerably to the cost (and hassle). Besides which, the difference in speed between a SCSI drive and an IDE/ATA drive is negligible in normal use, and it's really only servers that benefit from multiple device support. SCSI makes little practical sense for the average desktop system.

Serial ATA If you buy a new motherboard today, there's a good chance that it will have an alternative hard disk interface either alongside or as a replacement for traditional IDE/ATA channels. Enter Serial ATA, or SATA. This is, we are assured, the interface of the future, offering data throughput of 150MB per second. This betters the current and final leader in IDE/ATA technology, which peaks at 133MB/sec. The next version of SATA will hit 300MB/sec, followed by 600MB/sec, and possibly onwards and upwards from there.

Now this is all good stuff and much to be welcomed. However, the fact is that hard drives themselves are not yet sufficiently speedy to make the most of this new interface. Raw performance benefits are thus largely theoretical for now.

That said, if your motherboard currently has an IDE/ATA/33 or 66 interface (i.e. with a data throughput of only 33 or 66MB/sec, see the Speed #2 section on p54) and you intend to install a new hard disk, you might want to upgrade to SATA. This is easily achieved with a SATA expansion card. This gives you a couple of SATA sockets on a circuit board that slots into a spare PCI expansion slot on the motherboard. Even if you see no real-world benefits, you will at least have a SATA drive that could be reused in a future system. IDE/ATA drives may soon be obsolete and the motherboards of tomorrow will lack suitable sockets, so buying SATA now brings with it a spot of future-proofing.

On a point of interest, or at least note, the PCI socket itself has a maximum data throughput of 133MB/sec. This is slower than SATA's 150MB/sec throughput, so you wouldn't appreciate the full potential of the drive even if it could pump out bits and bytes at 150MB/sec. Which it can't. Again, see Speed #2.

There are two other advantages of SATA over IDE/ATA. First, the interface uses a much narrower cable than the flat, wide, ribbon-like IDE/ATA design. These cables are neater and easier to work with, and don't impede airflow inside the case to anything like the same extent. Secondly, because each SATA channel supports only a single drive, there is no need to daisy-chain drives on the same cable or worry about jumper settings.

TECHIE CORNER

IDE/ATA standards Just one IDE/ATA standard? That'll be the day! Here's a summary of the main specifications in the order in which they appeared. Forget what they mean, how they evolved and why they matter: when buying a new drive, just make sure you choose one that matches your motherboard's particular flavour of IDE/ATA support (time to check that manual again). Or check the stickers on your existing drives and buy like for like.

IDE	ATA-1
EIDE	Fast ATA-2
EIDE Ultra33	ATA/33
EIDE Ultra66	ATA/66
EIDE Ultra100	ATA/100
EIDE Ultra133	ATA/133
ATAPI	An IDE standard that supports devices other than hard disks, such as CD-ROM and DVD drives.

Oh, and ATA is sometimes called DMA (or UDMA) instead.

Internal versus external drives

You don't need to open up your PC or worry in the slightest about sockets if you opt for an external model.

An external hard drive is basically the same device as an internal model only housed in a case rather than installed in a drive bay. It needs to connect to the motherboard, of course, but your computer doesn't have any accessible IDE/ATA or SATA sockets on the outside of the case. Therefore, an external drive hooks up with the rest of the system through either a USB or a FireWire port (or, rarely, via an external SCSI interface but we won't worry about that here). External drives are thus only really an option if your computer has a USB 2.0 or FireWire interface, but we'll show you how to add this later.

External hard disks are portable, practical and probably not as pricey as you might imagine.

Pros and cons

External drives are always a little more expensive than their internal counterparts as you pay for a protective case, a button or two and perhaps a panel of blinking lights (for which read, external drives can be something of a rip-off). However, the advantages are truly considerable. An external drive is portable, which means you can use it at home and in the office and hook it up to just about any PC anywhere. Some are bulky as bricks but offer tremendous capacity, while others fit in your palm or pocket.

Because they simply plug into a port around the back of your PC, or perhaps into a USB hub, external drives save you the hassle of an installation routine (not that installing an internal drive is any great drama, as we will demonstrate). Most drives don't even require software drivers, so you can start using them immediately upon connection. You can also disconnect a drive at any time without having to reboot the computer. That's the joy of 'plug-and-play'.

It's always easier to find what's wrong with a device when you can see it (and give it a shake), especially if it has self-diagnostic measures built in. And it's much easier to take back to the shop if it's a DOA dud.

For large-scale backups, what could be easier? Indeed, it's perfectly possible to backup up your entire primary hard disk to an external device once a day (preferably overnight) and then carry it off for safe-keeping elsewhere. See pp26–9.

Some drives, particularly the smaller models, are bus powered. This means that they draw the current they need to operate from the USB or FireWire socket. This in turn means no need for power cables or plugs.

As for the disadvantages… well, you can't install Windows on an external hard disk and use it to run your computer (actually, in some situations, you can but not without difficulty and complications) so an external drive is no replacement for the primary, internal disk. They are also extremely nickable, prone to get left on trains and deeply attracted to coffee spillages.

External drives connect via USB (left) or FireWire (right). In terms of relative performance, they are more or less identical.

This mini-drive has a whopping 20GB capacity but is powered directly through the USB interface.

PART 3

ADDING A NEW DRIVE

Step-by-step hard disk upgrade

As we've mentioned, you can install a new internal hard disk either as a replacement for the old one, in which case you'll have to reinstall Windows, or as an ancillary drive, in which case you end up simply with more storage space.

Virtually all tower cases have space for a second hard disk but it pays to check before plunging ahead. Also, a second hard disk should be installed on the same IDE/ATA channel as the primary disk, which means that it must share the same ribbon cable. Check that the existing ribbon cable has a spare connector. If not, you'll need to get hold of a new one.

Installing a new hard disk is just the same as uninstalling an old one, although obviously in reverse. In the following example, we'll remove an existing disk in preparation for a replacement. To fit a secondary, additional disk, you would simply install it in a free drive bay and make the same power cable and ribbon cable connections, being sure to use the same ribbon cable as the primary disk and remembering to set the jumpers accordingly (see Step 6). If you're installing a SATA drive either as a replacement or an addition, connect it directly to a SATA socket on the motherboard.

This full-size tower case has no shortage of drive bays: three for 5.25-inch drives (typically CD and DVD drives) and no less than four for 3.5-inch drives. One of these is reserved for the floppy drive but that leaves plenty of scope for hard disk upgrades.

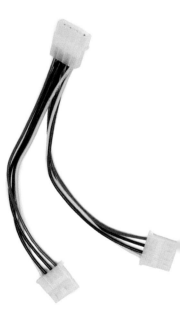

A splitter overcomes a shortage of power cables.

Before commencing any internal work on your PC, re-read the safety precautions on p33.

Make sure that you can access the drive bay. Sometimes this means removing a plastic cover on the front of the case. Also check how to secure the disk in place. Usually this is a simple case of inserting screws on either side of the bay, but occasionally a sliding rail mechanism is used instead. Begin by unplugging the four-wire power cable from the rear of the drive.

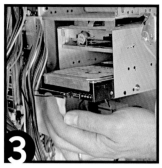

Now carefully remove the ribbon cable from the drive, leaving the other end connected to the motherboard.

Unscrew the drive from its bay...

And carefully remove the drive from the computer.

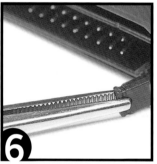

Now you need to set the jumpers on your new hard disk. This determines whether the device will be the master (or sole) device on this IDE/ATA channel, or the slave (see p56). If this is a replacement drive, it will certainly be the master; if it's a secondary drive sharing a ribbon cable with the existing drive, it will be the slave. Check the manual that came with the disk for instructions on how to set the jumpers appropriately. You may also find a jumper guide printed on the hard disk casing. Remember that you can also set the jumpers to the Cable Select position and let the cable sort out this master/slave nonsense.

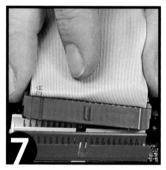

Slot the new hard disk into the vacant drive bay and reattach the power and ribbon cables i.e. reverse Steps 2–5. Be sure to match the Pin 1 stripe on the cable with Pin 1 on the drive. A secondary drive should be installed in a free drive bay close to and preferably beneath the existing drive (this makes it easier to attach the shared ribbon cable). Don't over-tighten the screws as they mustn't poke too deeply into the bowels of the drive. Also check that the ribbon cable is still securely attached to the primary IDE/ATA socket on the motherboard, or plug it in now if you're using a new cable.

PART

Formatting a new hard disk

Before you can use your new disk, you must partition and format it. The first procedure tells the computer how many separate 'chunks' of usable space there are on the physical disk – the norm would be one, unless you want to sub-divide the disk space – and the second determines which file system the operating system will use. A file system is 'simply' a means of organising data on the disk, and your choices are FAT32 (for Windows 98 and Me) and NTFS (for Windows 2000, XP and Vista).

Formatting with a Windows XP CD-ROM

In this example, we will assume that you've just installed a brand new hard disk as a replacement for an old disk. This means that you now have to install Windows before you can do anything else, which means formatting the new disk. The important thing is making sure that your computer can boot from the CD-ROM drive, which may require a BIOS tweak (see Appendix 1). Now place the XP CD-ROM in the drive and start the computer. The routine is very similar with Windows Vista.

Enter

The Windows Setup program should launch immediately and beaver away on its own for a few minutes in preparation. Eventually, you'll be asked what you want to do. Just press Enter to proceed.

F8

Enter

Hit F8 to agree to the license terms. If you're using an upgrade rather a full version CD-ROM, you'll have to prove your entitlement at this point. All you have to do is remove the Windows XP CD, place your old Windows disc in the drive, and press Enter.

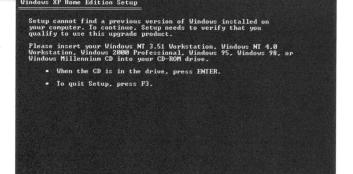

3

 Enter

The Setup program now identifies the new disk and invites you to install Windows. Press Enter to continue.

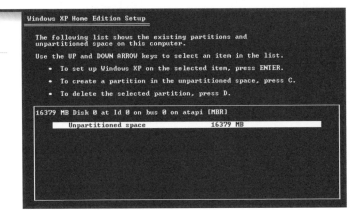

4

 Enter

Here you can choose which file system to format the drive with. The default – NTFS – is best for Windows XP, so hit Enter. You could choose to select the 'Quick' option but this bypasses an important check on the disk's physical integrity so we wouldn't recommend it.

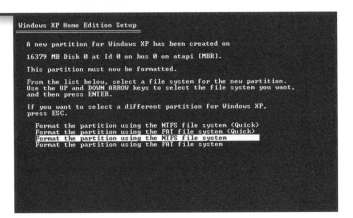

5

You'll be prompted to replace your Windows XP CD-ROM now if you had to remove it in Step 2. When the formatting is complete, the setup routine continues and Windows is installed.

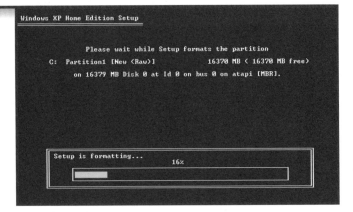

Formatting from within Windows

Let's say you've installed a secondary hard disk in order to increase storage space. In this case, you can format the device from within Windows. Simply open My Computer and look for the new drive letter (probably D: drive). Right-click it and select Format from the menu.

PART

Partitioning a hard disk

When you have a large hard disk at your disposal, it can be advantageous, although admittedly counter-intuitive, to sub-divide it. This is called partitioning. Essentially, to partition a hard disk is to split it into two or more independent sections that the computer treats like physically distinct disks. Each partition has its own drive letter, and each can hold data or an operating system.

Why partition?

There are three main reasons to partition a hard disk. The first is to install Windows on one partition and everything else – all your software and data – on another partition. The advantage is two-fold: a problem with Windows shouldn't affect anything else and can be treated in isolation; and keeping Windows on its own partition should (and we stress should) keep it running smoothly for longer. That said, it's a geeky and sometimes problematic thing to do (problematic because some software won't install properly on anything but the Windows partition) and we can't honestly recommend it.

The second reason is to aid your backup regime, particularly if you use a disk imaging tool. If you keep all of your important files and folders (or games) on a discrete partition, you can back this up quickly and in a single hit using Acronis True Image or similar. This is easier than backing up the entire computer, including Windows, every time.

A third reason is to run two (or more) operating systems on the same physical hard disk.

To partition a hard drive, you'll need a third party utility such as Partition Magic from Symantec (**www.symantec.com/partitionmagic**).

This computer actually has four hard drives but you can see that Disk 2 has been partitioned.

The same computer seen through the eyes of Windows. Now there are effectively five hard disks. Drive letters G and H relate to the partitioned Disk 2.

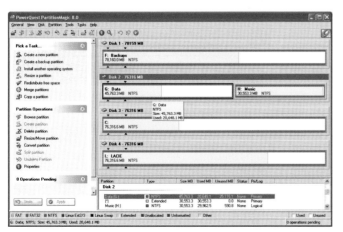

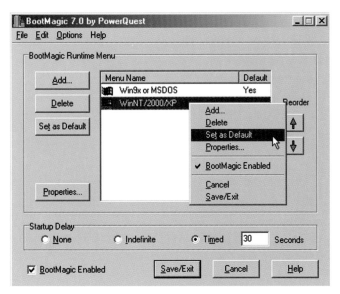

A boot manager lets you swap between operating systems.

Make life easy with a partitioning utility.

What you need to know

The language of partitioning is dense and confusing, and it seems that every possible action is subject to dozens of qualifiers. While utilities such as Partition Magic provide wizards to simplify common tasks, it is still advisable to understand the basic principles and terminology. Here is a very potted guide to the basics.

Master Boot Record A vital file that tells your computer where on the hard disk to find the operating system. Without this record, it would be unable to start, or boot. The MBR also includes details of any disk partitions.

Boot manager A program that lets you swap between partitions in order to run multiple operating systems on one computer. A good boot manager kicks in every time you restart and offers a choice; less flexible versions must be configured from within Windows before closing down. Windows XP and Vista have their own built-in boot utilities.

File system The File Allocation Table, or FAT, is a record of every file's location on the hard disk. This in turn depends upon the rules of the file system. As disks have grown in size, file systems have adapted and improved, and newer operating systems are designed to take advantage of these developments. The main file systems for Windows are as follows:

File system	Appropriate for
FAT	Windows 95a
FAT32	Windows 95b; Windows 98; Windows Millennium Edition; Windows 2000; Windows XP
NTFS	Windows 2000 (recommended); Windows XP (recommended); Windows Vista (essential)

You choose which file system to use whenever you create a new partition. Note that Windows 98 and Me cannot 'see' NTFS partitions, whereas Windows 2000, XP and Vista are backwards-compatible with FAT32.

Partition types Ancient computer wisdom decreed that a hard disk may have a maximum of four partitions. These are called the 'primary' partitions, and you can install a separate operating system on each. However, it's possible to cheat by turning a primary into an 'extended' partition, which may then be split into several 'logical' partitions. The really important point is that only primary partitions are bootable, so logical partitions are suitable for files and applications but not operating systems.

ADDING A NEW DRIVE

Dual-booting

When you have two or more hard disks or disk partitions, you can run two or more operating systems on your computer. This is the perfect way to try out an alternative to Windows, such as Linux, or to experiment with a new version of Windows. You might be thinking about upgrading to Windows Vista but you're unsure whether it's really for you. After all, lots of old software doesn't run under Windows Vista, and some older hardware won't work either. No problem: in a dual-boot environment, you can run Vista for everyday use and switch to XP whenever you need play an old PC game or use an old printer or whatever.

It's possible to dual- or multi-boot in many configurations but the easiest and, we think, the most profitable route is letting Windows itself make decisions during installation. To get started, you'll need to create a new logical disk partition of at least 15GB (but preferably considerably larger), as described in the previous section. Alternatively, you can use a secondary internal IDE/ATA or Serial ATA hard disk.

We'll look at two scenarios: here, upgrading to Windows XP from Windows 98 or Me; and later (see Part Nine) upgrading to Windows Vista or Windows 7 from Windows XP. But first a word about activation.

Windows Activation

Windows XP and Vista will only run for a certain time before you have to 'activate' your copy with Microsoft. This can usually be done over the internet, or failing that by phone. However, we strongly advise you against activating Windows when you first install it, particularly in a dual-boot scenario. You might decide after all that you want to replace your current version of Windows, in which case you would perform an over-the-top upgrade (simply installing your new version of Windows over the current version). You may decide that you don't like the new version, or perhaps too much of your hardware or software is incompatible with it. Or you may decide that you'd rather install your copy of Windows on a different computer. The point is that under normal circumstances you can only activate a copy of Windows XP or Vista once, so make sure that you are happy with it before taking this step.

There's no escaping 'activation' but you don't have to rush into it.

Upgrading to Windows XP (dual-boot)

When you install Windows XP in a clean partition, you get the chance to find out whether your current hardware and software works with the new operating system. Because what you end up with is a clean version of Windows, you will of course have to reinstall all your programs and probably download new drivers for your printer, scanner and other peripherals. If everything goes smoothly, you may decide to import your files, folders and settings from the earlier version of Windows and make this your primary or sole working environment. This is simple: use the

Windows XP CD-ROM to run the Files and Settings Transfer Wizard on the old version of Windows, and save the resulting file. You should be able to save it directly onto the new partition (probably D: drive). Now run the wizard again from within Windows XP – you'll find it on the Start menu under All Programs > Accessories > System Tools – and point to the saved file. Your files and program settings will be transferred to Windows XP.

Alternatively, and probably simpler, just install Windows XP over your old version of Windows. This will automatically preserve your files and settings.

New Installation (Advanced)

Next

The setup program will assume that you want to upgrade your current version of Windows. This is not what you want to do in this scenario; rather, you want to install Windows XP alongside Windows 98. Select New Installation from the Welcome to Windows Setup menu.

Advanced Options

I want to choose the install drive letter and partition during Setup

OK

Here, it is essential that you enter the Advanced Options dialogue and tick the box that lets you choose where Windows should be installed. Setup will now ask you a few questions about where you live and which language you want to use.

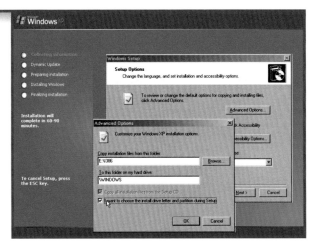

Select new partition or new hard disk

Enter

When you see this menu, select the new partition or disk. It will almost certainly be labelled D: unless you have several partitions/hard disk in your system (in which case be sure to choose the correct one). The point is that you don't want to install Windows on the current C: partition, as this would overwrite and wipe out your current version of Windows.

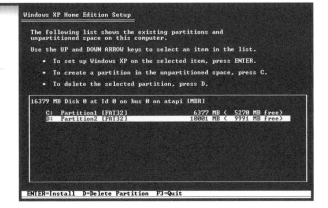

Format the partition using the NTFS file system

 Enter

You'll now be presented with the format options that we saw on p64. Again, use the arrow keys to scroll down to the NTFS option. Setup will now complete the installation of Windows on the new partition or disk.

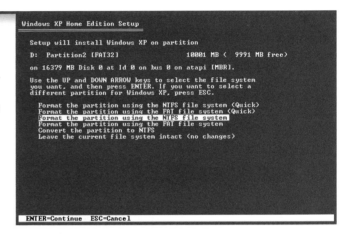

```
Windows XP Home Edition Setup

Setup will install Windows XP on partition

D:  Partition2 [FAT32]            10001 MB ( 9991 MB free)

on 16379 MB Disk 0 at Id 0 on bus 0 on atapi [MBR].

Use the UP and DOWN ARROW keys to select the file system
you want, and then press ENTER. If you want to select a
different partition for Windows XP, press ESC.

    Format the partition using the NTFS file system (Quick)
    Format the partition using the FAT file system (Quick)
    Format the partition using the NTFS file system
    Format the partition using the FAT file system
    Convert the partition to NTFS
    Leave the current file system intact (no changes)


ENTER=Continue  ESC=Cancel
```

 Windows XP

When, finally, the computer restarts, you will see the multi-boot menu. Indeed, you will see this every time you restart in the future. You can now choose which version of Windows you wish to work with. Note that the new Windows XP installation is designated the default, which means it will start automatically after 30 seconds unless you make a manual choice. If you prefer that your old version of Windows is the default...

```
Please select the operating system to start:

    Microsoft Windows XP Home Edition
    Microsoft Windows

Use the up and down arrow keys to move the highlight to your choice.
Press ENTER to choose.
Seconds until highlighted choice will be started automatically: 23




For troubleshooting and advanced startup options for Windows, press F8.
```

Start

Control Panel

Performance and Maintenance

System

Advanced Settings

 'Microsoft Windows'

OK

From within Windows XP, run through these steps to take control of the multi-boot menu. Here we are changing the default away from the new Windows XP installation. From now on, if left alone, the computer will eventually load the earlier version of Windows upon every restart. To start Windows XP instead, you simply have to select it from the multi-boot menu.

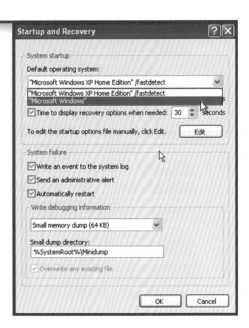

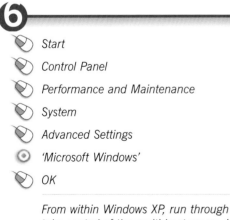

PART

Upgrading your CD drive to a DVD drive

The humble floppy disk is extinct and it looks like the CD drive is following suit: if you look through the optical storage section of any online computer shop you'll see lots of DVD drives but precious few CD drives. For example, at the time of writing, Dabs.com sells 177 optical drives, only two of which are CD drives.

So is the CD dead? Far from it: the rise of digital music means we're burning CDs like never before. We're just not using CD drives to do it. The reason is DVD. You can pick up a decent DVD drive for around £20. In addition to DVD playback and DVD disc burning, it will happily read and create CDs. If you're considering putting a CD drive into your PC, we'd strongly recommend that you go for a DVD drive instead.

DVD versus CD

The key difference between a CD and a DVD is storage space. A standard CD can store 700MB of data, which is 0.7 of a gigabyte, but a single-sided DVD can store more than 4GB. If it's a dual-layer disc, that figure doubles to a whopping eight and a half gigabytes, which is the equivalent of nearly 12 CDs. In many cases, a single DVD disc is big enough to store your entire photo, music or home video collection.

That extra storage space is good news for software companies. Windows takes a couple of gigabytes of storage space, so it won't

Modern DVD drives don't just play DVDs: they can record onto DVD and CD discs too, so you can use DVD for backup and make your own music compilation CDs.

fit on a single CD any more – but it will fit on a single DVD. Fewer discs means less packaging and lower manufacturing costs, so it's hardly surprising that almost all big software – Windows, Office and other similarly hefty programs – comes on DVD these days.

And then there are movies. As you might expect, a DVD player will play DVD movie discs. With modern PCs packing increasingly powerful graphics cards and sound cards, this means even the humblest PC can be an impressive home entertainment system.

DVD, Blu-Ray and HD-DVD

In the previous edition of this manual, we said that 'two new kinds of disc hope to replace DVD in everything from PCs to video players: Blu-Ray and HD-DVD'. We weren't impressed, predicting that 'one format will thrive and the other one fail. Unfortunately, nobody knows which one will be the winner, so … we'd suggest sitting this one out until a victor emerges.' We were right: HD-DVD has gone to the great technology graveyard in the sky, leaving Blu-Ray as the only DVD replacement around. So what is it and should you care?

Blu-Ray is a more advanced kind of DVD, which uses a blue laser instead of the red laser you'll find in a DVD player. Blue lasers have shorter wavelengths than red ones, and that means you can cram data much more tightly into a Blu-Ray disc than a DVD. The result is massively increased storage, with a Blu-Ray disc packing between 25GB and 50GB of data into a single disc. The film industry has been quick to take advantage of this, with Blu-Ray movie discs offering extremely high-quality pictures and sound together with extra features.

On the face of it, choosing Blu-Ray over DVD for your PC is a no-brainer due to the massively increased storage space. However, DVD drives and blank DVD discs are so ridiculously cheap right now that there's no really compelling reason to go for the newer, more expensive Blu-Ray format. It's a similar situation in the living room: while Blu-Ray offers better picture quality than DVD, you need to have an enormous television to notice any difference — and the films cost significantly more than they do on DVD.

You're probably wondering whether there's yet another technology poised to make Blu-Ray redundant. The answer, surprisingly, is no. While various technology firms are tinkering with various forms of storage, it's widely believed that Blu-Ray won't be replaced any time soon. Now that broadband internet is so common, digital distribution is taking over: instead of discs, we'll get almost everything via downloads. In 2005, Microsoft founder Bill Gates predicted that Blu-Ray is 'the last physical format there will ever be.'

TECHIE CORNER

Optical media Broadly speaking, there are two methods of storing data long-term on a computer: magnetic media, as in the hard and floppy disks; and optical media, as in a compact disc (recordable or otherwise). Optical in this context means that a laser reads light patterns reflected by the disc. In a recordable drive, the laser writes data to the disc by 'burning' pits in a malleable layer. This is quite a different process to that used in industry, where compact discs are pressed rather than burned, but the effect is much the same. Incidentally, as a rule (and a perfectly silly one at that) the term disc is generally used when referring to optical media like CDs and disk when referring to magnetic media. That's the convention we're following here. For more on CD technology, start here:
www.cdrfaq.org
www.pcguide.com/ref/cd

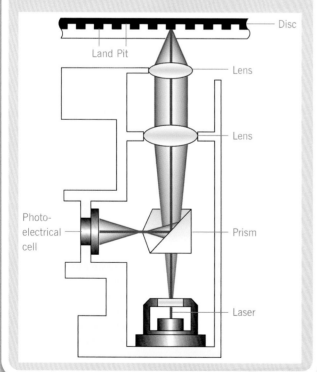

DVD drives: what you need to know

DVD drives are wonderful things. They can read data and music CDs, video and data DVDs, and many of them can create CDs and DVDs too. Inevitably, though, finding the best drive for you means wading through a little bit of alphabet soup. These are the most common kinds of DVD drives you'll find on sale:

DVD/CD-RW Also known as 'combo' drives, DVD/CD-RW drives can play DVDs and can read and write CDs — but they can't create DVDs of any kind.

DVD-RW These drives do everything DVD/CD-RW drives can do, but they can burn DVDs as well. Unfortunately this is where the alphabet soup gets particularly thick, as there are three main kinds of recordable DVD: DVD-R, DVD-RW and DVD-RAM.

DVD-R and DVD-RW are the same as CD-R and CD-RW: the R means recordable and the RW means rewritable. Recordable discs can only be written to once, but rewritable ones can be written to again and again. DVD-RAM is essentially the same as DVD-RW but uses a different format.

Last but not least there's another acronym to think about: DL. This stands for 'dual layer' and it means that the drive can use the extra storage capacity of dual-layer DVDs.

With us so far? Just to make things that little bit less

Virtually all DVD drives support virtually all DVD formats — but do be sure to buy compatible blank discs.

An external CD or DVD drive is basically an internal drive in a tough case with a USB or FireWire connection.

comprehensible, there are also different versions of each standard we've discussed, so a DVD-R disc isn't the same thing as a DVD+R disc. Thankfully most drives are designed in such a way that you don't need to worry about this, as they support both the plus and minus versions. That's why you'll see drives described with strings of letters such as DVD+/-R/RW/RAM/DL. Isn't technology wonderful?

Internal drives, external drives and interfaces

It's perfectly possible to put a DVD drive next to your existing CD drive, but we wouldn't bother: as DVD drives play and record CDs, there's no reason to keep your old CD drive — especially when the new one will probably be much faster and much quieter — unless you're planning to copy an awful lot of CDs. If you're simply replacing an existing drive, look for one that uses the same interface. For example, if your CD drive uses an IDE interface, look for an internal DVD drive with an IDE interface. If you're adding a drive to a new PC and the motherboard supports Serial ATA (SATA), go for a SATA one. It's faster and much less fiddly to install.

In addition to internal DVD drives, you'll see plenty of external drives advertised. In most cases internal drives are a better bet — they're cheaper and faster — but if you want to add DVD to a CD-packing laptop, an external USB drive is considerably cheaper than replacing a laptop's existing drive.

Step-by-step CD/DVD drive upgrade

Installing an optical drive is easy and it makes no difference whether it's ROM or RW, or CD or DVD. The key things are remembering to set the drive jumpers – when two devices share an IDE/ATA channel and ribbon cable, one must be the master and one the slave – and connecting the cables correctly. There is also the slightly fiddly business of running an audio cable between the drive and the sound card.

In actual fact, most modern CD and DVD drives can dispense with this cable and send an audio signal through the IDE/ATA cable. Look for 'Digital Audio Extraction' support in the spec. Even if it's not mentioned, there's every chance that your new drive will play audio just fine without a direct connection to the sound card.

However, it does no harm to use an audio cable if one is supplied. Most drives have two output sockets – digital and analogue – and which you use depends upon which type of input your sound card has (or motherboard, if the audio is integrated and you don't have a sound card). If you have neither a sound card nor a motherboard with an integrated audio chip, perhaps now would be a good time to skip ahead to the sound card section!

We'll proceed here on the basis of replacing one drive with another. If you are adding a second drive, simply snap off, prise off, unclip or unscrew the nearest drive bay cover to gain access to a free 5.25-inch drive bay. Also check that the old drive's ribbon cable has a spare connector within reach, or replace it if not.

Before commencing any internal work on your PC, re-read the safety precautions on p33.

First, disconnect the existing drive. Unplug the power cable, the ribbon cable (but leave this connected to the motherboard) and, if present, the audio cable that runs to the sound card or a socket on the motherboard.

Drives are usually secured in the bay with four short screws. Remove these now to free the device and slide it out of the case.

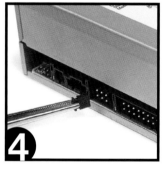

Before installing the new drive, check the jumper settings. If this is to be only drive on the secondary IDE/ATA channel (the hard disk should be connected to the primary IDE/ATA channel), it should be set to master. However, if this drive will share a channel and cable with an existing drive, it should be the slave. Again, you can use Cable Select positions if, and only if, you are using an 80-core IDE/ATA cable (see p56). Check the documentation that came with the drive if it's not clear how to set the jumpers.

5

Slide the new drive into the bay and secure it in place with the screws you removed earlier. Be sure that the fascia is flush with the front of the case.

6

Here we see the internal connections that must be made to the rear end of the drive. From left to right: audio cable, to connect to the sound card or motherboard socket; ribbon cable, to connect to the secondary IDE/ATA channel on the motherboard (note the striped edge that designates the Pin 1 position); and power cable.

7

Here, the audio cable is being connected to the CD input on the sound card...

8

And here we are plugging it into an audio input on the motherboard. You will do one or the other, depending on whether your computer has a sound card. If it does – and even if the motherboard also has an integrated audio chip – you will take the sound card route.

9

In this example, we can see two optical drives installed in neighbouring drive bays. Note the shared ribbon cable. This connects to the secondary IDE/ATA channel on the motherboard. Once again, we must stress that optical drives and hard disks should be connected to different channels.

TROUBLE-SHOOTER

Your new drive should 'just work' when you restart Windows. However, it will probably have come with some application software, including a CD or DVD recording program, and you should install this immediately.

● If your new drive refuses to play an audio CD – and your old one worked just fine – check that the internal audio cable is correctly connected. It's a fiddly little thing that can easily be missed. See Steps 7 and 8.

● If repeated buffer under-run threatens your sanity and you

have more coasters than cups, try getting the drive to record at less than its top speed. This usually solves the problem. Also leave the PC well alone while it's busy recording. Doing anything else at the same time drains memory and increases the likelihood of under-run.

● In Windows XP, check that the drive has been enabled for recording. Open My Computer, right-click the drive icon and select Properties. In the Recording tab, check the box labelled 'Enable CD recording on this drive'.

PART 4 Expansion cards

After decades of hardware evolution, today's PC has emerged with a plethora of different standards and interfaces, counter-intuitive design standards and an acronym soup of a language that purports to make 'sense' of it all. But not to worry: upgrading an expansion card remains one of the most effective ways to revamp a crusty old computer. It's easy when you know how – so let's go find out.

PART 4 A word about architecture

Today's motherboards continue to combine historical standards with the latest and fastest interfaces, but ISA is now virtually extinct.

As we have seen, the motherboard is the central component in your PC system, so much so that everything else connects to it one way or another. An interface is simply a gateway through which any two components or devices can 'talk' to each other. We've looked already at how internal drives use the IDE/ATA interface, talked about slots and sockets for processors, and plugged extra memory straight into the motherboard. Now let's turn to expansion cards.

Get slotted

Expansion slots are connectors on a motherboard used for attaching printed circuit boards (cards). The beauty of such a system is that you can immeasurably improve the performance of your computer without wielding a soldering iron. There are three main expansion slot standards (in order of age):

ISA (Industry Standard Architecture). ISA slots are black, long, slow and all but obsolete. You're most likely to find a modem in one. Or dust. You may have a couple inside your case but certainly won't find them on new motherboards.

PCI (Peripheral Component Interconnect). The PCI standard is faster than ISA and its slots (white, short) typically host sound cards, older graphics cards and perhaps a TV tuner. A USB or SCSI card can also be bolted on through the PCI interface to give a computer still more interface options. Three slots is an acceptable minimum, four better, and more are always welcome.

There's now a new flavour of PCI known as PCI Express (PCIe). This is available in several speeds.

AGP (Accelerated Graphics Port). This is a slot designed exclusively for modern graphics cards, specifically optimised for 3-dimensional effects and digital video. There is only ever one AGP slot per motherboard, and you'll only find it on Pentium II systems and above. However, a modern machine is no cast-iron guarantee of an AGP slot as some motherboards incorporate the necessary graphics chips directly within the motherboard itself. As with old PCI slots, AGP is now heading towards obsolescence thanks to PCIe.

Blank check

Expansion slots are positioned on the motherboard in such a way that one end of an installed card pokes through a slot in a panel around the back of the PC. These slots are usually covered with blanking plates but these can be easily removed. One factor to watch is that it's not uncommon for adjacent PCI and ISA slots to share a blanking plate, with the implication that you can install one or the other type of card but not both simultaneously.

Integration

We mentioned earlier that some motherboards incorporate more features than others within their own circuitry. For instance, a motherboard may or may not come with built-in audio, graphics and network controllers, which negate the need for a sound card, graphics card and network card respectively. The main attraction of this approach is price: it's cheaper to build and sell a PC with a bells and whistles motherboard than one bristling with add-on expansion cards. Because such motherboards don't require the same number of expansion slots, it's also possible to make motherboards – and thus computer cases – significantly smaller.

However, there are downsides. With fewer expansion slots, it's not always easy to add extra features. If you want to turn your PC into a television and digital video recorder, for instance, you would want to install a TV tuner i.e. a PCI-style expansion card that can pick up and record broadcast television signals. But what if your system doesn't have a free PCI slot? Your only option would be an external tuner that connects to the computer through a USB port. That's fine, but it involves an extra power supply and plug socket and will cost you more than an internal version.

There's also a concern about hardware failure. If an integrated graphics chip were to fail, how would you fare? Well, if the motherboard had a vacant AGP slot, you could simply install a replacement graphics card – and if it didn't, you'd be up the proverbial gum tree. The only way to restore pictures on your monitor screen would be to opt for a less adept PCI graphics card or to replace the motherboard.

Let's now look in some detail at three popular and worthwhile expansion card upgrades.

Blanking plates can be removed to open up access to expansion slots.

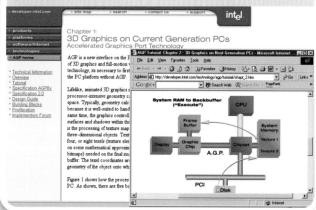

Integrated circuitry is convenient but the lack of expansion slots can make future upgrades tricky.

PART ④ Upgrading your graphics card

As PCs become a central part of our lives, we're using them for all kinds of interesting things: editing digital photos or digital videos, watching DVDs and, of course, playing games. However, each of these places serious demands on your PC's graphics hardware, and underpowered graphics cards can struggle to cope. If that's the case with your PC, a new graphics card can be a good investment.

One word of warning, though: if you want to play games on your PC and it currently struggles with solitaire, upgrading can be

The screenshot above shows two open windows at a resolution of 1,024 x 768 pixels; the one below shows the same windows but the resolution has been dropped to 800 x 600. Everything gets bigger, which is good for the eyes, but there's less room on screen for multiple windows.

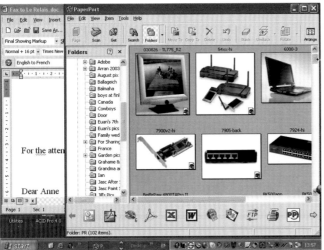

extremely expensive. High-end graphics cards cost as much as some computers and, in the case of older PCs, the rest of your system may be underpowered too. If you don't already have a fast processor and lots of RAM, a games console such as the Xbox 360 will be a smarter – and much, much cheaper – bet.

That said, the popularity of computer games has been responsible for some incredible advances in graphics technology, and many current cards are more powerful than PC processors were just a few years ago – which means they're great not just for games, but for anything that involves putting things on your screen. The influence of games has percolated into every aspect of computing, so for example Windows Vista uses the 3D power of graphics cards to deliver its ultra-shiny animated interface.

Resolving resolution Your PC's graphics card and monitor are inextricably entwined. The graphics card (or video card, as it's sometimes called) generates the picture and the monitor displays it, and you'll get the best results if the monitor and card are getting the best from one another.

For example, let's look at resolution, which describes how much detail appears on screen. Resolution is described in pixels, which are the individual dots of light that make up the on-screen picture. A resolution of 800 x 600, known as SVGA (Super Video Graphics Array) gives you 600 rows of 800 pixels, so the entire screen consists of 480,000 pixels. The higher the resolution the more dots, so 1,280 x 1,024 delivers 1,310,720 pixels. The more dots, the more you can squeeze onto the screen without losing detail. It's exactly the same as with digital cameras: the more pixels, the better.

The higher the on-screen resolution, the more you can cram into it. At 800 x 600 you can only really view one program or window at once, but at 1,280 x 1,024 it's quite possible to see several programs simultaneously – so for example as we write this, we're running at 1,280 x 1,024 and our screen shows our word processor, our email inbox and some little windows such as our clock, calendar and weather forecast.

So what does this have to do with graphics cards and monitors? You'll find that while graphics cards usually support a wide range of screen resolutions, there are physical limits to what a monitor can display. There's no point trying to run a 1,280 x 1,024 resolution on a 15-inch screen because even if it can display such a high resolution – which is unlikely – the on-screen text will be so small you'd need a microscope to read it. Conversely, a big monitor can be a bad investment if your graphics card isn't up to the job, so if your graphics card only supports resolutions of up to 800 x 600 there isn't much point in buying a 21-inch monitor that's designed to display at 1,600 x 1,200.

As a rule of thumb, if you've got a 15-inch display and don't fancy changing it then a basic graphics card that supports up to 1,024 x 7,68 is all you really need; but if you want to buy a big screen then you'll need a suitably hefty graphics card to go with it.

Here are the recommended optimum display settings

*Screen size **15 inch***
*Resolution **800 x 600***

*Screen size **17 inch***
*Resolution **1,024 x 768***

*Screen size **19 inch***
*Resolution **1,280 x 1,024***

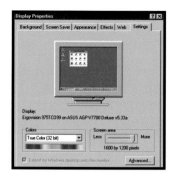

*Screen size **21 inch***
*Resolution **1,600 x 1,200***

What you need to know

Graphics cards are plagued with technical specifications and you need to understand at least the basics in order to make an informed purchase.

Interface Graphics cards plug into a slot on your PC's motherboard and, as we discovered earlier, your PC probably has either a PCI or an AGP slot. AGP is the better of the two, but you can't put an AGP card in a PCI slot or vice versa. If your PC came with a PCI graphics card, it's very unlikely that you'll also have a spare AGP slot – so if you want to use an AGP graphics card, you'll need to shell out for a new motherboard. Alternatively you could just buy a really good PCI card and save yourself a lot of effort!

Not all PCs include a graphics card or, at least, one that you'd recognise. Many use a technology called 'integrated graphics', which means the graphics are handled by a chip that's part of the PC's motherboard. Such technology is great for everyday PC work but it can run out of steam if you put serious demands on your system's graphics hardware, such as playing games. The good news is that many machines with integrated graphics systems also have a spare AGP slot; if you install a new graphics card in that slot, it automatically overrides the integrated graphics chip. The bad news is that older machines with integrated graphics might not have a spare slot. Upgrading your graphics would mean a new motherboard.

Some recent PCs include a third kind of interface: PCI Express. PCI Express offers even better performance than AGP and, in the very near future, most high-end graphics cards will use it rather than AGP. PCI Express also enables a technology called SLI (Scalable Link Interface) that enables two PCI Express graphics cards to work in tandem, provided of course your motherboard has two PCI Express slots. With SLI you can run up to four monitors at once, or use the two cards to power a single display for incredible gaming performance. It's impressive stuff, although such power is overkill for systems that don't also have extremely fast processors and lots of RAM.

For most graphics card upgrades you'd simply swap one AGP or PCI card for another of the same type. But even here, there can

Today's graphics cards use the AGP slot and come with their own memory chips.

be problems. The AGP interface is available in several versions that run at progressively faster speeds and so handle more data per second. These include AGP 2x, 4x and 8x. If your motherboard has a first or second generation AGP slot – AGP 1x or 2x – then installing an 8x-speed card would be a waste of time.

Furthermore, older AGP slots run at 3.3 volts whereas 4x and 8x slots run at 1.5 volts. The upshot is that you can't install a new card in an old motherboard and expect it to work. In fact, it *should* be impossible to do this – 1.5V cards have a differently keyed connecting edge designed to prevent erroneous installation in a 3.3V slot – but it's still well worth checking compatibility before you go shopping.

Power Before considering a graphics card upgrade, it's really important to make sure your PC's power supply is up to the job. That applies to all graphics upgrades, but it's particularly important if your system currently uses integrated graphics. Integrated chips use tiny amounts of power, but some high-end graphics cards are incredibly demanding. Always check the specifications to see how much power your potential purchase needs and make sure your PC can handle it!

Memory Graphics cards come with their own slice of memory onboard. How much dictates just what it can do and how quickly. Memory also determines how many colours the card can display. If you right-click on the Windows Desktop, select Properties and click on the Settings tab, you'll see your current card's colour depth setting. If you now try to increase the setting – say, from 256 to 16-bit – you may find that the resolution slider automatically adjusts to a lower setting. This is because cards can typically pump out a full colour range at a low resolution or a high resolution in fewer colours, but not both simultaneously.

Memory matters. The minimum a modern graphics card offers, typically 4MB, will get you to 1,280 x 1,024 resolution in 24-bit colour, and that is just fine for business work on Windows XP. However, for Windows Vista or gaming you'll need considerably more: Microsoft recommends a minimum of 128MB graphics memory for Windows Vista Premium and, as ever, it's worth taking the minimum requirement and at least doubling it.

TROUBLE-SHOOTER

Never upgrade a graphics card and a monitor simultaneously. From a diagnostic point of view, you only want to work with one suspect device at a time. If Windows will only start in safe mode, the card's refresh rate is probably set too high for the monitor. Lower the setting in Display Properties. Click Start, Control Panel and Display, and look in the Adapter tab. Your monitor probably has its own display settings, usually accessible through buttons on its casing, and you may wish to adjust the brightness or contrast to optimise the display. You can also adjust the image size to suit the viewable screen area.

A cooling fan is de rigueur for a fast graphics card.

Processor Yes, graphics cards also have processors. As you would expect, the faster the processor, the better the card is at rendering complex graphics. Look for the term 'graphics accelerator' or, for the ultimate hardware high, a GPU (Graphics Processing Unit). Add-on cooling fans are now commonplace and something of a necessary evil: we've seen, or rather heard, powerful graphics cards that display the most fantastic 3-D effects at high resolutions but sound like jet skis.

Dimensions In ye olden days, graphics cards were two-dimensional affairs, perfectly adequate for 'flat page' office-style work but hopeless for playing games or displaying digital video. Then along came 3-D graphics cards that sat in a slot alongside the existing 2-D model and kicked in when intensive video rendering was called for. This was clearly a daft set of affairs and so, in time, evolved the next generation of cards that combined 2- and 3-D functions. Badly. Some time thereafter, good combination cards emerged, and that's where we are today. Incidentally, 3-D isn't really three-dimensional; it's just clever trickery that adds the illusion of depth to video presentations.

VGA vs DVI The very latest monitors are digital whereas the monitor currently sitting on your desk is almost certainly analogue. What happens is that your computer produces a digital signal, and the graphics card converts it to analogue before sending it to the monitor. This is a tad silly because it inevitably involves some image degradation, but an analogue monitor has no way of processing raw digital data. However, a digital monitor can do just this. The computer's digital images are pumped directly to the monitor in their original format and the graphics card need no longer perform an analogue to digital conversion. Look for an interface called DVI (Digital Visual Interface) on the graphics card. This may co-exist with an analogue VGA (Video Graphics Array) output or it may be the only socket on the card.

You can convert a DVI output to an analogue output with a simple adapter so a digital graphics card is a good buy even if

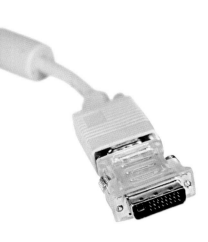

A simple adapter lets you connect an old analogue monitor to a new digital graphics card.

Here, the computer is connected to a TV set via an S-video TV-out connection. The red and white plugs are simultaneously feeding audio from the computer's sound card to the TV's built-in speakers.

you keep an analogue monitor for now. You never know when you'll need to replace it and your next model will probably be digital.

Ins and outs As well as feeding computer-generated images to a monitor, a graphics card may have other uses. Chief of these is probably a TV-out socket that lets you connect the computer to a TV instead of, or as well as, to a monitor. If your PC has a DVD drive, for instance, or if you have saved some of your own digital video footage on the hard drive, you could hook it up to the telly and enjoy the movies on the big screen.

The two common interfaces here are S-video and composite video (see Appendix 2). It obviously helps if your TV and graphics card share the same type of interface – i.e. they both have S-video sockets or they both have composite video sockets – but it's possible to convert an S-video signal to composite, and vice versa. You can also use a SCART adapter to connect a computer to a TV that has neither. Just one important caveat: television screens are low-resolution devices woefully unsuitable for working with a normal Windows environment.

Graphics cards sometimes also include video-in sockets, which you can use to capture video from devices such as camcorders and VCRs. You can also get graphics cards with integrated TV tuners that let you watch and record live television on the PC.

Invest in a dual-head graphics card if you want to run two monitors simultaneously without having to install a second graphics card.

Two heads better than one?

Odd though it may seem as an upgrade option, you might like to install a PCI card alongside an existing AGP card. The point is that you could then connect two monitors simultaneously and run them as a super-wide Windows desktop. For instance, you could keep your word processor and e-mail program open in windows on one monitor and reserve the other for full-screen web surfing. Windows 98, Me, 2000, XP and Vista all support dual monitor setups.

Alternatively, you can get dual-head graphics cards that support the same setup without requiring a separate PCI card.

Note that you can't necessarily run two monitors from a graphics card simply because it's equipped with both VGA and DVI sockets. These are often provided merely as alternatives i.e. you can use one or the other at any given time. That, however, is not always the case and sometimes you can indeed run dual monitors from such a card. Check the specifications.

Step-by-step graphics card upgrade

The beauty of expansion slot architecture is that internal cards can be installed and uninstalled with virtually no effort. Here we replace one AGP graphics card with another.

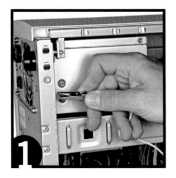

Before commencing any internal work on your PC, re-read the safety precautions on p33.

A single screw usually secures the graphics card to the case chassis. Remove this now. Support the card as you do so but try to avoid handling its components.

Many fast AGP cards are actually fairly heavy – cooling fans and heatsinks are the culprits – and so have retention mechanisms to support them in the slot. There may be a push pin arrangement or, as shown here, a clip rather like the retention clips used in RAM slots.

If present, release the retention mechanism carefully. Again, hold the card carefully and don't let it drop on the motherboard as you lift it from the slot! Remove the card from the computer case.

Take the new card from the antistatic bag in which it was supplied (hopefully) and reverse this procedure. Take care with the retention mechanism and be sure to screw the card to the chassis. Now carefully put everything back together, reconnect the monitor cable, and switch on the PC. All being well, Windows will automatically identify the new hardware and ask for its driver software. Pop the installation CD-ROM in the drive when prompted and follow the directions.

Display Settings can be accessed through the Control Panel or by right-clicking the Desktop, selecting Properties and opening the Settings tab. Here you can fine-tune your new display. The most important settings are screen resolution and colour depth (as discussed), and the refresh rate (see the Monitor section later). The idea here is to set the refresh rate to the highest level that the monitor supports. You should find this option by clicking the Advanced button and opening the Monitor tab.

DirectX and Windows Vista

Before Windows Vista came along, Windows couldn't take advantage of high-end graphics cards – but Windows Vista can and does. If your graphics card isn't up to the job you won't get the snazzy, semi-transparent interface and whizzy effects such as 3D windows.

The technology within Windows that handles 3D graphics is called DirectX and the latest version – DirectX 10 – will be Vista-only. Games designed for Vista will work with older hardware but, if you want the best experience, Microsoft says you'll need a graphics card that meets the requirements of DirectX 10.

Such cards are likely to be powerful – and pricey. At the time of writing NVidia had just unveiled the first graphics card compliant with DirectX 10, the GeForce 8800. It's undoubtedly powerful – the basic version has a 500MHz processor, 640MB of system memory and plugs into a PCI Express slot – but it'll also set you back £250.

PART 4 Upgrading your sound card

Time was when the average desktop PC emitted only feeble and occasional bleeps. But these days even the humblest domestic computer is a veritable home entertainment centre. A sound card is standard equipment in any new system, as are, unfortunately, cheap, tinny speakers that do it no justice whatsoever. More of them later but for now merely note that good speakers can enhance sound quality up to a point but the sound itself is generated internally. A powerful sound card is the starting point for aural satisfaction.

With a decent sound card onboard, your PC can eclipse your stereo in the audio stakes.

Why bother? Do you really want your PC to double as a stereo? Well, yes if you want to play audio CDs on your computer. Thanks to the phenomenal popularity of the MP3 file format and the widespread distribution (and piracy) of music on the internet, you could even build and play a music collection entirely on and from your hard disk. And then there are multimedia presentations like encyclopaedias and reference titles. And DVD movie soundtracks. And computer games. And sound files on web pages. And internet-based radio and TV channels. And so on…

Moreover, a sound card means that you can record your own music on your computer if you have the mind and/or the talent to do such a thing. Have you considered the benefits of internet telephony where long-distance calls on the internet cost a fraction of normal telephone charges? There's also the evolving world of voice recognition: speak into a microphone and smart software transcribes your words onto the page as text.

All of these examples require a sound card. The good news is that your PC almost certainly has one onboard already; the better news is that the quality and flexibility of sound technology has appreciated dramatically these past few years, yet even top of the range hardware is realistically priced. So, if your card is found wanting, give it the heave and slot in a new one.

First, of course, and as always, do a little research.

What you need to know

Figuring out which card best suits your needs is not too tricky if you keep an eye on the following considerations:

Interface Modern sound cards all use the PCI (32-bit) expansion slot. There's every possibility that your existing card is sited in an ISA (16-bit) slot but it's time to bid it a fond farewell. However, your motherboard may include an integrated audio chip, in which case you won't have a sound card at all. What you will have, at least if the chip is AC '97 compliant – an industry standard – is quite superb multi-channel sound and no pressing reason to upgrade. The only real trouble with integrated audio is that the ports are typically squeezed onto the motherboard's own input/output panel where space is tight. As a result, the microphone input may have to double-up as the centre/subwoofer output in a multi-channel set-up. What this means in practice is that you can't run a surround sound system (e.g. for music or movie playback) and keep a microphone connected (e.g. for voice recognition software) simultaneously. The port's function at any given time will be determined by the sound card's driver settings, which can be fiddly to configure.

A sound card, by contrast, usually provides a full array of inputs and outputs on the card itself and, if necessary, on an optional auxiliary port bracket or breakout box.

Incidentally, it is possible to use an external sound card. This is ideal if you're shy of opening your case, don't have a free PCI slot or want to add multi-channel audio playback to a laptop computer.

Modern sound cards use the more powerful PCI interface.

An external sound card provides multi-channel audio without surgery.

The full array of inputs and outputs on the card plus an external expansion hub (this is an alternative to a breakout box, which would require a free drive bay).

Multi-channel audio Cinema goers will be well aware of the three-dimensional 'surround sound' techniques used in today's movies, where the soundtrack comes at you from all directions. But you might be surprised to learn that you can achieve similar effects at home with a suitable sound card, especially when playing DVD movies on your computer. You'll need a whole bunch of speakers for the full effect (see p110) but there's nothing quite like it for realism.

On the other hand (there's always another hand), the vast majority of music around today was recorded in simple stereo. It's possible to 'up-mix' stereo sound into something approximating surround sound – each stereo channel is split up a bit and sent to different speakers – but results are, at best, variable. There's also the hassle factor of having to site satellite speakers all around the room. Don't underestimate this: there's no point whatsoever in connecting five (or seven) satellite speakers plus a subwoofer to your sound card unless you then position each speaker in just the right spot in your room to generate the illusion of 3-D audio. This means cables running everywhere.

Virtually all mid-range sound cards and motherboards designed with integrated audio support multi-channel output, but it's debatable just how useful this is unless you intend to spend a good deal of time watching DVD movies on your computer.

MIDI – or Musical Instrument Digital Interface – is, as the name suggests, an interface that enables a musical instrument (typically a keyboard) to connect to the sound card in order to play and record music. Or so you might think. In fact, a MIDI

'instrument' – or, more correctly, a MIDI controller – is not so different from a keyboard in the sense that it sends mute instructions to the computer. MIDI software then interprets this code and tells the sound card to make appropriate noises. Making music the MIDI way is both fabulously flexible – the MIDI file generated when you play a keyboard or other controller can be edited, modified, and applied to different sounds in an unlimited number of ways – and deeply counter-intuitive. One to master slowly, but potentially to good effect.

Many sound cards provide a MIDI interface that doubles up as a socket for a games joystick. Failing that, you can usually adapt a MIDI controller/instrument to connect via USB.

Wave table (WAV) A wave table card (see Techie Corner on p90) is essential for audio fidelity. The quality of a card's sound is measured in terms of bits, where more is better. Go for a 64-bit card if you intend to record your own music or are prepared to invest in speakers that make the most of the card's superior output; otherwise, a 32-bit card will suffice.

Duplex means that a sound card can make and record sounds simultaneously. Most conversations are duplex to some degree – we talk and listen at the same time – so a full duplex card is essential for PC chat and telephony. In fact, you'd be hard pressed to pick up a non-duplex card these days.

External connectors As we've mentioned, sound cards can provide a variety of interfaces, with or without the help of an expansion bracket or breakout box. The key considerations are:

The top edge of this internal sound card includes a digital SPDIF socket for connecting to the CD or DVD drive.

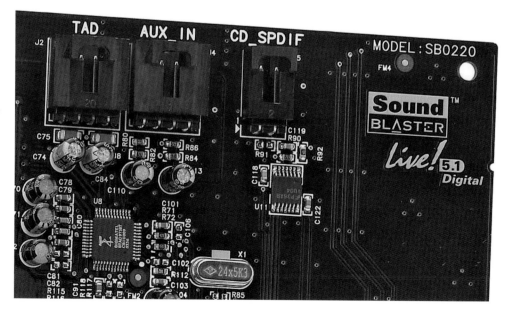

All the ins and outs you could ever wish for courtesy of an expansion hub, shown front and back. Of course, if you just need to connect a pair of stereo speakers, you can use the mini-jack connection on the sound card itself.

● *Speakers/line out* At worst, a single 3.5mm mini-jack will provide analogue stereo output. You can connect speakers here or run a cable to the auxiliary input on your hi-fi system for amplified sound. You may find three of these that together provide the six-channel output required for 5.1 surround sound (front left/right; rear left/right; centre/subwoofer).

● *Line-in* Another 3.5mm mini-jack socket that lets you connect an external device for PC recording. If you want to make a digital copy of your vinyl records or tape cassettes, for instance, you would connect your hi-fi to this input.

● *Microphone* Plug in a mic and do the karaoke. Or, in a more sober mood, use voice recognition software that transposes your spoken words into text on the page. You'll need a good quality microphone for best results and, in fact, you'll fare better with a USB model.

● *Game/MIDI* A dual-purpose interface for joysticks and MIDI instruments.

● *SPDIF* or Sony/Philips Digital Interface. A digital input/output standard. If your CD or DVD drive has a digital output, you should connect this to the digital input on your sound card. Or if your CD/DVD drive supports Digital Audio Extraction, the sound card's digital output can broadcast the audio signal directly from an audio CD (or from any file on the hard disk) without putting it through an analogue to digital conversion.

Step-by-step sound card upgrade

Upgrading a sound card is just as straightforward as replacing a graphics card. Easier, in fact. In this example, we'll remove the original card from its ISA slot and install a new PCI card.

Before *commencing any internal work on your PC, re-read the safety precautions on p33.*

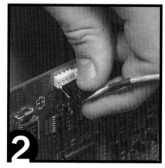

Note the *thin audio cable connecting the sound card to the CD or DVD drive (or both, or neither). If present, unplug this cable at the sound card end only.*

A single *screw secures the sound card to the chassis. Remove this now and set aside.*

TECHIE CORNER

Sampling Way back yonder, sound cards used a technology called FM (Frequency Modulation) Synthesis whereby the tone of, say, a violin was generated according to complex mathematical formulae. This worked just fine as far as it went but you'd never be fooled into thinking a Grapelli was in the room. A radically different technology called wave table synthesis was then developed. Here, actual recordings – samples – of musical instruments are digitised, stored in memory and called upon to reproduce truly lifelike music. It's still synthetic, of course, but it's the next best thing to housing a miniaturised orchestra in your PC.

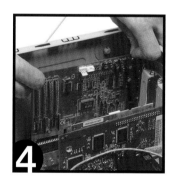

Carefully *remove the old sound card from its ISA slot. Hold the card by the edges and be sure not to damage its components with your fingers. This can be a fiddly business, particularly if there are other expansion cards either side, and it might take a little effort to get the card free. Do not rock it from side to side.*

Take *the new card from its antistatic bag and position it gently on but not in a free PCI slot. This is just to check which metal blanking plate on the chassis needs to be removed in order that the card can access the outside world.*

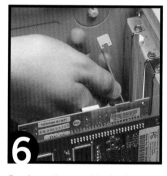

Replace *the card in its bag while you remove both the retaining screw and the blanking plate.*

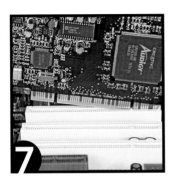

Gently insert the new card in the PCI slot, making sure to match its connecting edge precisely with the slot opening. Again, be sure not to touch the card's components. If necessary, use a gentle end-to-end rocking motion to ease it into the slot.

The idea is to install the card fully and levelly in the slot. This will take a little downwards pressure but not enough to bend the card or crack the motherboard!

Now secure the card to the chassis using the screw that held the blanking plate in place or one that came with the drive. You may also care to close up the ISA slot's hole with the spare blanking plate. Anything that keeps the dust down is good.

Reattach the audio cables to the appropriate connector on the card (consult the manual for directions). Carefully put everything back together, reconnect the speakers and switch on the PC. All being well, Windows will detect the new card, launch the New Hardware wizard and prompt you for the appropriate drivers. Have any CD or floppy disks that came with the card to hand along with your Windows installation disc and follow the instructions.

TROUBLE-SHOOTER

Never upgrade a sound card and speakers simultaneously! From a diagnostic point of view, you only want to work with one suspect device at a time.

● **No sound** when you play an audio CD? Did the speakers work just fine with the old card? Try plugging headphones into the CD-ROM drive (there should be a jack on the front) to make sure that both the drive and your CD playback software are working. If so, and if you have a suitable cable with 3.5mm jacks on either end, connect the headphone socket to the audio input on the sound card. If you can hear the CD through the speakers

now, the problem lies with the internal audio cable. Open the PC (after taking all the usual precautions) and ensure that it's correctly connected at both ends. Replace if necessary.

● **Just on** the off-chance, double click the speaker icon in the System Tray (the right-hand end of the

Windows Taskbar) and make sure that the CD drive has not been muted.

● **Also try** playing audio files saved on the hard disk. If necessary, use the Windows Find Files tool to seek out files with the extension WAV, WMA or MP3.

● **Have a look** in Device Manager (see pp23–4) and ensure that the sound card icon is not flagged with an exclamation or question mark (this would indicate a problem or conflict).

● **Modern** sound card software is often fiendishly complex. There will likely be a host of settings to play around with, probably some diagnostic tools too, and almost

certainly much less help in the manual than you would like. Look for an electronic manual on the supplied CD-ROM or consult the card manufacturer's website for further help.

PART  Mobile internet access

Back in the 1990s, the only way to get internet access in your home was by plugging a modem into a telephone socket and transmitting data through the old copper wires — slowly.

Over time, broadband became commonplace, both through ADSL (Asymmetric Digital Subscriber Line, which uses the same copper telephone lines in a new way) and cable (which uses the fibre-optic cables that bring telephone and TV services into homes). Bandwidth has increased, geographical access has improved, and it's never been easier for most of us to get onto the internet at decent speeds.

Recently, however, there has been a new contender on the block in the form of mobile broadband. Quite simply, this is a way of using fast mobile phone networks for internet access. You'll commonly hear the term 3G, which stands for 'third generation'. This means that mobile networks are capable of carrying data wirelessly, including internet traffic, at speeds similar to that of a basic wired broadband service. What this means in practice is that you can plug a mobile 'dongle' into your computer's USB connection and access the internet without the need for wires or a connection to your telephone or cable service. Mobile broadband is obviously appealing for laptops, when you need internet access on the move, but is also now a realistic contender for a home-based internet service.

A broadband dongle is basically a mobile phone without the phone! It uses the same mobile networks to bring internet access to your computer.

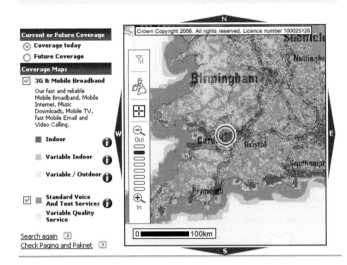

All mobile network operators provide coverage maps to show you what kind of speeds you can expect in your area. Check their websites for details.

Costs

There are two standard pricing models: pay a monthly fee and have unlimited access to the internet (around £15—30 per month with a long-term contract); or pay as you go, usually based on a fixed price per day (around £3—4). If you only use your mobile broadband service occasionally, the pay-as-you-go option can work out cheaper despite relatively high daily costs. However, if you're considering mobile broadband as an alternative to a fixed internet service, you'll certainly want a monthly contract.

Pros and cons

The advantages of mobile broadband over fixed broadband are essentially:

● no wires

● very easy to use

● available anywhere.

The disadvantages are:

● It is considerably slower than many high-speed broadband services, which means web pages take longer to load and downloads are slower.

● You can only use it when you are within range of a strong mobile signal.

● Network operators usually impose fairly stringent 'fair use' policies of around 3GB per month. This makes mobile broadband unsuitable for viewing videos (e.g. YouTube) or listening to streaming music. It's fine for web access and email but that's about it.

On that second point, mobile network operators have different levels of coverage across the country. You might have encountered a situation where you can't get a mobile signal on, for example, your Vodafone mobile phone when a friend has a strong T-Mobile signal. It's thus important to know that you can get a strong mobile signal wherever you are most likely to use your service, whether that's at home or in the office. Before buying a mobile service, ensure that the shop will let you return it and cancel the contract if you find that you can't get a strong signal — something that requires trial and error, unfortunately. The good news is that all mobile network operators offer very similar mobile broadband packages, so if one network doesn't work for you, chances are another will.

If you can, the best bet is to test signal strength with one or more 3G mobile phones. If you can get a strong 3G signal on, say, an O_2 mobile phone, you'll be able to use an O_2 mobile broadband dongle without difficulty.

Networking

Just as you can use a router to set up a home network with a fixed internet service, you can — sometimes — share a mobile broadband service in the same way. What you need is a wireless router that allows you to plug in a mobile dongle. The mobile broadband service can then be shared among your computers wirelessly (over Wi-Fi) or, if you prefer, with Ethernet cables. Most of the network operators offer such packages.

Many smart phones can be used as modems, which is an efficient way of staying connected to the internet when on the move.

Tethering

Another possibility is to use a 3G mobile phone as, in effect, a mobile broadband modem. This is when you connect the phone to a computer — usually a laptop — and use its 3G data capability for internet access. This is not really practical for home use as it ties up your mobile phone, but it can be useful when travelling. If you only need mobile internet access occasionally, it saves the hassle and expense of paying separately for mobile broadband.

Tethering is not always simple — the procedure varies from handset to handset — and it's not always free. For instance, if you have an iPhone, O_2 charges you £15 minimum to use it as a modem despite the fact that you're already paying to access the internet through the O_2 mobile network. That said, it's perhaps not unattractive compared to paying £10 or £15 per month for a separate mobile broadband contract.

Right now, mobile broadband offers a quick, easy way to get a computer online, with the added benefit of being able to use the service anywhere (subject to finding a strong 3G signal). However, until network speeds increase significantly — wait for 4G, or the fourth generation of fast mobile networks — and, crucially, until network operators lift their 'fair use' policies and allow us to use mobile broadband services just like fixed broadband services (without limitations), anybody who uses the internet for more than web browsing and email access is better off with ADSL or cable access.

PART

Adding USB and Firewire

All PCs now come with at least a couple of USB (Universal Serial Bus) ports on board and some, but by no means all, have FireWire (or IEEE-1394a, to be precise and pedantic). Both are fast interfaces ideally suited to connecting a range of external peripherals to your computer, and either can be added as a simple upgrade.

If you're wondering which interface is 'better', you're not alone. FireWire used to be much, much faster and more expensive than USB, which made it the natural choice for connecting digital video cameras to computers. However, USB then got a dramatic upgrade with the USB 2 spec (a.k.a. Hi-Speed USB) and overtook its rival. FireWire too has now been upgraded to IEEE-1394b (a.k.a. FireWire 800) which runs twice as quickly as the original interface and once again leaves USB in its wake.

USB is generally used for scanners, printers, keyboards, digital cameras, portable music players and the like. The faster USB 2 now makes it possible to hook up external hard disks and fast CD or DVD drives. FireWire is still the natural gateway for digital video – all digital camcorders have a FireWire interface – and is also well suited to external drives.

USB offers almost unlimited expansion capabilities. Go for the newer, faster USB 2 standard.

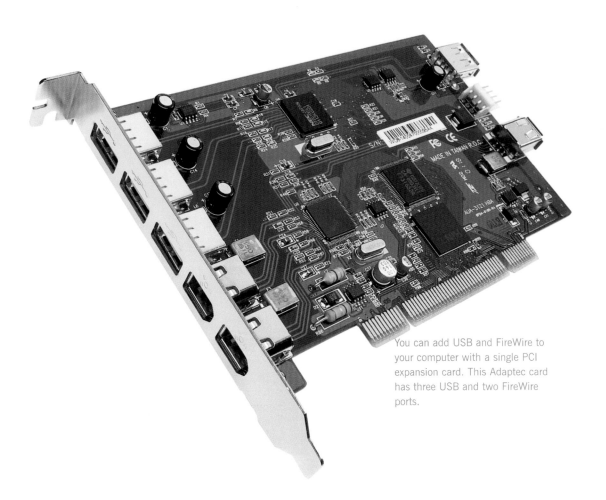

You can add USB and FireWire to your computer with a single PCI expansion card. This Adaptec card has three USB and two FireWire ports.

Check that your system can use USB before you take the plunge.

If your computer already has USB ports, we'd suggest upgrading to USB 2 if and when you feel the need for greater speed. FireWire remains a must for video enthusiasts, but do bear in mind that you'll need a very fast processor and bags of RAM to successfully edit your footage on a PC.

Perhaps the best upgrade of all is installing a combined USB 2/FireWire card. These are now readily available and open up all sorts of connection possibilities in one easy, affordable move.

One small caveat: the first release of Windows 95 and everything that went before it had no support whatsoever for USB, so an operating system upgrade to at least Windows 98 and, preferably, Millennium Edition or XP is in order first. Intel has a free software utility called USBready that can give your PC a complete once over for USB readiness. Download it here: **www.usb.org/about/faq/ans3#q1**

What you need to know

Speed An awful lot of data can pass through a USB or FireWire bus in a short time. The older flavour of USB (1.1) had a top speed of 1.5MB per second, but USB 2 runs at up to 60MB per second. Basic FireWire achieves a maximum throughput of 50MB per second, while the newer FireWire 800 standard increases this to 100MB.

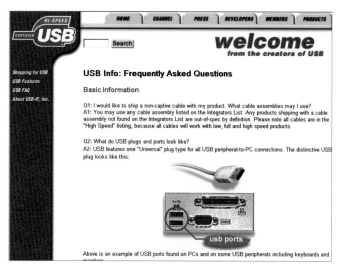

Flexibility You can connect up to 127 USB devices or 63 FireWire devices to a single port, but that's more impressive in theory than in reality. While FireWire devices can be linked together daisy-chain fashion – each new device simply plugs into the last one in the chain – USB requires the use of hubs, or expansion boxes with multiple USB ports. Many keyboards and monitors come with USB hubs built in.

Plug and play Windows will (or certainly should) recognise any USB or FireWire device as soon as it's plugged in and prompt the drivers immediately i.e. no rebooting. No fussing with jumpers or other fiddly hardware settings either.

One of the most useful devices of all is a so-called USB key or flash drive. This is basically a slice of memory attached to a USB plug which you can plug into any USB port and treat just like a miniature hard drive. Perfect for file transfers and the natural successor to floppy disks.

Hot-swappable Instead of having to reboot your PC every time you connect a device, you can plug and unplug USB and FireWire devices at will.

USB expansion hubs are essential if you want to connect several devices to a single port.

Portable storage space with a USB drive. Available in sizes from 16MB to 1GB and beyond. Always choose a USB 2 model for speedy transfers.

Just a few of the devices you can
connect to a PC via USB and
FireWire:

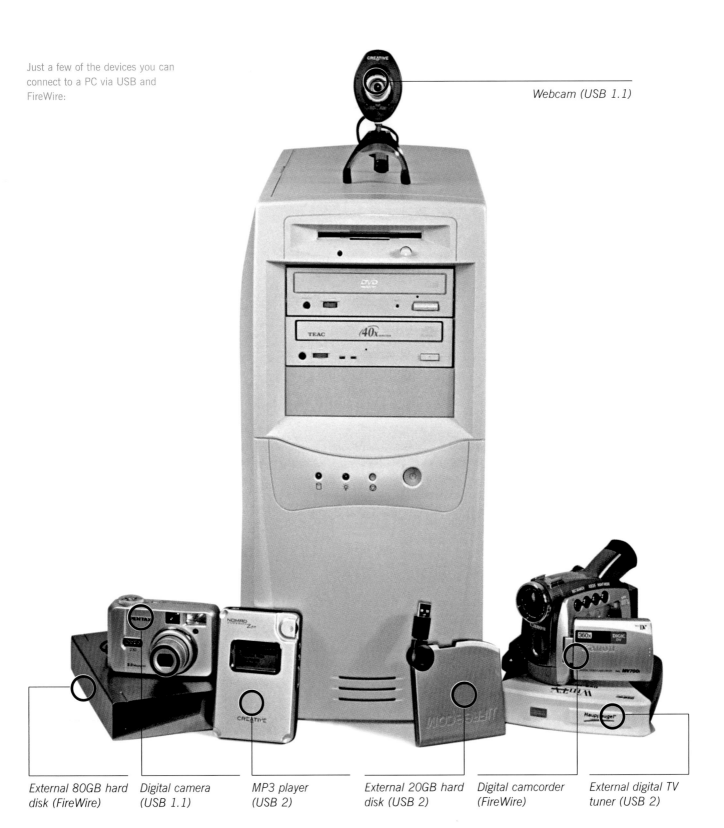

Webcam (USB 1.1)

External 80GB hard
disk (FireWire)

Digital camera
(USB 1.1)

MP3 player
(USB 2)

External 20GB hard
disk (USB 2)

Digital camcorder
(FireWire)

External digital TV
tuner (USB 2)

PART  Step-by-step USB card upgrade

USB controller cards typically come with two or four USB connectors and use the PCI expansion slot. Sounds simple? It is. Here's how. Note that the installation process for a FireWire card is identical.

Before *commencing any internal work on your PC, re-read the safety precautions on p33.*

Take the *new card from its antistatic bag and position it gently on but not in a free PCI slot. This is just to check which metal blanking plate needs to be removed.*

Replace *the card in its bag while you remove both the retaining screw and the blanking plate.*

TROUBLE-SHOOTER

There's nothing much that can go wrong providing you install the controller card correctly. However, here are a couple of things to look out for:

USB cables have different connectors on either end. The flatter, wider connector – Type A – goes to the USB port, and the squat, square Type B connector goes to the device. Never use a cable with Type A connectors on both ends to try to wire two

computers together. For one thing, such cables are illegal; for another, you'll blow up both PCs and burn down your house.

Don't buy a USB cable longer than 5 metres. It won't work. If you really need to cover a long distance, either add a powered hub every 5 metres or daisy-chain together up to five 'active extension' cables to boost the signal.

Take out *the new USB card again and gently insert it in the vacant PCI slot, making sure to match its connecting edge precisely with the slot opening. Be sure to hold the card carefully without touching its components. If necessary, use a gentle end-to-end rocking motion to ease it into the slot.*

Now *secure the card to the chassis using the screw that held the blanking plate in place. Carefully put everything back together and switch on the PC. All being well, Windows will detect the new card, launch the New Hardware Found wizard and prompt you for the appropriate drivers. Have any CD or floppy disks that came with the card to hand, along with your Windows installation disc and follow the instructions.*

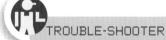

PART 5

Peripheral devices

A peripheral device is any component in a computer system that isn't actually the computer itself. If you take away the processor, memory and motherboard, all you're left with is a box of bits that falls some way short of a working PC. But the monitor, keyboard, mouse and printer are mere add-ons. So too are the hard disk, CD-ROM and floppy drive. Here we'll look at upgrading the most common external peripherals, beginning with the most important – and expensive – of them all.

PART 5 Upgrading your monitor

Because monitors are so pricey, manufacturers and retailers of budget – and even high-end – computer systems tend to cut corners here first. But while a 15-inch display unit may have looked just fine in the shop, do you now find yourself shuffling the chair ever closer each day just to see what's going on? Has the picture lost some of its sparkle and colour depth? Have you taken up digital photography or computer gaming and found that your ageing monitor no longer cuts the mustard? It's time to save your eyesight and go for a bigger, better model. Choose wisely and it will serve you well for years – and, unlike the rest of your system, it won't be obsolete as soon as you get it home.

What you need to know

There are two main types of computer monitor – CRT (Cathode Ray Tube) and LCD (Liquid Crystal Display). Here's a brief summary of the pros and cons.

Screen size The screen size of a monitor is a diagonal measurement from corner to corner. However, while a 17-inch LCD model will indeed have a viewable screen of 17 inches, as you would hope and expect, the same size of CRT monitor typically offers a *viewable* screen size of only 16 inches or less. This is because the quoted

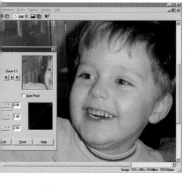

If digital photography is a hobby, you'll need a good monitor to see the results at their best.

15" LCD = 15" viewable area

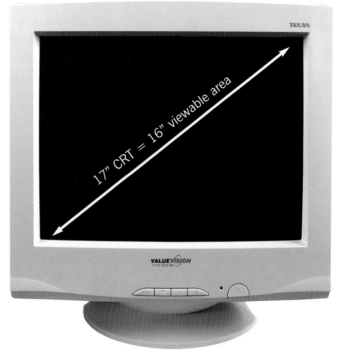

17" CRT = 16" viewable area

figure is a measure of the cathode ray tube itself, part of which is always hidden from view by the monitor housing. Indeed, we've seen 17-inch monitors that offer just a fraction over 15 inches of visible screen. Look for an 'actual screen area' figure, or whip out a tape measure and make your own comparisons.

Distortion Thanks to clever manufacturing techniques, CRT screens are now much flatter than they once were. This helps to reduce distortion, especially around the edges. Best of the bunch are those imaginatively called 'flat', as opposed to 'flat squared' or 'spherical' (avoid). LCD screens are perfectly flat so distortion issues don't arise.

In fact, there are several different manufacturing techniques and monitor standards. The two terms you are most likely to encounter are shadow mask and aperture grill. The first incorporates a perforated sheet of metal that focuses electron beams on to the screen, often used in FST (Flat Square Tube) models where the curvature of the glass is minimised. The second replaces the perforated sheet with a series of vertical wires through which the beams are channelled. These are held in place by two horizontal wires that can usually be seen (just), if you stare at the screen hard enough. Some people find this irritating but the aperture grill approach means that almost completely flat glass can be used to make a monitor.

Resolution We discussed resolution on p80, where we pointed out that the graphics card and monitor should be matched to produce the best quality picture. However, CRT monitors generally run well and look good at a full range of resolutions whereas LCD screens are optimised to work at a single resolution.

Colour and contrast You'll often find that creative types – graphic designers, illustrators and so on – are the first to invest in shiny new technologies, and yet many design firms have CRT screens instead of LCD ones. There's a really good reason for this: while LCDs get better and better by the day, good CRTs usually offer better colour reproduction and contrast. That doesn't matter for playing games, doing spreadsheets or browsing the internet, but it's essential when you're designing things on screen that will end up in print: the colours on screen need to be identical to the ones that will appear in the printed advert, brochure, poster or illustration.

TECHIE CORNER

CRT and LCD – the difference! Trusty old cathode ray tube technology works by firing a beam of electrons at the screen in order to stimulate red, blue and green phosphor dots. By continually drawing lines across the screen, the beam paints a picture across the entire viewable area. Then it does the same thing over and over again many times per second (the refresh rate).

In an LCD monitor, a liquid crystal solution is suspended between two sheets and an electric current switches individual cells (pixels) on and off to block light or let it pass through. In TFT (Thin Film Transistors) models, a tiny transistor controls each pixel. Or, to cut a long story short, CRT works just like your television and LCD just like your digital watch. For full details, look here:
www.pctechguide.com/ 42CRTMonitors.htm
www.pctechguide.com/ 43FlatPanels.htm

CRT Screen

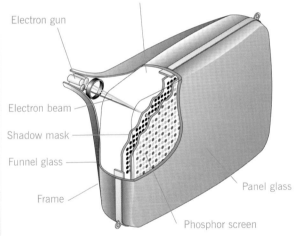

Inner magnetic shield
Electron gun
Electron beam
Shadow mask
Funnel glass
Frame
Panel glass
Phosphor screen

LCD Screen

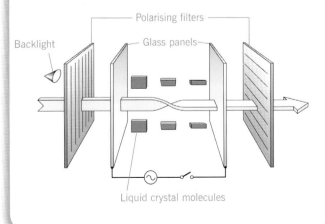

Polarising filters
Backlight
Glass panels
Liquid crystal molecules

Refresh rate A measure of how many times per second the monitor redraws the image on screen. As a rule, the higher the resolution, the harder it is to maintain a high refresh rate; as another, a high refresh rate means less visible flicker, and that means no headaches or eyestrain. Look for a CRT monitor capable of sustaining a refresh rate of 85Hz at a resolution of 1,024 x 768 and at least 75Hz at 1,280 x 1,024. (Refresh rates are not so important with LCD monitors because of the different display technology: around 60Hz is acceptable.)

Dimensions No comparison here. CRT monitors are big, bulky and heavy; LCDs are neater, much shallower and relatively lightweight. If you're pushed for space or don't fancy bashing a hole in your wall to accommodate the rear end of a CRT monitor, stretch the budget and splash out on LCD. Alternatively, consider 'short neck' CRT monitors where a premium price buys a much reduced tube depth.

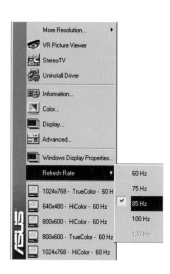

Viewing angle CRT screens can be viewed from just about any angle – try it and see – but you need to be sitting pretty straight on to an LCD monitor to see the full picture. Not a big issue, perhaps, and the viewing angles are improving all the time, but LCDs are not ideally suited to communal use. Then again, does your family really sit around the PC on a regular basis?

Analogue or digital? Both CRT and LCD monitors are available with the DVI (Digital Visual Interface) interface, although it's much more common on the latter. We strongly recommend a DVI monitor. You might not notice a dramatic improvement in image quality but at least your monitor will be compatible with your next graphics card or computer.

Price LCD monitors used to be *much* more expensive than CRTs but mass production has brought the prices tumbling down and now they are pretty much standard equipment with new PCs. Also, when you're making comparisons, remember that a 15-inch LCD offers practically the same visible viewing area as the average 17-inch CRT.

There's no getting away from it: LCD monitors are infinitely sleeker and sexier than their CRT cousins.

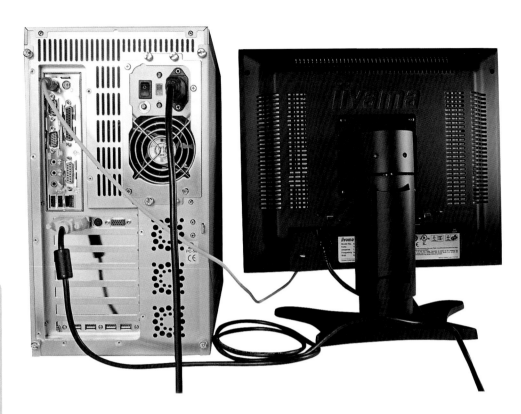

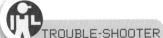

TROUBLE-SHOOTER

No picture? It sounds obvious but make sure that the monitor is plugged in and switched on. **Also check** that the graphics card isn't trying to produce an image at a higher resolution and/or refresh rate than the monitor can handle.

Is the brightness set to zero? It sounds unlikely but it can happen during experimentation with the monitor's own controls. **Failing that**, reconnect your original monitor and see if the picture returns. If so, it's a safe bet that your new monitor is a dud – but do seek out the trouble-shooting section in the manual and eliminate all possible problems before sending it back. **Dead pixels** It's a fact of life that virtually every TFT LCD monitor sold comes with a dead pixel or two. These look like tiny dots on the screen, and are black or coloured depending on whether a transistor has failed in the off or on position. However, unless your screen is peppered with them to the extent that it detracts from normal use – a rare occurrence indeed – don't worry about it. Besides which, most monitor manufacturers will merely point you to the small print that explains that a few dead pixels are permissible according to the terms of the sale.

Installing your new monitor

On one hand, this is a simple case of switching off your PC, unplugging the old monitor, plugging in the new one, and rebooting. If necessary, use a DVI adapter to connect a digital monitor to an analogue graphics card, or vice versa. Windows then detects that something has changed and launches the New Hardware Found wizard, at which point you'll be prompted to install the monitor's driver. But (you just knew there would be a but), it takes a little more effort to get a perfect picture.

Get tweaking First off, you'll want to experiment with the monitor's own controls. Modern monitors typically have a couple of buttons that control elements of the display, such as brightness, contrast and position (you can adjust the image width and depth to fill the available screen space). Most provide an on-screen display that makes it very much easier to see what you're doing.

As we've seen, the graphics card is responsible for generating the image that appears on screen, and now is the time to tweak its settings to best effect. For instance, you might want to boost the refresh rate to take advantage of your new monitor's increased capabilities. Click Start, point to Settings, click Control Panel, double click Display and open the Settings tab (or right-click the Desktop, select Properties and open Settings from there). Here you can set the resolution (screen area) and colour depth (the maximum number of colours). Click the Advanced button to access further options. Be sure to check and, if necessary, adjust the refresh rate in the Adapter tab. Set it to the highest rate that your monitor can support at the resolution you've chosen (consult the manual for details). It's generally easier on the eyes to compromise with a lower resolution and a higher refresh rate than the other way around. Remember that LCD monitors are designed to work at one optimum resolution.

Play around with the display settings and any supplied utilities to make the most of your new monitor.

PART 5

Upgrading your keyboard and mouse

Too many coffee spills made too many sticky keys? Cat got your mouse? Have you outgrown those flimsy, undersized devices so clearly thrown in as an afterthought with your new computer system? Do you want some extra bells and whistles in the shape of shortcut keys and internet buttons on your keyboard and a couple of programmable buttons on your mouse? Or have sore wrists and the onset of RSI (Repetitive Strain Injury) driven you to consider an ergonomic approach?

What you need to know
Very little, in truth, but a few pointers won't go amiss.

Interface Keyboards and mouse both use a small 6-pin PS/2-style plug and socket or, very rarely, a larger 5-pin DIN. Although you can buy adapters to convert one to the other, it's easier by far to source kit that's immediately compatible with your PC. Alternatively, if you're running Windows 98 or later, consider USB devices. Many USB keyboards have additional sockets that allow you to connect a couple of low-powered devices directly to the keyboard rather than to the back of the computer or to a separate hub. A USB mouse would be the most obvious contender. USB mice are also more responsive and smoother in operation.

Keys and buttons Today's keyboards come with somewhere between 101 and 107 keys as standard. Any reference in the specifications to 'Windows 95' guarantees the inclusion of three

How do 26 letters and 10 digits add up to 100-plus keys?

Scrolling wheels, programmable buttons, funky colours, with or without wires. What more could you want from a mouse?

extra keys that provide quick access to the Start menu and context-sensitive menus (equivalent to a right-click with the mouse in most applications). Some keyboards even have a built-in trackball, which can save a lot of to-ing and fro-ing between the keyboard and the mouse, while many others feature 'hot keys'. These provide shortcuts to programs, instant access to features like speaker volume, and back/forward/stop buttons for browsing the web. In fact, the possibilities are vast. You'll find that some keyboards are designed more for office work and others for playing music and videos. Regardless, you can usually reprogram hot keys to perform the functions that are most useful to you.

Mice can be similarly adept. All have two clickable buttons, some have three, and most now have a central wheel nestling between the left and right buttons. You may find this awkward to use at first but it's a terrific boon for scrolling swiftly through documents and web pages. Indeed, we'd unhesitatingly recommend the wheel as sufficient reason to upgrade an old mouse. Beyond this, you can get mice with additional buttons which can be programmed to do useful things. If your mouse has a thumb-operated button along the side, for instance, you could make this minimise all open windows or click the back button in your browser or do pretty much anything else you like.

Ergonomics 'Ergonomic' is a marketing term, not a standard and definitely not a science. That said, ergonomic keyboards are designed to maintain a more natural hand and wrist posture, thus helping to prevent symptoms of RSI like carpal tunnel syndrome. The first time you try one, it will feel decidedly odd and distinctly unnatural – but persevere and you'll likely be hooked. Our advice is to seek the testimony of friends and colleagues. Toying with a keyboard for 30 seconds in a shop really doesn't tell you anything.

Those handy Windows keys are useful shortcuts.

Do your wrists a favour with an ergonomic design.

This cordless Bluetooth kit includes a base station for easy (ahem) connectivity with other Bluetooth-enabled devices.

Optical mice run fluff-free for ever.

A trackball is a motionless mouse.

Cordless One rather tasty upgrade option is a cordless keyboard and mouse. Most cordless devices use RF (Radio Frequency) technology whereby every press of a key or click of a button transmits a signal to a small receiver connected to the PC. More recently, Bluetooth-enabled keyboards and mice have been widely marketed. In either case, the end result is a neater desk. Cordless devices are also ideal if you have a computer connected to your TV and you want to control the on-screen action from a distance.

Optical mice This style of modern mouse has a light sensor on its underbelly that detects motion and relays this to the computer. No more de-fluffing.

Trackballs Instead of sliding a mouse around a mat, a trackball stays stationary while you move the screen cursor by manipulating a big ball, just like the arcade games of yore. Some people love them; others wouldn't give them desk-room.

TECHIE CORNER

Under the (key) covers
There are two main manufacturing methods for keyboards. Switch-based devices have micro-switches under every key and click satisfyingly with every key press. Capacitive keyboards incorporate a single sensitive membrane beneath the keys. Every tap makes an electronic connection that sends a signal to the computer via a microprocessor. No clicks here – the keys generally have a smooth, quiet action – but capacitive keyboards tend to last longer because there are fewer bits to break. Then again, unlike switch-based keyboards, they cannot usually be repaired if they go wrong. Such is life.

Tablets As an alternative to the mouse, or even as an add-on, consider a graphics tablet. With these, you draw and tap on a flat tablet with a cordless pen in order to mimic the actions of a mouse. Tablets are designed primarily for use with drawing and photo-editing applications but can also be a most natural – and accurate – way to control the on-screen cursor.

You can use a pen and tablet instead of dragging a mouse around a mat.

Installing a new keyboard and mouse

What can we say? If you're replacing one PS/2 device with another, turn off your computer, unplug the old, and plug in the new. The only thing you really need to watch is that you plug the mouse cable into the mouse socket, usually colour-coded green, and the keyboard cable into the keyboard socket, usually colour-coded purple.

If you're adding a USB device, do just the same but connect the new hardware to any free USB port on the computer or, if you have one, a USB hub. Windows will then recognise the addition and ask you to install the driver software. Pop the supplied CD-ROM in the drive and follow directions.

Thereafter, you can activate fancy features and program extra keys and buttons with the supplied software utility. Failing this, open the mouse and keyboard configuration tools in Windows. Click Start > Settings > Control Panel and then Mouse or Keyboard. In Windows XP, the route is Start > Control Panel > Printers and Other Hardware.

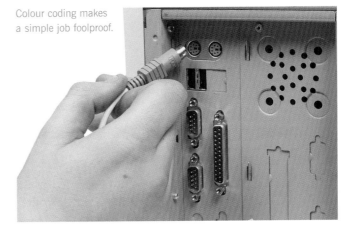

Colour coding makes a simple job foolproof.

PART 5 Upgrading your speakers

Decent speakers can make even the crummiest sound card sound better than it deserves to, but a top-notch sound card is wasted on those tiny, tinny units usually bundled 'free' with computers. So, be you music lover or musician, computer games player or DVD movie fan, invest in a decent set of bins if you want to rock the house.

What you need to know

Hi-fi buffs will have little trouble with speaker specifications but the rest of us need a little help.

Subwoofers and satellites A subwoofer is a big-speaker-in-a-box that sits on the floor and boosts the bass signal. Satellites are smaller but still full-range speakers positioned left and right of the listener in order to produce a stereo effect. Such a setup is described as 2.1 (two satellites plus a subwoofer), 4.1 (four satellites plus a subwoofer), or 5.1, or 7.1, or whatever.

Surround sound This is the effect created when a second set of speakers is positioned behind the listener, one to each side, to complement a pair of stereo speakers positioned left and right of the sound source. A separate subwoofer handles the bass tones and, in a 5.1 setup, a further satellite is positioned directly in front of the listener. A sound card capable of surround sound then pumps different elements of the multi-channel audio signal to different speakers. The enveloping effect can be quite spooky.

Digital input Most sound cards output an analogue signal – they have to convert the computer's native digital signal to analogue in the process, which is daft – but some have digital outputs, usually labelled SPDIF (Sony/Philips Digital Interface). If yours is thus equipped, it's worthwhile getting digital speakers to complement it.

Stereo speakers are fine for listening to music but you might want to invest in a 5.1 sound system if you plan to watch DVD movies on your PC. This setup goes further still in the surround sound stakes with no fewer than seven satellite speakers.

TECHIE CORNER

Going overboard
Computer audio technology, both analogue and digital, continues to evolve apace. We haven't even touched on the scientific stuff, such as signal to noise ratios and frequency responses. The bottom line is this: if you really want to use your PC as a sound system, you are truly spoilt for choice and should research the multitude of options carefully; but if you just want a decent sound quality for playing CDs and the odd game, a mid-range, mid-price multi-channel sound card and a decent set of 4.1 or 5.1 surround sound speakers will blow your socks off. To find out much, much more, go here:
www.dolby.com

You can expand your options with a digital decoder. However, this is overkill for a straightforward PC system.

Satellite speakers usually connect to the back end of the subwoofer.

Separate decoder Some speaker systems are available with a separate standalone decoder. Such a unit usually has multiple inputs and is most useful in a home entertainment environment where you want to connect, say, a DVD player, TV, hi-fi, portable music player and PC to the same set of speakers. A decoder can also accept a raw, encoded audio signal from a computer's DVD drive (or from a basic DVD player, come to that) and decode it into the multi-channel signals required to drive a surround sound setup.

USB Sound cards normally convert the digital signal from audio CDs and MP3 files into an analogue signal, and pipe it to the speakers. As we've mentioned, digital sound cards skip this conversion and broadcast a 'cleaner' digital signal. However, it's also possible to buy digital speakers that connect to the PC through the USB port, thereby bypassing the sound card altogether. You have to be pretty committed to aural fidelity to spot the difference, and they're not the easiest things to configure, but we thought we ought to mention them. Incidentally, USB speakers will only work with audio CDs if your CD/DVD drives support Digital Audio Extraction, see p74.

Spaghetti This is what you get when you install a 4.1, 5.1 or 7.1 speaker system. Be prepared to trip over more wiring than you thought possible and be sure to follow the setup directions carefully.

Installing your new speakers

Plug them in to the audio out channel(s) on your sound card, connect the power supply to a wall socket, and switch them on. Sounds too simple to be true? Well, yes and no. No, because hooking up stereo speakers to your PC really is as straightforward as that. The main thing to watch is where the PC has two sets of speaker sockets: one set nestled in the motherboard's input/output panel (the same panel that holds the mouse and keyboard sockets) and another on an expansion card. In such cases, the computer has integrated audio and a separate sound card: see p17 for an example. The sound card is always the one to go with here.

But yes, connecting speakers can also be absurdly complicated when surround sound is involved. You'll first have to run cables from the sound card to the subwoofer, possibly via an external decoder, and from there make all the satellite speaker connections. This is definitely a job to be undertaken with the speaker supplier's manual in hand.

High-tech speakers need to be positioned correctly and configured with software.

PART  # Upgrading your printer

Inkjet printers have long been bundled 'free' with new computer systems. Unbelievable value, screamed the ads, but the reality was unbelievably duff print quality. If you ran your business cards off on one of those ... well, colleagues would accept them politely but mark you down as a cheapskate amateur.

How times have changed. Even the cheapest inkjet on the market today, bundled or otherwise, is a remarkably adept device. But there's a sting in the tail, as we shall see.

Prints charming More on the detailed specs in a second but do take a moment to consider why you need a printer and what you want it to do for you. The first decision is choosing between an inkjet and a laser. If crisp, clear text is paramount, particularly for business, then a laser printer is a must. But if you'd like some colour in your life, an inkjet is the obvious solution. Or at least it was until recently. Colour laser printers have plummeted in price and you may now find a model that justifies a little additional outlay. However, colour lasers are still much better suited to printing colour documents than to colour printing per se, particularly when it comes to photographs. This may change, but for now we'd recommend a colour laser for spicier business stationery but a good inkjet is still essential if you want to print digital images at a high resolution (i.e. top quality).

A modern inkjet printer can produce stunning colours at a high resolution.

Some printers are geared up to print on a wide variety of media – envelopes, various paper sizes and weights, transparencies, address stickers, labels for your home-burned CDs and so forth – while others are pretty much A4 and US letter size or nothing. Some run on batteries for under-the-arm instant portability; others can print direct from a digital camera without a computer in sight. There really is a printer out there for every purpose and the prices just keep on falling.

What you need to know

It pays to research the market carefully and we'd recommend reading a few comparative group tests in computer magazines to see what's currently hot and what's not. Such is the pace of evolution that last month's super-duper photo-realistic miracle of modern engineering is invariably this month's overpriced smudger. Here's a guide to the main considerations.

Interface There are now four connection choices: traditional parallel port; newer USB, at either speed, for faster data processing; newer-still Bluetooth for wireless connectivity; and a network interface for sharing a printer with multiple computers. For 'normal' use, a fast USB 2 interface is now the default standard.

Go for a USB printer if your PC supports it.

From portable to professional, there are printers to suit every output.

Consumables Inkjet printers use ink supplied in replaceable cartridges, and lasers use powdered toner. As a rule, colour inkjet printers are cheaper to buy than monochrome laser printers but more expensive to run. Irritatingly, the cheapest printers often use the most expensive cartridges – and therein lies the sting in the tail. Do the sums: a giveaway inkjet that costs more than its own purchase price to refill each time is not much of a bargain.

You think we're joking? Far from it. There are £29 printers out there that cost considerably more to replenish with fresh ink. The long-term running costs can also be staggering: one recent study found that a £40 printer could cost nearly £1,800 to run over 18 months.

Be aware that if you're tempted to refill old cartridges with cheap ink – and there are plenty of companies who'll happily sell you a kit to do just that – you can save a pretty penny but you'll almost certainly invalidate the printer's warranty. You'll also get in a mess. By all means try out your local high street refill company

Insist on an inkjet printer that uses separate black and coloured ink cartridges.

TECHIE CORNER

Print technologies

The two grand impact printers of yesteryear were clattering, clumsy affairs. Dot-matrix models struck pins against an ink-impregnated ribbon – the greater the number of pins, the better the quality of the letters – while daisy-wheel machines hammered protruding characters on a rotating disk. Neither type could print pictures

and both are now all but obsolete, certainly on the domestic desktop (which is not to say that you won't find them bashing out despatch notes in warehouses around the world: if staff have to shout, there's an impact printer at work).

Laser printers use light to generate a charged image on a drum and heat-fuse powdery black toner on to paper. Inkjet printers

squirt tiny globules of ink straight at the page. This used to mean that pages came out all sopping wet and soggy, but no longer. It's all so much more refined these days, and a good deal more flexible. Even the cheapest inkjet printer suffices for homework projects and printing out web pages, and the humblest laser can produce professional quality text.

High-quality paper is a worthwhile investment for photographic reproduction.

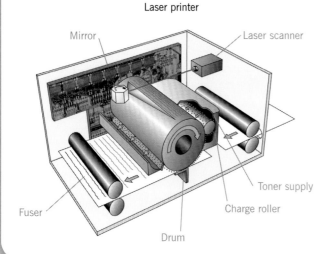

Laser printer

Mirror

Laser scanner

Fuser

Drum

Charge roller

Toner supply

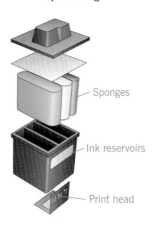

Inkjet cartridge

Sponges

Ink reservoirs

Print head

and see if you're happy with the resulting quality. An alternative is buying 'compatible' cartridges that install in your printer just like manufacturer-branded originals but cost considerably less.

Be sure to choose a printer that uses separate black and colour ink cartridges, as there's nothing more wasteful than throwing out perfectly good colours just because the black runs out (and vice versa).

Resolution This is a rating of the level of detail in a printed image, measured in terms of dots per inch. Look for at least 600dpi or 1,200dpi. Beware references to 'enhanced' or 'interpolated' resolution, as this involves software sophistry and is not a true reflection of a device's ability. Also check that a quoted resolution of 600dpi means 600 x 600 (i.e. 600 dots per inch horizontally and vertically). Sometimes, 600 x 300 resolutions are misleadingly described as 600dpi.

Memory Laser printers have to buffer data from the PC as they work and so incorporate RAM chips. The bare minimum is 512KB but 2 or 4MB makes for faster, more reliable performance. Many models' memory can be upgraded, which could be helpful if your work rate shoots up or you print a lot of graphics.

Speed Most manufacturers claim that their printers are capable of churning out X pages of Y-sized paper with Z% ink coverage per minute. That would be just fine if they all used the same criteria, but they don't. Sadly, it's up to you to get out the calculator and do the maths. However, do you really care how

If your laser printer is slowing you down, see if you can upgrade its memory. ·

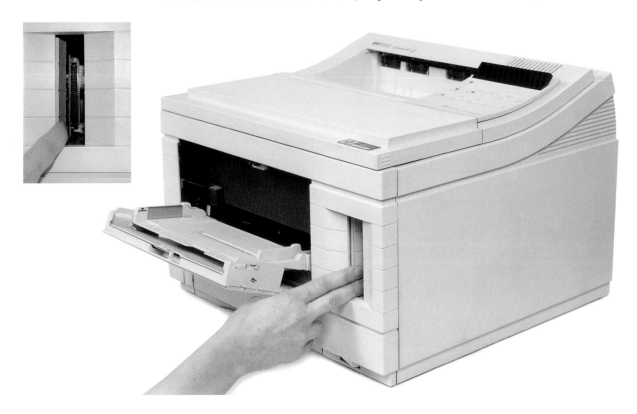

fast your printer is? Most domestic tasks are hardly 'mission critical' so we'd suggest concentrating more on quality than on speed.

Media Virtually all laser printers work just fine with cheap, plain paper (so-called laser paper is just a little whiter and brighter). However, it is worth investing in specialist papers to get the best results from an inkjet. Don't feel that you necessarily have to buy same-brand, though; a little experimentation with alternative papers often pays dividends.

Duty cycle This is the manufacturer's measure of a printer's maximum workload. A monthly duty cycle of, say, 12,000 pages means just that: don't print any more than 12,000 pages in any given month if you want the device to continue performing at its peak. Clearly, this has much more relevance in an office setting than at home.

Lifespan How long is a piece of string? Keep refilling an inkjet printer when it runs dry and it should last 'forever' – or at least until you upgrade your operating system and discover that it no longer supports your now-obsolete device! The photosensitive drum in a laser printer must be periodically replaced, usually at quite some cost. Look for a drum lifespan of somewhere between 15,000 and 30,000 pages, and be sure to factor this in when making price comparisons. Sometimes, the toner cartridge and drum are combined in a single unit.

Software You may find a whole heap of application software in the box. Inkjets typically come with a photo editing package and something along the lines of a make-your-own-greetings-cards utility. But don't be swayed by the software alone: it's not nearly as important as the hardware specifications.

Printers, particularly inkjets, often come with a full range of applications.

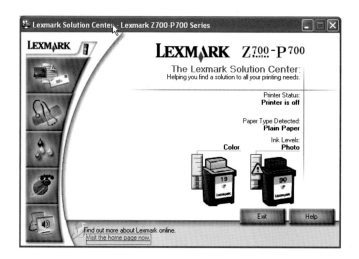

Installing a new printer

All printers have a pre-installation routine that generally involves removing strategic strips of packing tape, loading the ink cartridges or toner, bolting on feeder and output trays, and perhaps running a self-test procedure. Follow the manual's instructions to the letter.

Thereafter, the routine depends upon whether it's a parallel or a USB model. In the latter case, Windows will detect the device as soon as it's plugged in to a USB port and ask for the installation CD-ROM. However, some printer manufacturers insist that you load driver software *before* connecting the printer. Again, read the manual carefully.

Adding a printer in Windows XP

In Windows XP, there's a handy Add Printer wizard on hand to step you through installation. As it says at the outset: 'If you have a Plug and Play printer that connects through a USB port ... you do not need this wizard.' That's the beauty of USB: plug in a device and Windows either works with it immediately (if the drivers have been installed previously) or prompts to install the drivers first time around. With the old parallel interface, none of this is possible. However, the wizard makes reasonably light work of installation.

Start

Control Panel

Printers and Other Hardware

Add a printer

Next (on the Add Printer wizard's opening screen)

Automatically detect and install my Plug and Play printer

Next

Begin by connecting the printer. Be sure to uncheck the Plug and Play box.

Use the following port: LPT1

Next

For obscure reasons, Windows knows the parallel port as LPT1. Since that's where your printer is connected, select it from the list. It should, in fact, be pre-selected for you by default.

Your printer

 Have Disk

You can either select your printer from the list and click Next, in which case Windows will install a driver from its own database; or click Have Disk and use the installation CD-ROM that came with the printer. The latter is better, for the driver is likely to be more up to date (i.e. less buggy). Either way, this will get the printer working.

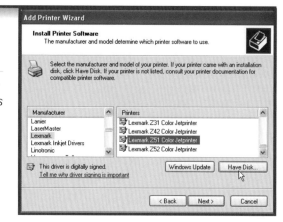

 Printer name

 Yes

 Next

Finally, give your printer a name or accept the proffered suggestion and decide whether or not you want it to be the default printer. The default printer is the one that all applications will use without question. If you only have one printer, of course, it will be the default device by, er, default.

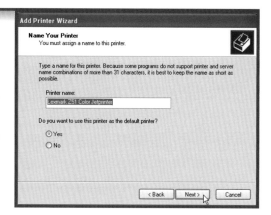

Adding a printer in Windows Vista

Although Windows Vista looks very different to earlier versions of Windows, adding printers works in exactly the same way as on its predecessors – unless you have a USB printer, in which case it's even faster and easier than before. Let's see it in action.

If you aren't connecting a USB printer, connect it to your computer (or if it's a wireless printer, switch it on) and then click on Start > Control Panel. Look in the left-hand column and you'll see a section headed Hardware and Sound. Click on Printer.

2

Vista will now display the list of installed printers – you might find entries such as 'fax' in here, but you can ignore them. Look immediately above the list and you'll see a toolbar. Click the *Add a Printer* button in the toolbar.

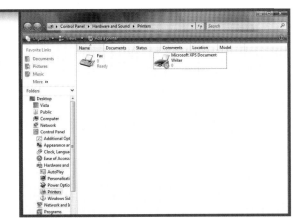

3

We're on familiar territory here: it's a wizard, and it's essentially Windows XP's Add Printer Wizard. Simply choose which kind of printer you want to install – a local printer, or a Bluetooth or network printer – and the wizard will take you through the necessary steps.

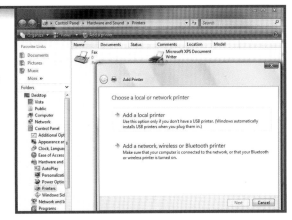

4

With USB printers, Vista makes things exceptionally easy: just plug the printer into a spare USB port and you should see a pop-up balloon in the bottom right of the screen. 'Installing device driver software', it says and that's exactly what it's doing.

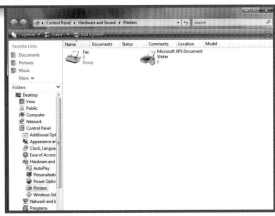

5

After a few seconds, the balloon will change: this time it tells you what printer you've connected and that everything's gone swimmingly. If you look in the Control Panel window you'll now see that your printer has appeared in the list, with a big green tick to show that it's the default printer. The next step? There isn't one: you're finished!

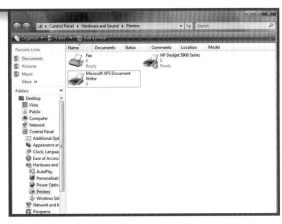

PART  Upgrading your scanner

A scanner takes a picture of a piece of paper and turns it into a digital image file that you can view and edit on your computer. There, it's as simple as that. So what might you use one for?

Well, you could scan a paper document into your PC and then fax it through the modem. Or you could print out a hard copy or two and thus emulate a photocopier. You might scan recipes, magazine articles, newspaper clippings or handwritten notes and preserve them forever on your hard disk, or perhaps email them to friends as file attachments. You could scan your snapshots, remove the red-eye and embarrassing ex-partners with an image editing program, and publish them on your website or in a newsletter. You might even scan every shred of paper in your possession and index and archive it all neatly on disc, so creating a truly paperless home/office. The uses for a scanner are indeed many and varied.

Like printers, 'free' scanners are often bundled with new computers to add the illusion of value but invariably they're second rate models. Plus any scanner more than a couple of years old is going to be vastly outclassed by today's generation.

Flatbed is the most common design for scanners. However, there are plenty of alternatives, including truly portable pen-sized models.

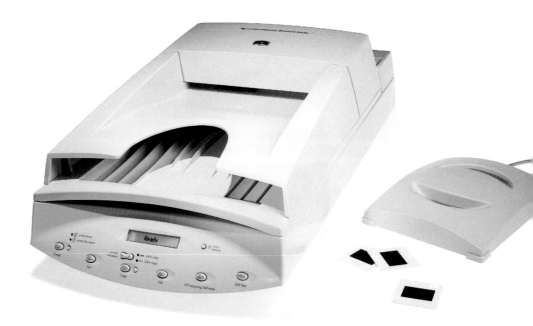

An ADF attachment saves time and effort when making multiple scans.

What you need to know

The language of scanner technology is unfamiliar to most but in fact there's nothing too complicated.

Design Scanners come in all shapes and sizes but flatbed models are by far the most popular. These look just like mini photocopiers: you lift the lid, place a document face down on the glass plate, close the lid and initiate the scan using software on your PC. Any flatbed should handle an A4 page with room to spare, and the lids are often cleverly hinged or completely removable in order that bulky objects such as books can also be scanned.

Alternative designs include handheld scanners that you manually sweep across the page and sheetfeed models where you feed pages through a roller mechanism one at a time.

Interface SCSI was once common but usually meant having to install an adapter on an internal expansion card, which was fiddly and expensive. USB is now the interface of choice but the slower parallel port also suffices.

Resolution The detail of a scanned image is measured in terms of dots per inch. More is better. Look for at least 600 x 1,200dpi true, or optical, resolution (as opposed to interpolated resolution – usually a much higher figure but not a true reflection of a scanner's capability).

Colour depth This describes how many colours a scanner can distinguish. Older scanners stuck at 24 bits, which equates to recognising nearly 17 million colours, but new models scan at 36 bits and are moving to 42 or even 48 bits. The greater colour depths help scanners to deal with bright and dark images as well as distinguish finer colour nuances. For scanning magazines and photos at home, a 30-bit scanner is more than adequate.

TWAIN In order for scanners to communicate with a wide range of software applications, they virtually all support a common standard called TWAIN (Technology Without An Interesting Name, according to urban legend). This means that even a word

processor or spreadsheet program can import an image straight from a scanner.

An adapter lets you scan film transparencies and slides as easily as printed pages.

ADF Strictly an optional extra, Automatic Document Feeders feed documents through a flatbed scanner one page at a time. Very useful for high volume work.

Transparency adapter This is a bolt-on accessory with a built-in light that enables a scanner to scan photographic transparencies.

OCR If you scanned the page that you're reading right now into your computer, you might think that you could immediately cut, copy and paste the text. But you'd be wrong. A scanned page is merely an image that makes no distinction between words and pictures. OCR, or Optical Character Recognition, is the process of turning a scanned image into editable text. Essentially, software 'reads' the image and determines which bits are words (and, crucially, which words) and which bits are design elements and pictures. OCR is almost never 100% successful but the best programs let you proofread as you go along to correct mistakes. Most scanners come with at least a 'lite' OCR package in the box.

Speed As with printers, some scanners are marginally quicker than others. The interface makes the biggest difference: SCSI scanners are quick but rare; parallel scanners should be avoided; USB 1.1 scanners are ideal; but USB 2 (Hi-Speed USB) scanners are best of all.

Software Look for at least a basic image manipulation program with your new toy. After all, you're going to want to tweak all those scanned images. For real ease of use, some scanners have a one-touch button that fires them into action without fussing with software. Others start working as soon as you open or close the lid. However, in most cases you'll run a TWAIN-compliant application on your PC and control the scanning process from there.

Installing your new scanner

You install a USB scanner in exactly the same way as any other USB peripheral: connect it to a free USB port on your PC and install the driver from the supplied CD-ROM when prompted.

Scanners come in parallel and SCSI flavours but USB is a good compromise between speed and convenience.

PART 5 Multi-function devices

As you'll no doubt have noticed during a previous excursion to any computer shop, there is an alternative to buying a separate printer and scanner. We're talking, of course, about multi-function devices, or MFDs. An MFD neatly combines print and scan functions in a single box.

One of the immediate advantages is that most MFDs also work like photocopiers: lift the scanner lid, place your document face-down on the glass plate, press the Copy button, and out pops a (scanned and printed) hard copy.

What's more, many MFDs also have built-in modems, which means they can both send and receive faxes. If you remember what we said earlier, a modem can handle faxes just as easily as an internet connection. A fax-capable MFD simply takes advantage of this. In fact, faxing with an MFD is usually a much simpler process than fiddling with modem software on the screen: the scanner takes a photo of your document, you type in a telephone number, and the modem sends the document through the phone line to any fax machine on the planet.

An MFD can be a printer (inkjet or laser), a scanner, a photocopier and a fax machine. They cost less – much less, in fact – than the combined cost of separate devices and they offer tremendous convenience, not least because they require only one plug and one cable connection to your PC. So is there a downside?

Well, the printer component in any MFD is by far the most important and it used to be true that MFDs tended to offer inferior print quality when compared with dedicated printers. But that's no longer the case. We'd merely advise that you check the specs carefully and judge an MFD just as you'd judge a standalone printer. The only real trouble with a decent MFD is the risk that a minor hardware failure in just one element could see the whole shebang shipped off for repair, leaving you sans printer, scanner, copier and fax. Still, balance that with the convenience and cost advantage and you may well feel that an MFD is too good to resist.

A fax-capable MFD may be the only office peripheral you need.

PART **6**

Home networking

Although you can prolong the useful lifespan of a
computer almost indefinitely with well-chosen upgrades,
there may come a time when you just can't resist starting
afresh with a brand-new system. Or perhaps you buy a
new PC for the kids, or invest in a laptop. Whatever the
reasons, it is becoming increasingly common to find two
or more computers in the household – at which point,
when you tire of running between them transferring files
on floppy disks, it makes practical sense to link them
together.

PART  The basics of home networking

The benefits of networking are manifest and significant. Any computer on the network can access files stored on any other computer's hard disk; they can share a single printer regardless of which computer it happens to be connected to; and, most important of all, they can share a single connection to the internet. This means that you can have two or more computers online together without having to invest in additional phone lines.

What you need to know

Wired and wireless There are two kinds of home network: wired networks, as the name suggests, use wires to connect computers together and wireless networks use radio waves. Wired networks are the cheapest and quickest kinds of network to set up, so we'll look at them in detail first.

Speed The most common connection standard used in home networking – or Local Area Networking (LAN) – is Ethernet. This is generally available in three speeds:

● 10Base-T (Ethernet) Data is transferred at a maximum rate of 10 megabits per second

A couple of Network Interface Cards plus a cable equals one home network.

- 100Base-T (Fast Ethernet) Data is transferred at a maximum rate of 100 megabits per second
- 1000Base-T (Gigabit Ethernet) Data is transferred at a maximum rate of 1,000 megabits per second

For home use, 10Base-T is ample, 100Base-T desirable and 1000Base-T overkill.

Interface Many modern PCs are now network-ready but Ethernet can easily be added by means of a Network Interface Card (NIC). Most cards are sold as '10/100', which means they can run at either Ethernet or Fast Ethernet speeds. NICs always use the PCI interface.

Wiring Ethernet cables come in two main flavours: coaxial and twisted pair. Some NICs have connectors for both but the most common option for home use is a twisted pair cable with RJ-45 connectors on either end. An RJ-45 connector looks like a larger version of the RJ-11 connector on your modem cable or telephone. Always buy 'Category 5' cables because they support all speeds of Ethernet and can be reused if you ever upgrade a network from 10Base-T to 100Base-T or 1000Base-T.

Hubs and switches A hub is a box that sits between networked computers to facilitate the free flow of data. Hubs are generally pretty dumb and play no active part in managing data flow, but some incorporate switches that 'intelligently' control the traffic. A switch can avoid networking bottle-necks but it's certainly not essential for a small home network.

Topology Local Area Networks can be set up in many ways. By far the simplest is a peer-to-peer arrangement, in which each PC is an equal partner on the network. The alternative is a client-server model where one computer – the server – controls all the action. This is definitely overkill and over-complicated for home use.

Software As we shall see, it is easy to set up home networking without using any extra software if your PC runs Windows Millennium Edition (Me), XP or Windows Vista.

An RJ-45 Ethernet cable.

A peer-to-peer network is perfect for hooking together two PCs but a hub adds expansion possibilities.

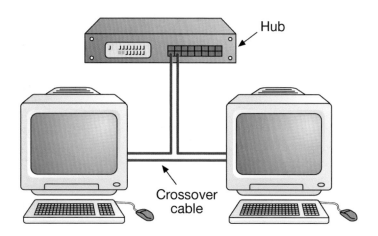

Hub

Crossover cable

PART 6

The Network Setup Wizard

Although it's possible to create a basic network by running a cable between two PCs, if you've got a broadband internet connection then it's a good idea to use a device called a router. This does two things: it's a broadband modem that connects your PC to the internet, but it also enables you to connect several PCs together and to share your broadband connection with each of them. In this tutorial, we'll show you how to share your broadband connection on a Windows XP machine.

First steps: Connecting your broadband router

When you've got a router, connecting to the internet couldn't be easier. It's just a matter of connecting one cable to the wall socket for your broadband connection, running an Ethernet cable to your PC, and plugging the power supply into the mains. Once you've done that, configuring the connection is very simple. Windows automatically detects the router, so all you need to do is enter your ISP's account information. Here's how.

1

Every router is slightly different, but the principles are the same – in this case we're using a NetGear router, but you'll find the procedure is almost identical no matter what model or manufacturer you've chosen. Once you've connected your router and switched it on, open your web browser and enter the following address:
http://192.168.0.1
This will connect to your router so you can configure your broadband connection – but you'll need to provide a user name and password before you can access the settings. On NetGear routers the defaults are 'admin' and 'password'. Remember to change them later so other people can't get in.

You'll now see the router's settings screen. In the case of our NetGear kit, the bit we want is in the Basic Settings section, shown here. Your ISP will give you the necessary information to input here, such as your login details and password. In most cases you can ignore any settings that your ISP hasn't provided information for.

When you've entered your details, a pop-up window will show the router's progress as it attempts to log in to your broadband account. This can take a few moments. In this screen, our router says everything's working fine.

And here's the proof: NetGear routers automatically connect to and display the NetGear website so you can see that your broadband connection is working. That's our internet connection set up – now, let's share it.

Using your router for home networking

Once your router's connected to the internet, you can share your connection with your other PCs – but you can also use it to share files between different computers. As we'll discover, it isn't difficult to set up and it's very easy to use.

Click on Start > Control Panel and look for the Network Setup Wizard icon. This Wizard enables you to make the necessary changes to your system for networking without having to wade through stacks of dialog boxes and obscure menus, so it's a real time saver. Double-click on the icon and click Next to continue.

It's very important that before you run the Wizard, everything you need to connect is switched on and plugged in. That's because the Wizard can automatically detect your network hardware and make the appropriate changes, and it can't do that if it can't find anything to connect to.

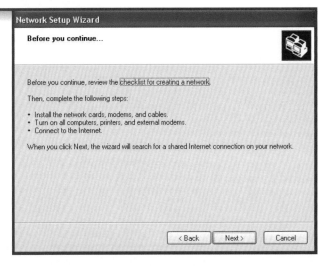

Straight away the Wizard spots that we have an internet connection, and asks us if that's the connection we want to use. It is, so click on Next.

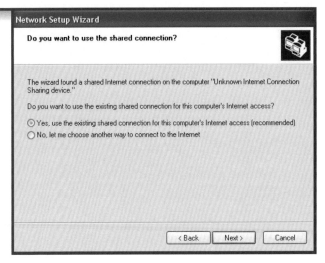

Every computer needs to have a unique name, and you can change the default settings here. You can provide two names: a full description and a short name. The latter name is the one that will be displayed to other computers on your network.

This screen asks you to give your workgroup – Microsoft's name for a local network a name. The default is MSHOME and there's no need to change it unless you plan to run lots of different networks in the same building.

This step is crucial: in addition to sharing your internet connection, you can also share files and printers – which means other computers on your network can use your printer or access files you've shared. If you don't turn on file and printer sharing, they won't be able to do that.

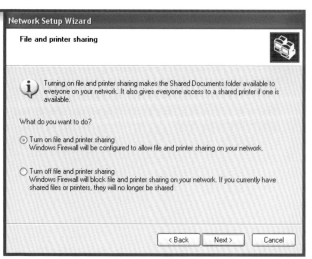

7

We're ready to go: this screen simply tells you that Windows XP is ready to make the necessary changes to your system, and it gives you a summary of the options you've chosen so far. Click on Next to make the changes.

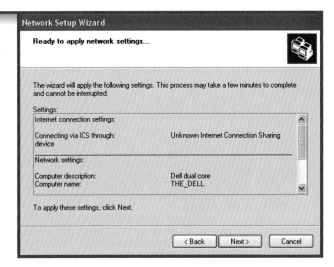

8

Time for one of Windows' cute little animations, which gives you something to look at while the appropriate changes are being made. Depending on the speed of your system, you'll see the animation for anything between a few seconds and a few minutes.

9

If you're connecting to other Windows XP machines, it's just a matter of running the same Wizard on those PCs, but this screen also enables you to create a Network Setup Disk that makes the necessary changes to machines running older versions of Windows. If you don't need to do that, check the 'Just finish the wizard' button and click Next.

And that's it. Windows now gives you two links that will explain more about the Shared Documents folder and network sharing in general, or you can click on Finish to exit the wizard.

We've repeated the process for our other PC, so it's time to test our network. Click on Start > My Network Places and you'll see a map of your network. Your PC is on the left (in this screenshot it's the one called 'The_dell') and any other machines on the network will appear in this window. As you can see, we have another machine: Liz-PC. You can always tell the difference between your machine and network ones: folders on your PC use the standard folder icon, but ones on your network appear with a little pipe below them.

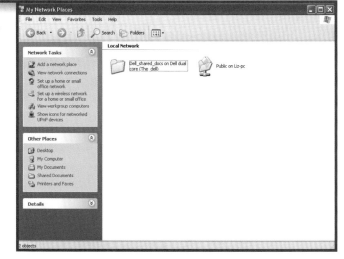

Accessing a network folder is as easy as accessing one on your own hard disk: just double-click on it and it will open. In this screenshot, we've double-clicked on the Liz-PC/Public folder that appeared in My Network Places, and we're now browsing its contents – so if we wanted to look at one of the pictures on that machine, we'd open the Pictures folder and double-click on the image file we wanted to look at. Simple!

Sharing files

Sharing files is one of the best things about networking. For example, last night we were browsing our digital photos on a laptop, and while the laptop was with us on the sofa the actual photo files were on the desktop PC upstairs. However, it can be a potential problem too. If you're not careful, it's possible for other people not only to view the files on your PC, but to change them too. That's fine if you want them to be able to do that, but it's not so good if the kids have just deleted all the Excel spreadsheets that you use to do your tax return.

The good news is that Windows makes it very easy to control how files are shared, and by default it only shares files you put in your Shared Documents folder. The rest of your hard disk remains off-limits.

Even when you do share files, you can control what people can and cannot do with them. If you right-click on your shared folder in My Computer and click on the Sharing tab you'll see a section headed Network Sharing and Security with two tick boxes: share this folder on the network, which means other users can view your files and copy them to their own PCs – this will be ticked if you've followed our walkthrough so far – and a second box, Allow Network Users to Change My Files. If you tick this second option then not only can other users view and copy your files, but they can edit, rename and even delete them. If you'd rather not let the kids have full control over the files in your Shared Documents folder, untick the box and click on Apply.

Although it's possible to share any folder over your network by right-clicking on it, choosing properties and then applying options in the Sharing tab – we'd advise against it, especially at home. It's all too easy for someone to accidentally delete something important. In most cases, it's a better idea to stick with a single Shared Documents folder and simply copy the files you want to share into that.

Networking in Windows Vista

Windows Vista makes networking even easier. While some things are identical to Windows XP – for example, installing your router and configuring your broadband connection is the same simple process in Vista as it is in XP, albeit with slightly nicer looking pictures – setting up a network is much, much quicker.

The key is the Network and Sharing Center, which you'll find in Control Panel > Network and Internet. Instead of messing around with Wizards, setting up a local network in Vista is just a matter of turning on Network Discovery, File Sharing and Public Folder sharing on both PCs, hooking them together and waiting for Vista to introduce them to one another.

Windows Vista makes networking simple – and it's about time too.

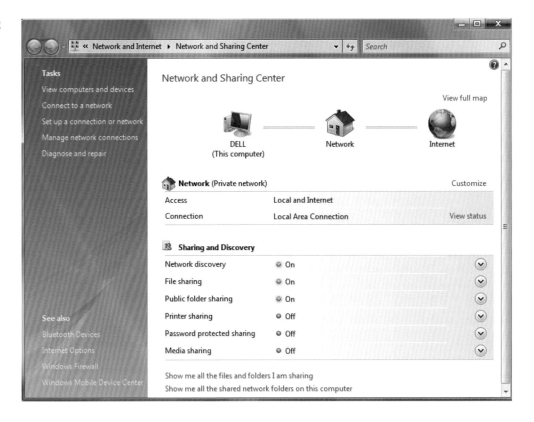

Wireless networks

We've already discovered how you can use a router to share your broadband connection with several PCs – and if you buy a wireless router, you can do it wirelessly. Instead of connecting your PCs together with cables, it's just a matter of installing wireless adapters in each of them. Wireless adapters are available as PCI cards (for desktops), PC Cards (for laptops) or USB adapters (for both desktops and laptops), and wireless routers are available for both ADSL and cable broadband connections.

Wireless networks – often called Wi-Fi – are ideal for homes: because they use radio transmissions instead of cables you don't need to drill through walls if you want to use computers in other rooms, and in many cases you can browse the net from your shed if the signal's strong enough.

Setting up a wireless network isn't much more difficult than setting up a wired one, and the equipment isn't much more expensive than wired networking equipment. However, wireless networking does raise some important issues that you might want to take into account.

Wireless security

The single best thing about wireless networks is that they work through walls. Unfortunately, the single worst thing about wireless networks is that they work through walls. As we write this we're within range of two wireless networks: our own and our next-door neighbours'. They can't connect to our wireless network but we can connect to theirs. That's because our wireless network is secure and theirs isn't.

It's very easy to secure a wireless network: when you buy a router, it has a range of security features built-in. For example, you can set a complicated password for your network, so anyone who doesn't know the password can't get on to your network; for extra security you can even create an 'access list' of computers. That turns your wireless router into an electronic bouncer: if a computer isn't on the list, it doesn't get into your network.

There are very good reasons for securing a wireless network, although they might not be obvious. For example, while the average person doesn't have the technical know-how to hack your system and steal your important files, if your network isn't secured it's child's play for anyone within range to connect and then use your internet connection. That's bad news for two reasons: they're getting free internet access that you're paying for and, more seriously, they could be up to no good. If they're caught, you could end up with the blame.

Why letting other people use your net connection is a bad idea

Whenever you connect to the internet, your ISP gives you a unique address, which is the internet equivalent of a telephone number. This address, known as the IP address, is logged – so if you try to hack into the Pentagon or look at illegal content, you can be traced. Although ISPs don't spy on you, they do keep logs of IP addresses and their activity, and the police can compel them to hand over those logs if they believe a crime has been committed. When you use a wireless network, the IP address is assigned to your router and to any machine connected to it. That means that if someone else connects to your network, anything they do will still appear to come from your IP address.

Of course, you're a perfectly law-abiding, upstanding member of the public – but what about the people next door or people you haven't met? Although wireless networks don't extend too far, they do extend into the street – and, as a lot of companies have discovered, that means people can sit outside in their cars and take advantage of wireless internet access for dodgy purposes. In the US, a number of people have been prosecuted for doing just that.

There's another, less dramatic reason not to share your broadband connection with other people: in most cases, your ISP's terms and conditions state that you can't share your broadband with anyone who doesn't share your building.

Wireless standards

There are two main wireless standards: 802.11b, and 802.11g. They both work in the same way but 802.11g is much faster than 802.11b and uses slightly different technology, so a wireless card that only supports the b standard won't be able to connect to a g network. However, most wireless cards now support both standards: look for products that are described as 802.11b/g and you'll be able to connect not just to your own wireless network, but public wireless networks too.

There's a third standard, 802.11n. This is even faster than 802.11g, and it uses a technology called MIMO – multiple inputs, multiple outputs – to improve signal strength and speed. However, at the time of writing, the 802.11n standard hasn't been finalised. That hasn't stopped companies selling 802.11n hardware, but beware: until the standard has been agreed by all the main players, you might find that so-called 'pre-n' hardware doesn't work properly with other firms' 802.11n products. Always make sure that any pre-n hardware can be upgraded (for free) when the final, official standard is published. If in doubt, don't buy it.

If that wasn't confusing enough, some manufacturers also offer their own versions of existing standards, so for example you'll see wireless products advertised as 'Super G' that offer much faster speeds than 802.11g is supposed to deliver. Such products do work, but they only work with other products that use the same technology – so if you buy a Super G router but a standard 802.11g wireless network card, you won't get any benefit from the Super G technology.

Wireless speed and range

According to the blurb, 802.11b kit delivers connection speeds of 11Mbps while 802.11g kit ups that to 54Mbps. That's much faster than a broadband connection, but the figures are somewhat misleading. The figures you'll see on the box are maximums and you'll never achieve them in the real world.

There are two reasons for this. The first is that the speed is shared by however many machines are connected, so if you have two computers accessing an 11Mbps connection simultaneously then they get 5.5Mbps each. The speed also drops with distance

– 802.11b's range is around 150 metres, but the signal strength drops dramatically long before that point, particularly if the signal has to pass through walls or other obstacles. The further you are from the wireless router, the slower your connection will be.

The second reason why the quoted speeds are over-optimistic is due to 'overheads'. Some of the data transferred between a wireless device and a wireless router is about the connection – essentially the router is asking 'is anybody there?' and your computer replies 'yes, I'm over here!' That chatter is essential to establish and maintain any wireless connection, but it takes a lot of data – typically 40 to 50% of the network connection. So your 11Mbps connection drops to around 5.5Mbps before you even get started and, when you connect a second PC, the speed halves again to around 2.75Mbps – and it gets even slower the further away you are from the wireless router.

Does any of this matter? Yes and no. Even 2.75Mbps is fast enough for sharing a 512Kbps broadband connection, but there's not much point in spending money on a 22Mbps broadband connection if your wireless kit can't deliver it to your computer. That's why it makes sense to get the fastest wireless kit you can afford: the difference in price between 802.11b and 802.11g kit isn't dramatic, but if you're getting a fast broadband connection that you want to use with multiple computers then the faster kit is worth the extra expense.

Who needs cables? Take your laptop to the garden.

Connecting to a wireless network

Whether you're connecting to a wireless network at home or one in an airport or coffee shop, all the software you need is inside Windows – or at least, it has been since Microsoft launched the second Service Pack for Windows XP. In this walkthrough we'll use Windows Vista, but the process in XP is much the same.

If your computer came with wireless networking built-in (something that's very common with laptops) then the necessary hardware drivers should be pre-installed on your system. If you've added wireless hardware to your system yourself, though, you'll need to install the necessary drivers from the CD that came with your kit. Until you do, Windows probably won't recognise your hardware and you won't be able to connect to any wireless networks.

When you're in range of a wireless network, if your wireless network adapter is switched on then Windows will notify you with a pop-up in the bottom right corner of the screen. Right-click over the network icon in the System Tray to see the available options.

The option we need is the top one, Connect to a Network. Click on this to see a list of available networks.

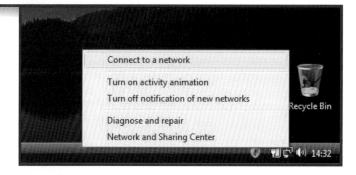

Windows will now show you not just what networks are in range, but whether they're security protected (i.e. whether they need a password) and how strong the signal is. In this case we'll connect to the security-protected network at the top of our list: to do this, double-click on the name of the network you want to join.

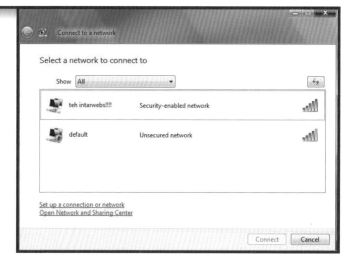

4

You'll now see a brief animation while Windows attempts to connect to the wireless network. If it's password protected, you'll need to enter the appropriate details at this point; if you don't know the password you won't be able to connect at all.

5

Mission accomplished: we're connected. A pop-up in the bottom of the screen tells us what network we've connected to and how strong the signal is.

6

On Windows Vista you can see more information by clicking Start > Control Panel > Network and Internet > Network and Sharing Center. This gives you a diagram showing how you're connected and what you're connected to and it also tells you what networking features are enabled. In this screenshot, our wireless network includes a shared internet connection, so we can browse the internet from anywhere we can get a wireless signal.

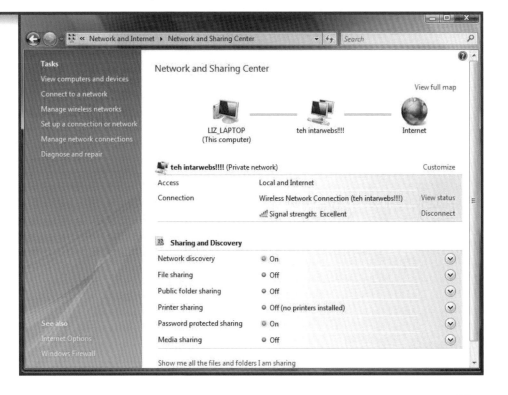

PART  **PC maintenance**

Computer hardware is a curious mix of solid-state components with no moving parts to break or seize and precision-engineered, finely-tuned devices that require regular maintenance and cleaning to work at their best. Things can and do go wrong, so here we consider some sensible preventative measures to stop potential problems in their tracks, some basic trouble-shooting techniques, and a maintenance regime designed to keep your PC running smoothly.

PART

Windows utilities

As you may expect, Windows comes equipped with an array of useful tools designed to optimise its performance. While many people swear by the likes of Norton SystemWorks or McAfee Office, others never spend a penny on third-party utility software. Let's look at what Windows has to offer.

Defragmenting your hard disk improves performance.

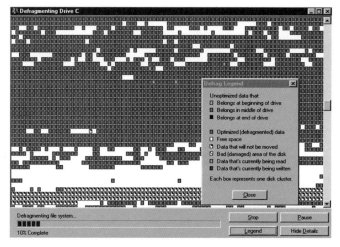

Disk Defragmenter

The data on your hard disk is stored in lots of small packets. Although this is an efficient use of space, one side effect is that individual files can get split apart and stored piecemeal all over the disk. This process is known as fragmentation and it only gets worse with time. Every time you open a fragmented file, Windows has to track down all the different bits and pieces and stick them back together again – a time-consuming and wasteful business. However, with a utility called Disk Defragmenter, you can restore all files to their former glory and buck up system performance at a stroke.

If you are using Windows 98 or Me, it's important to close down all system activity before you begin: any attempt by a program to write data to the hard disk causes Disk Defragmenter to start from scratch. Close all running programs, such as your word processor, browser or email program in the usual way, and disconnect from the internet. You should end with a clear Desktop and no buttons on the Taskbar. Then look at the System Tray – the part of the Taskbar next to the clock – for icons that show which programs are running in the background. Right-click each icon in turn and select Exit or Close. You should be left with just the clock and speaker icons.

Close down all programs before running Disk Defragmenter.

Finally, press the Ctrl, Alt and Delete keys simultaneously. This reveals any other open, but hidden, applications. Highlight each item in turn – with the exception of Explorer and Systray – and select End Task. With versions of Windows from XP on, you can continue to use your computer while defragmenting.

Now click Start > Programs > Accessories > System Tools. Here you will find Disk Defragmenter. Start the program and select the drive you wish to optimise (usually the C: drive).

Tell the program which disk to work on.

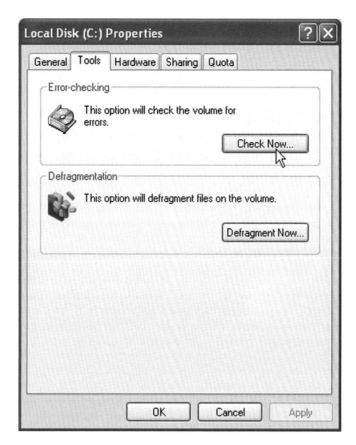

In Windows XP, the disk-checking utility is accessed by right-clicking a drive in My Computer.

ScanDisk

Whenever your PC crashes or closes down unexpectedly, you may notice that it runs through an error checking process next time you start it up. This is ScanDisk looking for, and hopefully fixing, file problems on the hard disk. However, you can also run ScanDisk on demand. Here's how.

In Windows 98/Me, click Start > Programs > Accessories > System Tools > ScanDisk. There are two options here: a Standard test, which is reasonably quick and checks all your files and folders for errors; and a Thorough test, which takes much longer but also examines the physical integrity of your hard disk. If you're having problems with your PC – perhaps a document won't open – the Standard test is usually enough, but we'd recommend a Thorough scan once in a while as part of a periodic system maintenance regime.

Check the box marked 'Automatically fix errors' to speed things up. You can set the parameters of what ScanDisk will and will not do in the Advanced dialogue box but the default options are just fine. As with Disk Defragmenter, leave ScanDisk to work in peace. If it finds any lost clusters (parts of files), it saves them with the extension .CHK in the root directory (the topmost folder in Windows). These may safely be deleted. If, however, ScanDisk reports any 'bad sectors', back up your files immediately. Although Windows will not now write any new data to these unusable areas of the hard disk, it may be a sign of impending disk failure.

Windows XP operates slightly differently. Open My Computer to see your drives, then right-click the drive you want to check (usually C: drive). Select Properties from the menu, open the Tools tab and click the Check Now button.

Let ScanDisk automatically fix any problems it finds.

Disk Cleanup

Programs take up a lot of space but so can individual files, particularly web pages saved to the hard disk by your web browser. Disk Cleanup can automatically remove a good deal of this debris.

As with Disk Defragmenter and ScanDisk, Disk Cleanup is found in the System Tools menu. The program offers several options: simply check each box in turn for an explanation of what it does. Do be cautious about emptying the Recycle Bin, especially if you've just deleted a bunch of files. Sure as eggs is eggs you'll wish you hadn't permanently consigned that complete record of your household finances to oblivion three seconds after you push the button.

The Temporary Internet Files area may be quite large. This is your browser's cache – an area of your hard disk set aside for keeping copies of the web pages you visit. If you delete its contents, your browser will have to reload each page from scratch next time you revisit a favourite site instead of plucking some or all of its elements from the cache. This may slow down your surfing a little but the cache soon fills up again and the effects are short-lived. Besides, many web pages are updated frequently so having an old copy on your computer isn't really much of an advantage.

Disk Cleanup explains what it's going to do before it starts.

Maintenance Wizard

The problem with ScanDisk, Disk Defragmenter and Disk Cleanup is, of course, that you'll never remember to use them. That's why Windows includes Maintenance Wizard, a utility that lets you set up an automatic schedule for running one, two or all three programs at regular intervals. Once again, find it by clicking Start > Programs > Accessories > System Tools, and then run Maintenance Wizard in custom mode. Note that it's best to schedule these tasks to run at a time when you're not using your computer, like the middle of the night. You also have to ensure that no running programs will interfere with Disk Defragmenter (see above), so close down anything that's not absolutely essential and deactivate any screensaver before you bed down. Oh, and don't forget to leave your computer switched on and running.

Maintenance Wizard is not available in Windows XP.

If you're prone to forgetfulness, what you want is a Wizard.

Registry Checker

The Registry is a database of Windows settings. Without the Registry, Windows won't start or run at all; and if the Registry gets corrupted, all manner of errors can crop up. It's well worth while making a manual backup of the Registry before undertaking any work on your computer, be it a new program installation or a hardware upgrade.

Click Start > Programs > Accessories > System Tools > System Information. Now click the Tools menu button and select Registry Checker. Accept the proposal to make a backup of the current Registry file.

Alternatively, in Windows Me and XP you can back up the Registry simply by making a System Restore point (see p147).

Registry Checker isn't available in Windows XP but only because XP includes some rather more robust tools that automatically protect the Registry from damage.

Add/Remove Programs

Ah, if only life was simple and you could install and delete software at will and with ease. Well, sometimes you can, but only sometimes. The trouble is that there's no single, catch-all, foolproof method for ridding a system of unwanted applications. Some come with their own uninstall utilities while others rely on Windows to do the work. Still others display a thoroughly leechlike determination never to be deleted.

A 'true' Windows program should install smoothly and do away with itself just as easily. However, in practice, bits and pieces of programs are often left behind, notably empty folders and scattered cryptic files. Most worrying are orphaned entries in the Windows Registry, a record of all that makes your system tick. Conflicts and confusion in here can be serious. Windows XP controls rogue programs far more effectively than its predecessors, to the extent that it objects in the strongest possible terms if you try to install something that hasn't been tested and automatically backs up and restores any critical system files that are altered during installation or use.

But why bother getting shot of old software? Why not just let it be? Three reasons:

1 Old programs take up disk space. Sooner or later, you're liable to need it, so it's better to manage this as you go along.

2 You might not realise it but many programs run continuously in the background even if you never actually use them to do anything useful. This eats into available RAM and has a detrimental effect on performance.

3 Every additional program on your system increases the risk of conflict with another, more useful program. As a rule, tidy

Add/Remove Programs clears out the clutter. Unfortunately, it doesn't always work perfectly.

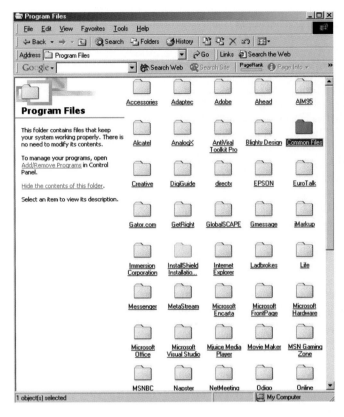

How many of your programs do you actually use?

systems run more smoothly and you may find that simply uninstalling some half-forgotten software miraculously cures no end of unexplained ills.

So, click Start > Programs and see just what you've got onboard. Point at any superfluous programs and see if an Uninstall option appears. If so, select it and follow the step-by-step instructions. At the end of the process, you may be warned that some elements of the program must be manually removed. Make a note of any details supplied. The leftovers are usually a top-level folder in the Program Files menu and perhaps one or two sub-folders within. Now click My Computer, select your hard disk, click Program Files and find the folder(s) that you jotted down. These may now be dragged straight to the Recycle Bin. Incidentally, Windows Millennium Edition has the touching habit of refusing you access to Program Files on pain of the sky falling in. Just override it.

Where a program doesn't come with its own uninstaller, click Start > Settings > Control Panel > Add/Remove programs. This brings up a list of programs that Windows can automatically delete. Just highlight the program and click Add/Remove.

System Configuration Utility

You know the way that certain programs start automatically every time you turn on your computer? This behaviour may be highly desirable, as with anti-virus software, or may be intensely irritating. To stop them in their tracks, there are three possibilities:

1 Look in the program's own Preferences or Options (or similar) menu and see if you can uncheck a 'Start this program with Windows' (or similar) option.

2 Click Start > Programs and look in a folder called Startup. This contains shortcuts to programs that start with Windows. To remove a shortcut, right-click it and select Delete.

3 If neither approach solves the problem of persistent programs, click Start > Run and type 'msconfig'. Now click OK to launch the System Configuration utility. In the Startup tab, you'll find a list of programs and background utilities. Look for the offending item and uncheck the box.

Most well-behaved programs let you decide when and whether they start.

Nobble programs that start without your permission with the System Configuration utility.

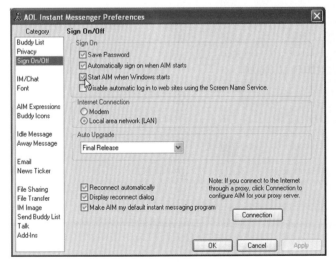

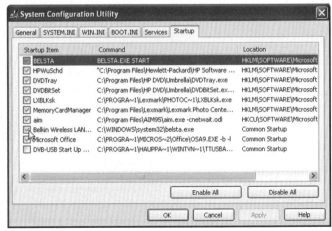

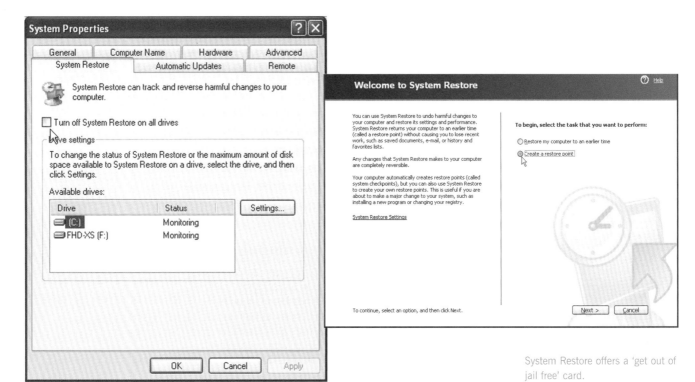

System Restore offers a 'get out of jail free' card.

System Restore

Windows Millennium Edition, XP and Vista include a background tool called System Restore. This takes regular 'snapshots' of the system and allows you to roll back in time in the event of trouble. For instance, if you install a rogue program and Windows starts crashing, you can restore your system to the way it was before the installation.

It sounds magical and, up to a point, it is. We'll mention it again in the trouble-shooting section but for now you should ensure that it's actually active.

In Windows XP, right-click the My Computer icon on your Desktop, select Properties and open the System Restore tab. In Windows Me, right-click the My Computer icon on your Desktop, select Properties, open the Performance tab, click File System and then click Troubleshooting. Here you'll find an option to disable the utility. Be sure not to.

You can make a manual checkpoint at any time, and we strongly suggest you do so before installing new software or hardware. Click Start > Programs > Accessories > System Tools and launch System Restore. Click the Create a Restore Point button and follow the directions. You can now revert to this checkpoint should anything go awry in the future (see p155).

Performance options in Windows XP

As we've mentioned, Windows XP demands a fairly hefty hardware configuration to run smoothly. If your system is anywhere close to the minimum requirements – see p22 – you may see a considerable benefit by switching off some of the fancier display effects. Right-click the My Computer icon, select Properties and open the Advanced tab. Now click the Settings button in the Performance section and check the Adjust for best performance option.

Performance options in Windows Vista

Windows Vista contains essentially the same performance options as Windows XP, but you'll find them in a different place. To adjust system settings for best results click on Start > Control Panel > System Maintenance > Performance Information and Tools. Along the side of the window, you'll now see links to the various options: Manage Startup Programs, Adjust Visual Effects, Adjust Indexing Options, Adjust Power Settings, Open Disk Cleanup and Advanced Tools. This last option tells you if Windows has detected any performance issues and also gives you access to a huge range of reports so you can see not just what your system's made of, but how reliable it is and whether you need to fiddle with any system settings.

Bid farewell to fading menus and mouse shadows for a boost in raw performance.

PART 7

PC MAINTENANCE

Viruses – a special case

However you cut it, computer viruses are a fact of life. At best, they're a hassle; at worst, downright destructive. You have to be something of a moron to release one 'into the wild', so to speak, but there's no shortage of them in the world. And so all we can do is accept that viruses are with us in abundance and take adequate precautions.

Update your anti-virus software frequently.

If you suspect you've been infected, scan your system without delay.

Don't be fooled by silly hoaxes – check them out on the web.

Protect and survive

Viruses are basically programs like any other. They typically have two parts: a means of getting into your system and a reason for doing so. Once inside, a successful virus might scramble your data, sit quietly in the background doing nothing at all until triggered by a key date, or instantly email copies of itself to everyone in your address book. Some viruses are created by geeks for the supposed kudos of being clever with code; others are written by malicious saboteurs bent on wreaking havoc across company networks or the internet itself. In all cases, your first and necessary line of defence is to install an anti-virus program. This attempts to identify inbound nasties in one or both of two ways: by spotting and isolating known viruses (highly effective but not much use against brand new bugs that aren't yet in its database); and by looking for suspiciously virus-like behaviour (a good safety net, although far from foolproof).

Moreover, because new viruses appear all the time, you must update your anti-virus program regularly. If it has an auto-update feature, all to the good: allow it to call home for updates whenever you're online. Otherwise, make it a point of principle to manually update it at least once a month, and preferably once a week. Some developers now release daily updates. Remember, an out-of-date anti-virus program is next to worthless, so don't assume that you're safe just because your new computer came with an anti-virus program pre-installed.

Get wise to hoaxes

Equally important is making sure that you don't contribute to the spread of these pests yourself. Never pass on a virus warning without first checking whether or not it's a hoax. If a rampant email virus can bring a network to a standstill, a flurry of hoax warnings is almost as damaging. So, if you get a virus warning in your email inbox, pause and consider before forwarding it to anybody else. Does it exhort you in the strongest possible terms to tell everybody you know 'WITHOUT DELAY!!!!'? Does it proclaim that unspeakable things will happen to your hard disk if you get infected? Does it read like the work of an idiot trying to get a rise out of the world? Then it's almost certainly a hoax. Check it out at Vmyths.com (**http://vmyths.com**) before you pass it on.

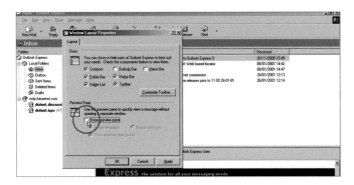

Switch off the Preview Pane option in your email program for better security.

MVSCS97 MaCrO Virus MaKer WORD97!! AlevirusS>C>S

OK

Quite what pleasure virus writers derive from their dark art is a mystery.

Periodically check for Windows updates and install any security patches.

Sensible steps

Aside from installing and updating anti-virus software, there are various things you can do to minimise the risk of infection.

Switch on your anti-virus program's background scanning features to ensure that all files are checked at the point of being opened.

Check for security updates and patches for your email program. If you use Microsoft's Outlook or Outlook Express, go here:
http://windowsupdate.microsoft.com
(It will only work if you are using Internet Explorer version 5 or better.)

Don't download files from strangers on the internet and delete, without opening, any unasked for email attachments. Don't even sneak a peek at mystery messages in your email program's Preview Pane, as this alone can be enough to do the damage. For maximum security, switch off the Preview Pane option altogether. In Outlook Express, click Layout in the View menu and uncheck the Preview Pane option.

Be wary of Word documents (files with the extension .DOC) and Excel spreadsheets (extension .XLS), as these could harbour macro viruses.

Never open an executable file type unless and until you've scanned it for viruses *and* been personally assured by the sender that it's safe. Extensions to look out for include: .EXE, .VBS and .JS.

Don't beg, steal or borrow dodgy software.

Beware of files that try to hide their true extension e.g. BritneySpearsNaked.jpg.vbs. Many a mug would assume that this is a harmless image file but the .VBS extension gives the game away: it's a script virus.

PC MAINTENANCE

Taking precautions

A little foresight and rudimentary background knowledge about the various things that can do a computer system harm goes a long way towards averting serious problems. We covered static electricity at the very outset and we'll take the liberty of assuming that you already know that water and electricity don't mix (i.e. don't play with your PC in the bath. Don't laugh: we know of one finance director who dropped his laptop in the bath; luckily for him, he survived – but his laptop didn't). Here are some other essentials.

A lightning strike could fry your computer – so better get protected!

Magnetism

If it wasn't for the magic of magnetism, your PC's hard disk couldn't permanently store data. Nor could floppy or Zip disks transfer files from here to there and back again. But while magnetism is undoubtedly a force for good, it can also do inordinate damage to your data when allowed to interfere with the strictly controlled conditions present in your computer system. It pays, therefore, to ensure that magnets in any form and data stored on magnetic media (as opposed to optical media like CD and DVD discs) do not come into contact with one another.

For instance, never stick a magnetic paper clip holder on your PC case lest it interfere with the workings of the hard disk. Keep floppies well away from magnetic sources like printers, fridges, cars, mobile phones, hi-fi speakers – and, of course, plain magnets. It's also unwise to stack them on top of the PC case. As we've mentioned before, a magnetic screwdriver may be perfect for retrieving lost screws but it shouldn't be allowed anywhere near the inside of a computer.

Power surges

You may well have a good idea of just how regular, or smooth, your electricity supply is. Then again, you may have no idea. Peaks and dips are sometimes made evident by an unexpected brightening or dimming of the lights, but a serious peak, or spike, can do a computer serious damage.

Now, all reputable PC manufacturers build some form of surge protection into the power supply controlling the current that flows into the system but it's unwise to rely on this alone. If you consider that you're at risk from sudden voltage spikes, or if you simply want an added layer of protection, consider a heavy-duty surge protector. This is a circuit breaker sited between your computer and the electricity supply that stops any spike in its tracks.

There are several different designs but the most effective deploy a metal-oxide varistor (MOV) that routes the surge straight to earth and thus out of harm's way. Unfortunately, these can be worn down over time and a single large surge may kill an MOV outright. This is fine – after all, it's the job of a surge protector to take the bullet for your computer – but, rather bizarrely, some units don't actually tell you when the MOV is dead. To avoid an unwarranted sense of security, be certain to buy a surge protector with a warning light that clearly displays whether or not it's working!

Power cuts

Spikes aren't the only power problem to afflict the computer user. Who hasn't experienced a sudden power cut and lost a minute, an hour or a day's work in a flash? Such incidents generally prove a great crash course in the importance of saving your work regularly as you go along but it's a lesson we could all do without. The answer is to invest in an uninterruptible power supply (UPS) of some sort. A UPS is essentially a battery unit that draws its charge from the mains supply and takes over power supply duties the instant a power outage occurs. Different models offer different levels of protection – some may provide only a few minutes power while others can keep a PC running for an hour or two (plenty of time to leap out of bed in the middle of the night, drive to the office and salvage that vital company backup job) – but the principle is simply to give you sufficient time to save your work and close down the computer in an orderly manner.

A surge protector prevents sudden spikes in current – or lightning strikes – from reaching and potentially destroying your hardware. This model sits under the monitor.

A backup battery lets you carry on working in the event of a power failure.

8

PART

Trouble-shooting

Although it's certainly true that your computer system is on a fast-track to obsolescence almost as soon as you get it home from the store, the good news is that hardware reliability these days is generally very high. Today's inkjet printer should still be technically capable of churning out full colour pages long after the manufacturer stops making the ink cartridges it requires. Also, most problems are evident immediately rather than, say, six months down the line. A new processor either works or doesn't work: it doesn't 'sort of work'. (For just this reason, incidentally, an expensive extended warranty is usually a waste of money.) You may be lucky and never experience a hardware problem; then again, your shiny new PC may be dead on arrival. Here we look at how to begin the trouble-shooting process.

PART 8 | Trouble-shooting in general

The first and entirely natural reaction to a computer problem is often one of panic, compounded by the realisation that we haven't been quite as rigorous with our backing up regime as we might have been. What happens if it never works again? Have all our files and documents disappeared forever? It's at such moments that we wish that we had taken a college course in advanced computing and that we had never become so reliant upon the infernal contraption in the first place.

Checklist

It's obviously beyond the scope of this book to cover every eventuality – which is why we wrote the *Haynes Computer Troubleshooting Manual* – but here are some general approaches that just might resolve your woes. First off, though, just relax. Put the kettle on. Go for a walk or sleep on it. Then calmly, rationally and logically think through the problem. Computers are fantastically complex at heart but also ridiculously simple in the sense that one bit plugs into another and can be easily replaced.

1   Are your PC and all its peripherals plugged in and switched on? How about any switches on the cases – could these have been inadvertently knocked to the off position? Be sure to check the power supply too – could a fuse have blown somewhere, either in the main fuse box or in the device's

Updated drivers can cure many known problems so check the manufacturer's website.

own plug? Perhaps your surge protector has given up the ghost and cut the power as a safety precaution? If your USB mouse, keyboard, printer or whatever are connected to a hub, try connecting them one at a time to a USB port on the computer itself to establish whether the hub is at fault. Many a call to technical support – and a resulting red face – could have been spared by these simplest of all checks.

2   Check that all cables are in place. It may mean crawling around behind your system but it's not uncommon for a USB cable to fall out of its socket and render a device inoperative. Cables themselves can also fail, albeit rarely, so it's well worth while experimenting with a spare cable before assuming that a device is a dud.

3   When did your PC or the suspect peripheral last work without trouble? Can you undo any changes that you've made in the meantime? Hardware conflicts (see Techie Corner on p161) are common and temporarily uninstalling a newly-connected component can often fix a problem or at least pinpoint its probable cause. Poorly written software applications are also notorious for thoroughly confounding the most carefully arranged system settings, so uninstall any recent additions (see p145).

4   If you're running Windows Millennium Edition, XP or Vista, try the System Restore utility. This is a way of reverting the computer's configuration settings to an earlier, trouble-free time. Click Start > Programs > Accessories > System Tools > System Restore and check to see when Windows made its last 'checkpoint'. Roll back to this checkpoint and see if the problem goes away. If so, all you have to do is work out what you did in the interim to cause all the bother. If not, try an earlier checkpoint. Don't worry about your files and documents, incidentally, as these are unaffected by System Restore.

System Restore can take you back in time to a point before your troubles began.

5   If your computer won't start normally, try starting it in Safe Mode instead. This loads and runs a bare-bones versions of Windows in which many features are unavailable, but it gives you a chance to carry out repair work (including running System Restore, uninstalling software and carrying out a virus sweep). To access Safe Mode, press the F8 key while the computer is starting.

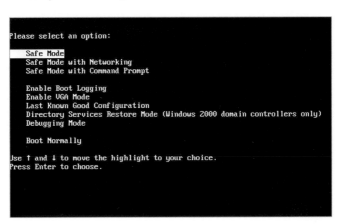

Safe Mode lets you troubleshoot Windows from within.

6 Also check Device Manager (pp22–4) for clues about any troublesome hardware. A device with a problem will be flagged with a yellow exclamation mark. Try removing any such device from the system. If the problem goes away, reinstall it. If the problem comes back, replace the device.

7 When Windows won't start at all, even in Safe Mode, try booting the computer from a start-up floppy disk or a bootable CD-ROM (such as the Windows XP disc). If you can do this, you can be fairly sure that the problem lies with Windows, not your hardware. Now would be a very good time to check that you have backups of all your important files, for the next step is not to be taken lightly: reinstalling Windows. You can either perform an over-the-top installation, in which Windows is reinstalled over the existing copy (and your files and folders should be preserved unharmed); or a clean installation, in which Windows is installed afresh (and all existing data, including your files and folders, is deleted in the process).

8 If you took our advice earlier and you make regular images of your hard disk, you could try restoring the most recent image file now. This works like the ultimate System Restore, as it replaces your current hard disk with an exact copy of the way it looked at the time the image was created. Be careful, though. Restoring an image file completely overwrites your current version of Windows and all your file and folders, so you lose any files created between the time of the image and the present. It is therefore vital to back up such files onto recordable CD or any other removable media now. You should also consider that an image won't get you out of a hardware problem. If your computer keeps crashing or refuses to boot because the memory is faulty, restoring an image will have zero impact. Finally, while restoring a disk image may be one way of curing a virus infection, there is a possibility that the virus will attack the image file itself during restoration. In the worst case, this could wipe out your healthy disk image as well as your infected Windows installation. Our advice is to rid yourself of the virus first. Visit any of the anti-virus companies' websites for advice.

9 If a specific device is at fault, don't forget to read the manual. There's no better place to find specific help, and you'd be surprised at just how many potential problems are unique to one particular peripheral. In these cost-conscious days, chances are that the full manual (as opposed to that wafer thin 'quick installation guide' that fell out of the box) is an electronic file rather than a proper printed affair. It may have been installed on your PC when you first loaded the software or you may have to find it on the installation CD-ROM.

10 Also visit the manufacturer's website and look for a Support or FAQ (Frequently Asked Questions) page. You may even find a discussion forum where you can search for similar issues and/or post a personal request for help. Quite possibly,

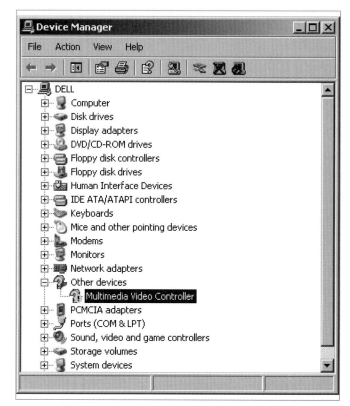

Suspect hardware is flagged in Device Manager.

the fault that you're currently experiencing is well known and a cure is already on hand in the form of a downloadable software 'patch' or bug-fixer. You'd think they'd tell you about this, would you not, especially if you registered your product when you first acquired it, but we've lost track and count of important – even essential – bug fixes slipped quietly onto support websites without any fanfare whatsoever. Of course, this assumes that your computer itself is working and has an internet connection, or that you have access to a working machine.

11 In a similar vein, try searching the web at large for help. For instance, enter a few relevant keywords into a search engine like Google (**www.google.com**). This is particularly helpful if the computer keeps freezing and throws up a 'fatal exception' or 'stop' error (the so-called Blue Screen of Death), in which case you should search for the error description or reference number. Newsgroups are also a fabulous resource. The easiest way to access and search them is again via Google: go to **http://groups.google.com** and search away.

12 If the problem is related even tangentially to Windows or another Microsoft product, you might find the answer you need in the Microsoft Knowledge Base (**http://support.microsoft.com**). This is a massive, searchable online database of questions and answers. Again, type in a couple of keywords and see what you get. As with any search, results are best when you provide accurate, pertinent information, such as the text of an error message.

13 To identify or eliminate a problem with a hardware device, the most effective procedure is one of substitution. If your keyboard should die, say, your first question would be: which is at fault – the keyboard itself or the interface on the computer? To find out, plug in a working keyboard or experiment with the malfunctioning keyboard on another computer, or, preferably, do both. The same applies to any peripheral, from the monitor to the mouse or a printer or scanner.

14 Where it gets slightly tricky is with internal components, particularly when the cause is not evident or if the computer won't start at all, as it's not so easy to whip out a hard drive or processor and test it out elsewhere. Even here, though, there are things you can do. The key is stripping the system down progressively until you reach the point where it works. Observing all the usual safety precautions (p33), proceed as follows:

a) Check that all internal cables are in place and firmly connected. Pay special attention to the processor fan's cable connection to the motherboard.

b) If you have more than one memory module, remove all but the module in the DIMM 1 slot. Restart the computer. If that doesn't do the trick, replace the module in DIMM 1 with one of the others, and try again.

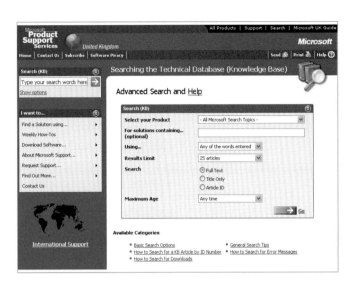

The Knowledge Base is an invaluable one-stop shop for help.

c) Remove the sound card and any other expansion cards with the sole exception of the graphics cards. This eliminates any possible short circuits. If the computer now works normally, replace each card one at a time until you identify the culprit. Obviously – at least we hope it's obvious – you must turn off and unplug the computer between each operation.

d) If it still won't start, disconnect the floppy and CD/DVD drives from the motherboard and unplug their power cables. Leave only the hard drive connected (and double-check its power connections).

e) Still no go? Swap the hard disk's ribbon cable with another and try again.

At this point, if the computer still refuses to start, you have either a broken PSU or motherboard, or dead memory modules or hard disk drive. Further elimination testing is required to definitely establish the problem. However, if you have access to another PC, try removing the hard disk from the faulty machine and installing it temporarily as a secondary (slave) device in the working system. This way, you can test whether the drive itself is functional and, if so, copy all your files and folders to the primary drive or to some form of removable media.

PART 8

Trouble-shooting specific problems

It's obviously beyond this manual's scope to cover every hardware eventuality. Indeed, it's beyond the scope of *any* manual, even those daunting 1,000+ page tomes that claim to teach you how to build a PC from scratch (but not necessarily how to switch it on). However, here are a handful of the more common problems to afflict the average computer system.

Hard disk

Insufficient disk space If Windows tells you that there's insufficient disk space to complete an operation or to save a file, you need to clear out some clutter sharpish. See p145 for tips on uninstalling old software and making more space. Better still, pre-empt the problem now. Click My Computer, right-click on C: drive, and select Properties. If the disk is more than 75% full, it's time to start making economies.

Permanently busy If your hard disk appears to be permanently busy (lots of whirring noise and a constantly blinking light on the PC's case), chances are you don't have enough system memory and Windows is using the disk as a RAM substitute. Add more memory (see pp39–43).

Unexpected disk noises may be a sign of impending failure. Back up your work onto removable media (recordable CDs, Zip disks, a tape drive or similar) immediately *before* switching off your PC, and seek professional advice.

Optical drives

Disc won't eject? Restart the PC and try again. If the tray still won't open, *switch off the power*, flatten out a paperclip and poke it into the small hole on the drive's case to release the mechanism.

Problem CDs If one particular CD won't work properly, perhaps sticking during playback or freezing the system, try cleaning it with a soft cloth. If it's scratched, it's probably irreparable, although it's certainly worth trying to run it in somebody else's computer before giving up hope. If, however, you start experiencing problems with many or all your CDs, the drive itself has a problem. Buy a lens cleaning disc to shift internal dust.

Suddenly no sound from your audio or multimedia CDs? Check the PC's volume settings are not muted (double-click the loudspeaker icon near the clock in the Windows System Tray and/or run any sound card diagnostic software). If this doesn't work, the audio cable connecting the drive to the sound card has probably become detached. Open up the case (after taking all the usual precautions – see p33) and reattach it.

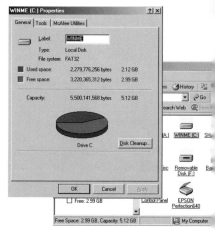

If your disk is getting full, now is the time to start making economies.

Turn to your sound card's diagnostic utilities to trouble-shoot audio problems.

Set the refresh rate as high as your graphics card and monitor will allow.

DVD disc won't play? Check that it has the same regional code as your DVD drive. Windows itself can't play DVD movies so you need a DVD player program. Is this installed?

Monitors

Unusual patches of colour on the screen, especially near the edges, are probably due to some magnetic influence. Use the degauss button or software utility to remove excess magnetism and move any magnetic sources – including speakers and the PC case itself – further from the monitor.

Flickering If you can see any flickering in the screen image, the refresh rate is too low. This way lies headaches and a most uncomfortable user experience. See p104 and make sure that the refresh rate is set to at least 72Hz (or higher if your monitor supports it).

TECHIE CORNER

Disk disaster

Hard disks don't go on for ever (although most are still spinning quite happily come the time for an upgrade) but, short of a catastrophe like complete destruction or theft, it's almost always possible to recover data from a badly damaged disk. Many companies worldwide specialise in data recovery, and some will even attempt a diagnosis through a modem link. The problem is that it's always an expensive option. That's why it pays to archive your old data on Zip disks or recordable CDs or similar.

However, if you simply must recover current data, the procedure depends upon the severity of the problem. If you've accidentally deleted the odd file or reformatted an entire disk and now wish you hadn't, or if a virus wreaked havoc, specialist software alone can sometimes recover your data. In the case of physical damage, a disk that's still working from an electro-mechanical point of view – i.e. still spinning – is relatively easy to work with, but even a device badly damaged by a power surge or fire can sometimes be persuaded to yield usable data. Not one to try at home you understand: call in the experts.

Modern printers typically have a host of configurable options.

Games and other software can play havoc with your display settings so go back to basics. Click Start, point to Settings, click Control Panel, and then double-click Display to access the options.

Printers

Poor print quality? This could be down to your choice of paper or some problem with the software settings. Experiment with different paper types and weights and be sure to run any diagnostic program that came with your printer. Also try printing at different resolutions.

Toner If your laser printer's toner is almost exhausted, remove the cartridge and rock it gently from side to side. This re-distributes the remaining toner and may see you through until you can buy a refill. Note that shaking an inkjet's ink cartridges does no good whatsoever.

Inkjet cartridges can move fractionally out of the correct alignment, leading to blurred, bleeding or fuzzy prints. Run the appropriate software utility to fix this.

Blurrred Is what you see on screen most definitely *not* what you get on paper? Check that the correct paper size is selected in the print setup settings and be sure to select portrait or landscape views as appropriate.

Paper jams are less common these days than once they were but can still stop a printer dead, particularly if you use a paper type or weight that the printer is not designed to accommodate. Consult the manual for instructions on how to open the unit and extract the mangled sheets.

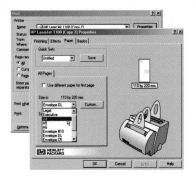

Are paper size and layout settings correct?

Modems

Connection Can you hear your modem in action as it dials up your Internet Service Provider (ISP)? Adjust the volume control on an external model until you can hear it chirruping when it tries to make a connection. For an internal modem, click Start > Settings > Control Panel > Modems and adjust the volume in the Properties section of the General tab. So long as you can hear *something*, the modem's not entirely lifeless and the problem is likely to be with the telephone line or, more commonly, a temporary hitch with the ISP.

Has your modem suddenly stopped working? If you've recently added a new extension handset or fax machine somewhere in your house, there may now be too many devices trying to share the same line. Try temporarily unplugging any additions and see if your modem comes back to life.

Diagnostics Try running the Windows diagnostic utility. Click Start > Settings > Control Panel > Modems and select the Diagnostics tab. Highlight your modem and click More Info. Windows now tries to contact the modem and reports back with any problems. 'Port already open' is the most common error message, and invariably means that some software application – perhaps a fax or voice-mail program – is messing up the settings. Close down all running programs and try again.

Pump up the volume to hear if your modem's alive or dead.

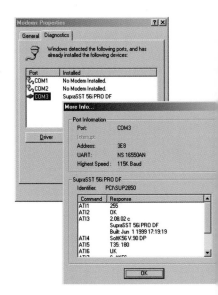

Windows will have a stab at rooting out modem troubles.

Are you connected If you *think* that you're online but can't access any websites or send and receive email, make sure that you're really connected. In Windows 98 and Me, click Start, click Run, type 'winipcfg' (without the quotes), and hit Enter. In Windows XP and Vista, click Start, click Run, type 'cmd' and then type 'ipconfig' in the popup window. If you see an IP Address that's not just a string of zeroes, you are indeed online and it's likely that the problem is a blip with your ISP. If not, your modem is failing to connect. For serious diagnostics, look here (and yes, this does rather presuppose that you can get online, in which case why do you need a modem trouble-shooter?): **http://support.microsoft.com/default.aspx?scid=kb;EN-US;q142730**

An IP address is a guarantee that you're online.

TECHIE CORNER

IRQ-some When hardware devices talk to the rest of the computer, they use one, more or none of the following: Interrupt Request (IRQ), Input/Output address (I/O), Direct Memory Access (DMA) and Memory Address. The first of these, IRQ, frequently leads to conflicts where two devices fight over access to the processor and system resources. Thankfully, Windows can configure most modern 'Plug-and-Play' devices (including *all* PCI expansion cards) automatically, but older ISA expansion cards may have jumpers that need to be set correctly.

In the event of a hardware conflict (warning signs: a new peripheral device or expansion card doesn't work or Windows starts freezing and/or crashing inexplicably), get along to Device Manager and look for evidence.

Click Start
Click Settings
Click Control Panel
Click System
Click the Device Manager tab.
Expand the list of hardware by

clicking the + signs and look for anything marked with a (!) – an indication that Windows suspects a problem. Highlight any such devices and click Properties for details.

The most common state of affairs is when two devices try to share a single IRQ. Windows will then prompt you to (temporarily) disable one in order to use the other. This very rapidly becomes a pain, so a better solution by far is to reassign their IRQ addresses. Sounds complicated? Not really – but the precise solution depends on the specific problem. Note too that Windows can share a single IRQ address between certain devices, so just because two bits of hardware have the same IRQ doesn't necessarily mean that you need to fiddle unless one or the other doesn't work or there's a (!) warning in Device Manager.

Look here for a detailed exposition of IRQ and its system stablemates:
www.pcguide.com/ref/ mbsys/res

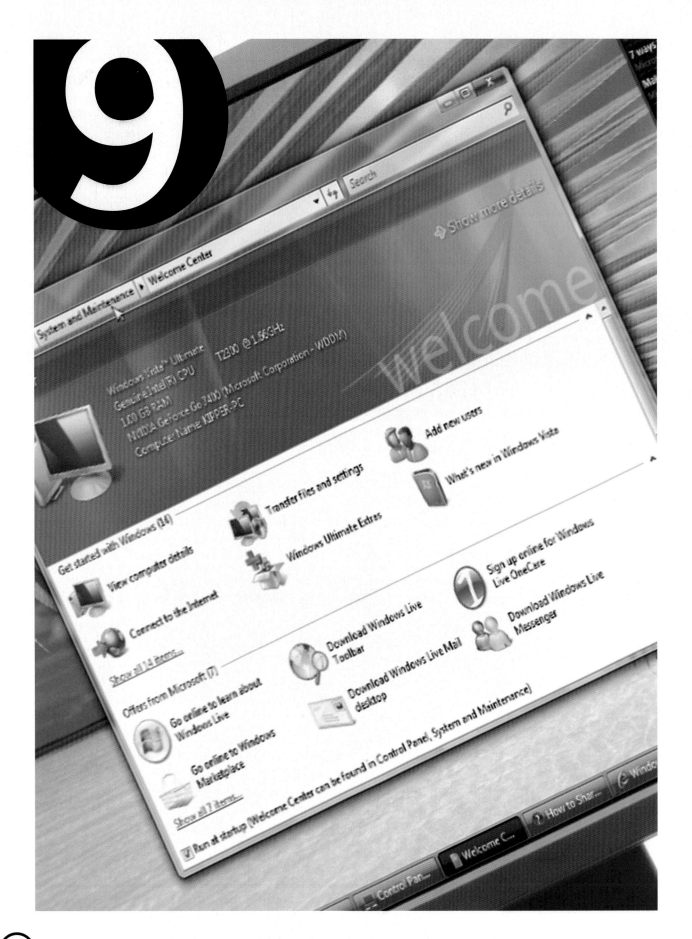

PART 9

Windows Vista & Windows 7: a user's guide

In January 2007, Microsoft unveiled the 'best Windows ever': Windows Vista. According to the hype, it made your system smoother, safer and sexier than ever before, and if you didn't rush out to upgrade immediately you were missing out on all kinds of wonders. However, cynics said Vista was nothing more than a prettier version of Windows XP with flakier habits. And now along comes Windows 7, the next 'best Windows ever'. Let's have a look at both.

PART  # A Vista overview

The most obvious change in Vista is the new user interface, which looks as if it's made from glass. It's very pretty and uses your graphics card's 3D power to deliver transparent windows, 3D effects and pin-sharp text. It looks good on anything from the smallest screen to the biggest plasma display. It's been reorganised too, and the result is that PC newcomers will find Windows Vista less intimidating – although XP experts will need a few days to get used to it, because familiar items have been moved. It's worth the effort, though, because Vista's way of doing things is faster and more logical once you get used to it.

The other big change is search. In Vista, search is everywhere: you can search from the Start Menu or from the toolbar in any folder window, and the result is that you can find things without wading through folders and subfolders. You can save searches too, so for example if you search for pictures with particular tags you can save the results as a Search Folder for instant access in future. Of all the things in Vista, the integrated search is our favourite: whether you're looking for a file, a folder, a program or a note, you can find it instantly.

Last but not least, there's security. Vista includes a firewall to stop programs connecting to the internet without your knowledge, Windows Defender to stop spyware sneaking on to your system, vastly improved security when you're browsing the web, and an annoying but important feature called User Access Control. Any time you try to install a program or tweak system settings, UAC pops up to ask whether you're sure – and if you don't say yes, the program won't install or the system settings won't be changed. It's mildly irritating when UAC interrupts a perfectly reasonable activity such as changing Control Panel settings, but it means programs can't install themselves or muck up your PC without your knowledge.

Those are the biggies, but Vista has more tricks up its sleeve. The superb Parental Controls feature enables you to keep the kids away from particular programs, web sites and gruesome games, and you can also use it to limit the time the little ones spend on your PC. Depending on which version of Vista you go for, you also get Media Center software, DVD creation tools, encryption to scramble sensitive files, backup and restore tools, and a useful feature called File Versioning that enables you to step back in time to recover a file that you've accidentally deleted, overwritten or edited. However, not all versions of Vista are created equal.

Vista versions

Windows XP was straightforward enough: you had Windows XP Home for home users, Windows XP Professional for business users, and Windows XP Media Center edition if you bought (or built) a Media Center PC. However, Vista comes in not one, not two, not three, but five different versions – six if you include the Starter edition that will be sold in developing countries – and that's before you include the 64-bit versions. So what's available and how much does each version cost?

Windows Vista Home Basic: As the name suggests, this is a basic version of Vista for home users. You get most of the important features including improved security, search and parental controls, but you don't get the snazzy new user interface or goodies such as media centre software, DVD burning and so on. We'd advise against buying this version.
Expect to pay: £106 (£61 as an upgrade)

Windows Vista Home Premium: This gives you the same features as Basic plus the new interface, DVD burning, media centre software, the Mobility Center for laptops and tools for Tablet PC users. The movie software can handle high-definition video (the one in Basic can't) and you get some basic backup tools too. This is the version you'll find on most home PCs and it's the best version for everyday home use.
Expect to pay: £124 (£61 as an upgrade)

Windows Vista Business: As you'd expect you don't get some of the home-friendly tools such as DVD Maker, high-definition movie-making or Media Center, but you do get a complete set of backup and restore tools and business-friendly networking features.
Expect to pay: £171 (£143 as an upgrade)

Windows Vista Ultimate: This version of Vista takes Home Premium and adds even more goodies: the backup and restore tools from the Business Edition, drive encryption to safeguard sensitive files, business-friendly networking and Ultimate Extras, which will be free, downloadable add-ons delivered via Windows Update and available to Ultimate owners only. This is the version we'd recommend for people who use their PC at home and at work.
Expect to pay: £160 (£150 as an upgrade)

There are several different versions of Windows Vista, ranging from the rather horrible Home Basic edition to the all-singing, all-dancing Ultimate Edition.

Windows Vista Enterprise: This is essentially the big-business version of Vista, designed specifically for large corporate customers.
Expect to pay: n/a

32-bit and 64-bit Vista: The standard versions of Vista are designed for 32-bit machines and 32-bit applications, which covers the majority of hardware and software. However, many modern machines have 64-bit processors – so should you buy the 64-bit version of Vista? We don't think so: you'll need 64-bit drivers for all your hardware, which could be tricky and you won't get the benefits of 64-bit computing if you don't have software that takes advantage of 64-bit processors. For now, we think the 32-bit versions are the best ones for the majority of PC owners.

Vista System Requirements

Vista has two sets of system requirements: Vista Capable, which means a PC will run Vista adequately but not spectacularly, and Vista Premium Ready, which we think is the minimum specification you should have before deciding to upgrade. The differences are:

Vista Capable: 800MHz processor, 512MB of RAM, graphics card with 32MB of memory
Vista Premium Ready: 1GHz processor, 1GB of RAM, graphics card with 128MB of RAM

As ever, those requirements are minimums: we wouldn't recommend running Vista on a machine with less than 1GB of RAM, and if you want to take advantage of the snazzy, glass-effect interface, a graphics card with 32MB of RAM is hopelessly underpowered. RAM is the biggie, though: the more you have, the happier Windows Vista will be.

If you're upgrading, you also need to know whether you can install Vista as an upgrade – which keeps your files and programs intact – or whether you'll have to do a clean install, which means you'll need to back up your files and reinstall all your programs. As if the different versions weren't confusing enough, they can't all be installed as upgrades. Here's what you need to know.

If you have ...	You can do an upgrade installation of ...
Windows XP Home	Basic, Premium, Business or Ultimate
Windows XP Professional	Business or Ultimate
Windows XP Media Center	Premium or Ultimate
Windows XP Tablet PC	Business or Ultimate

It's not a huge problem – we'd recommend a clean install wherever possible to make sure you're starting from a clean slate – but it's worth bearing in mind, especially when there's a big difference between the normal price and the upgrade price. It's worth remembering too that if you're using an upgrade version you'll also need to keep copies of your old Windows XP installation discs or, if you've got a laptop without installation discs, you'll need to use your laptop's backup disc creation utility to create some.

PART **9** # Upgrading your PC to Vista

If you're impressed by Vista's features and think your hardware has enough power, there's one more step before you should reach for your credit card. The Upgrade Advisor scans your system and checks two key things: whether your hardware is powerful enough to run Vista properly, and whether drivers are available for your various devices. Simply download the Upgrade Advisor from **http://tinyurl.com/o5bq4**, plug in any external devices such as USB drives or other peripherals and run the Advisor.

When the Upgrade Advisor has finished, it will tell you of any potential problems and it will also recommend which version of Vista you should consider. Don't worry if it recommends Home Basic and you'd rather have the Premium edition: just click on Premium in the left-hand panel to see if there are any potential problems that might prevent Premium from running properly on your PC.

Not all problems identified by the Upgrade Advisor are deal-breakers, though. For example, if you say you're interested in Home Premium, the Advisor will say you need a TV tuner card – which is true if you want to use Media Center to watch or record live TV. However, if you don't want to do those things you don't need to rush out and put a TV tuner card in your system.

It's essential that you run Upgrade Advisor before installing (or ideally, buying) Vista: if the installer encounters serious incompatibilities, such as a PC that can't cope with the basic system requirements, it will refuse to install Vista on your system.

Running the Upgrade Advisor before you install – or better still, buy – Windows Vista is essential. If Vista encounters any serious hardware incompatibilities it won't install until you fix them.

The Easy Transfer Wizard

If you've got an old PC running Windows XP and a brand spanking new one running Vista, the Easy Transfer Wizard can copy all your important stuff from your XP machine to your Vista one. It copies user accounts, folders, files, program settings, internet settings and bookmarks, email settings and your address book, and it's very easy to use: run the Windows Vista DVD on your old PC and choose Easy Transfer Wizard from the welcome screen. The Wizard creates a file containing all your items on the old PC, and it's just a matter of connecting the old PC to the new one and copying that file from the old PC to the new one. If both PCs have network cards, use Ethernet, as it's by far the fastest way to transfer data between PCs. If they don't, use a direct cable connection or transfer the Wizard's file to CD or DVD.

Installing Vista

There are three ways to install Vista: an in-place upgrade, which keeps your old programs, files and settings; a clean install, which wipes your old version of Windows as well as your files and folders; and a clean install on a freshly formatted hard disk or a hard disk partition, which wipes everything. The first option is the least hassle but it's also the most dangerous: if the installation process crashes, you could lose your data; and if your PC's riddled with problems, the installer will copy them across to Vista.

That leaves the two kinds of clean installation. Installing over the top of Windows XP is fine provided you've got installation CDs for all your programs and backups of your important files, and it gives you a clean slate so you can be sure Vista is running at peak performance. The third option is good too – not least because it enables you to create a dual-boot system, so you can have Windows XP and Windows Vista on the same system – but you'll need to use a third-party program such as Norton PartitionMagic (**www.symantec.com/en/uk**) to split your hard disk into two 'partitions'. That divides your hard disk into two sections, each of which your system sees as a separate drive – for example, on our system we've partitioned our C: drive into two separate partitions. Our C: drive is still there and that's where we have Windows XP – but the second partition appears as Drive E: and that's where we've installed Vista.

Transferring files from a Windows XP machine to a new Vista one couldn't be easier: simply run the Easy Transfer Wizard from the Vista installation disc on the old machine, and run it again on the new one.

Walkthrough:
Installing Windows Vista on an XP PC

1

Put the Windows Vista installation disc in your drive. After a few seconds, the Install Windows menu should appear (if you've disabled AutoPlay on your system, launch it by double-clicking on the disc in My Computer). If you've already run the Upgrade Advisor you can skip the 'check compatibility online' option and click on Install Now.

2

The installer will now ask whether you want to check online for installation updates. This is a good idea, as Windows Vista's installer may have been updated since your CD or DVD was manufactured.

3

Before you can continue, you'll need to enter the product key that came with your copy of Vista. Leave the 'Automatically activate ... ' option unchecked unless you're certain that you'll be keeping Vista on your system. If you don't activate Windows now, it will nag you every day so there's plenty of time to do so later.

4

You now have two options: Upgrade, which replaces your existing copy of Windows XP with Windows Vista and keeps your files and folders intact, or Custom, which enables you to specify whether Vista should be installed in a different folder, a different disk or a different hard disk folder. If you choose the latter option and select a clean install, the installer will wipe your system before installing Vista.

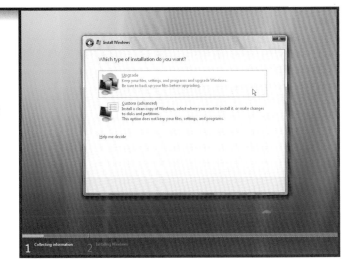

5

Time for a cup of tea. The installer will now copy the necessary files to your PC, unpack them and install Windows Vista on your computer. This takes a while, even on a fast PC.

6

When you see this screen you're nearly finished. The installer needs you to create a user account, so you'll need to specify a user name and password. It's possible to create an account without setting a password, but it's a very bad idea.

7

Now you have two more decisions to make: the official name of your computer – which only matters if you'll be connecting to a network – and much more importantly, the wallpaper that should appear on your desktop. Select a picture and click Next.

8

The installer will now ask you what security settings Vista should use. Unless you really know what you're doing, click on Use Recommended Settings. You can always tweak the settings in Control Panel later on.

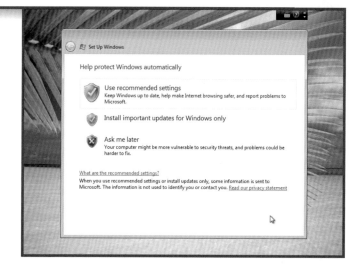

9

You've only one more decision to make: where your PC currently lives. Vista uses this screen to decide how much security it should apply to networking features, so a computer in a public location will have much more strict security settings than one in a bedroom.

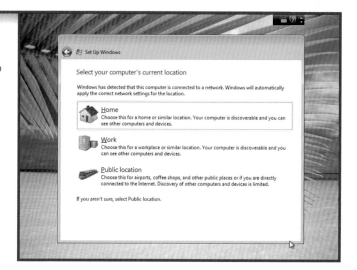

And that's it: if you click on the Start button in the bottom right of the window, Windows Vista will appear in all its glory.

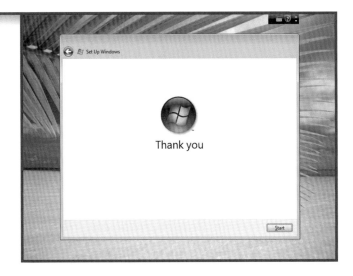

Congratulations: you've successfully installed Windows Vista and you're ready to start exploring. In the next section we'll give you the guided tour.

PART 9 Windows Vista: the guided tour

Now that Vista is up and running on your PC, it's time to discover its many wonders. In this section we'll give you a guided tour of the most important new features.

Aero Glass

Unless you're running Home Basic, the Aero Glass interface is the first thing you'll see when you run Vista: it's like the old Windows XP interface, but shinier and cleaner-looking. If your system is sluggish, turning off Aero Glass can boost performance.

The Welcome Center

Every time you run Vista you'll see the Welcome Center, which tries to persuade you to go online and buy Microsoft things. The top half of the screen provides easy access to common tasks, the bottom half attempts to take you shopping, and the checkbox at the bottom stops it from annoying you in future.

Flip 3D

Switching between windows using Alt + Tab still works in Vista, but Flip 3D is better still. Press the Windows and Tab keys together and you get a snazzy 3D version, which makes it easy to see what each program is doing. Keep pressing Tab and let go when the window you want to switch to reaches the front.

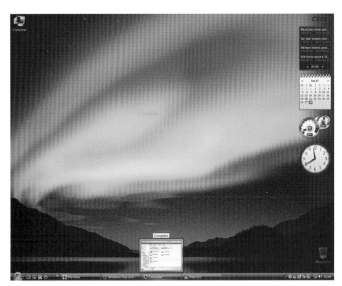

Taskbar Thumbnails

No longer do you have to open a program to see what it's up to: just hover over its button on the Taskbar and a thumbnail window will pop up. It's particularly handy when you want to keep tabs on internet downloads but don't want to stop what you're doing.

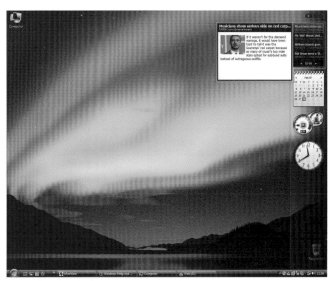

The Sidebar and Gadgets

If you wish you can display the Windows Sidebar at the edge of your screen and fill it with Gadgets, little programs that do handy things such as tell the time, show how much of your PC's horsepower is being used or check the internet for news headlines.

Search

Search is everywhere in Windows Vista, and you can start a new search from the Start Menu or from the search box at the top right corner of every folder window. Simply type what you're looking for and Windows Vista will find it. You can even save your search results as a Search Folder for instant access in the future: when you do this, clicking on the search folder will run your search again and show you the results in seconds.

Breadcrumb Navigation

When you open a folder, look at the top – Windows Vista uses internet-style breadcrumb navigation to show exactly where you are, so in this screenshot we're in Computer > Vista > Users > Vista > Music. To move back one or more steps, just click on the appropriate part of the breadcrumb trail – so if you wanted to go back two steps to the Users folder, you'd just click Users in the navigation bar.

The Start Button

Windows XP's Start Button has turned into a shiny globe and the Start Menu itself has changed slightly. As before you get the list of programs on the left, but instead of popping out endless menus when you click on All Programs the left window becomes a scrolling list. Along the right, you'll see various handy options: the Documents, Pictures, Music and Games links take you to those folders, while the rest of the options enable you to do useful things such as launch Control Panel or the Help System. You'll also see a search field at the very bottom of the Start Menu, which you can use to find files, folders or programs without having to wade through any menus.

DVD Burning

You no longer need standalone software to burn CDs or DVDs from within Windows Vista: you can do it from any folder. However, the discs created using this method are data discs, so if you want to make music CDs you'll need to create them in Windows Media Player. If you want to burn DVDs and you have the Home Premium or Ultimate editions of Vista, you can use Windows DVD Maker; if you don't have those versions you'll need to buy additional software.

Parental Controls

Windows Vista's parental controls – in Control Panel > User Accounts and Family Safety – are superb. You can filter internet traffic to stop the kids from seeing unsuitable sites, you can limit the time individual users can spend on your PC, you can specify whether certain games – such as gory shooting games – are off-limits, and you can block specific programs to keep the kids out of your money management software. Best of all, the parental controls are per-account. That means you can have different user accounts for different children and apply different levels of control to each.

Media Center

The Premium and Ultimate editions of Windows Vista include Windows Media Center, which turns your PC into a serious multimedia system. Before Vista came along, the only way to get it was to buy or build a dedicated media centre PC, which wasn't cheap. It's a music jukebox, photo viewer and DVD player, and if you install a TV tuner card into your PC, it can display live TV and even act as a very clever video recorder. Unlike most software Media Center is designed to look good on TVs as well as on computer monitors.

Networking

Changing networks settings in Windows XP can be a pain, not least because many of the features are far from straightforward. Windows Vista's Network and Sharing Center makes things much easier, so for example in this screenshot you can see that our various network settings are displayed using green and grey buttons. Green means something is switched on – in this case, network discovery, file sharing and public folder sharing – while grey buttons means those features are switched off. You also get a nifty diagram showing how your PC is connected to other PCs or to the internet.

User Account Control

User Account Control (UAC) is designed to prevent people from tinkering with your PC, and to stop software from sneakily changing your system. It works in two ways: if you're logged in as the system administrator and you attempt to install software or change system settings, UAC will ask if you're sure; if you're not logged in as the administrator, you'll be asked for the administrator password. If you don't know the password, you won't be able to continue – in this example, the kids can't change the parental control settings because they don't know dad's password.

PART

Windows 7:
a preview

At the time of writing, the latest version of Windows – Windows 7 – has recently launched. It's too early to reach a conclusion but it's worth noting that the early reception for Windows 7 has been much, much better than the three-year experience of Windows Vista!

The fact is that Microsoft got things badly wrong with Vista. It simply failed to live up to expectations, both in terms of raw performance – many computers can't run its lovely Aero Glass user interface – and in unnecessary complexity. Far from making things simpler, many people found – and still find, despite updates – Vista confusing. Meanwhile, Microsoft's major competitor, Apple, made significant advances, helped enormously by the popularity of the iPhone. The iPhone introduced a whole new audience to Apple's way of doing things; and once you've used the iPhone – which is indeed a wonderfully designed device with virtually no learning curve – making the jump from a Windows PC to an Apple Mac suddenly seems a lot more appealing.

Bottom line: for the past three years, if you have had a computer running Windows XP, you have had no compelling reason to upgrade to Windows Vista. XP was a massive leap forward from its predecessor Windows 2000 and remains immensely popular. So what now? Is Windows 7 worth the switch?

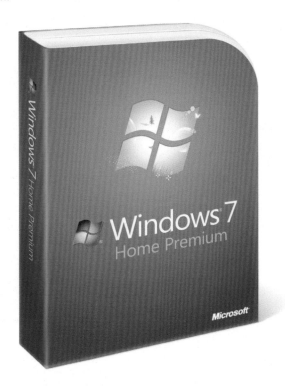

With Windows 7 you can choose from Home Premium, Professional or Ultimate varieties.

Windows 7 looks much like Windows Vista – until you look a little closer.

To upgrade or not to upgrade

The short but, in our view, accurate answer is: no. That's for one very simple reason, namely this: you cannot perform an in-place upgrade from Windows XP to Windows 7. Instead, you can 'migrate' your operating system from one to the other, but migration is not a straightforward upgrade. Migration will preserve your files and data but it does not leave your programs in place. This means that you'll have to reinstall all your applications from scratch.

Can you face doing that? Do you still have all your old installation discs and serial numbers? What about all the patches and updates you might have applied in the meantime? If you are up for such a challenge, feel free to migrate. But our advice is to stick with Windows XP.

In our view, it is simply ridiculous that Windows XP users cannot upgrade directly to Windows 7 in the same way that you can upgrade to Windows Vista. Indeed, given that Windows 7 is built on the Windows Vista architecture, there seems to be no good reason at all why a Windows XP PC cannot move straight to Windows 7, so long as it meets the minimum hardware requirements. However, that's the state of play.

Moreover, you face some choices even if you have a PC running Windows Vista. It seems daft but you cannot upgrade from certain versions of Windows Vista to Windows 7. If, for instance, you want to change from Windows Vista Ultimate to Windows 7 Business – arguably a downgrade – Microsoft only allows you to migrate, not to upgrade. If you want an easy upgrade, you must purchase the equivalent edition of Windows 7 i.e. Ultimate. Perhaps there are sound technical reasons for this; perhaps not. It certainly seems odd that Microsoft should sow such confusion without good reason.

Or does it? One of the biggest criticisms levelled against Windows Vista was the baffling array of editions that confused the consumer. Which flavour did you need? It was never clear. You might therefore hope that Windows 7 would ship with fewer options and a clearer marketing strategy. But no, not a bit of it. At launch, the choices are as follows:

Windows 7 version	Who for?
Home Basic	Emerging markets only
Starter	Only pre-installed on netbooks not sold as an upgrade product
Home Premium	Most home users
Professional	Small business users
Enterprise	Big corporate customers
Ultimate	Anybody who wants everything that Windows 7 has to offer

Bizarrely, Microsoft has swapped the meanings of Home Basic and Starter. With Windows Vista, Home Basic was a cut-down consumer product and Starter was the cheap version for emerging markets; with Windows 7, these roles have been reversed. This means that you can effectively ignore Home Basic as an upgrade option. Note too that Windows 7 Starter will only appear on relatively low-powered netbooks so you can ignore it too. And, unless you are a major corporate customer buying hundreds of copies of Windows, you can ignore Enterprise as well!

Full or upgrade?

As usual, Microsoft sells 'full' and 'upgrade' versions of each version of Windows 7. You qualify for the cheaper upgrade version if you are installing Windows 7 on a PC that's already running an older version of Windows or if you can produce an old Windows installation disc on demand during the installation process. Only if you have no evidence of having purchased an earlier version of Windows do you need to pay for the full version.

As mentioned above, you can't simply upgrade from any version of Windows Vista to any version of Windows 7. Here's how it works:

Version of Windows Vista	Version of Windows 7		
	Home Premium	Professional	Ultimate
Home Basic	Upgrade or migrate	Upgrade or migrate	Upgrade or migrate
Home Premium	Upgrade or migrate	Upgrade or migrate	Upgrade or migrate
Business	Migrate	Upgrade or migrate	Upgrade or migrate
Ultimate	Migrate	Migrate	Upgrade or migrate

Remember, from Windows XP, you can only migrate to Windows 7; an in-place upgrade is not an option.

Pricing

As for the cost, here are Microsoft's retail prices at the time of writing (these may be discounted by computer shops):

	Upgrade version	Full version
Windows 7 Home Premium	£79.99 (rising to £99.99 in 2010)	£149.99
Windows 7 Professional	£189.99	£219.99
Windows 7 Ultimate	£199.99	£229.99

There is also, for the first time, a Windows 7 Family Pack. At a cost of £150, you get the Home Premium product with a licence to install it on up to three PCs. That's not a bad deal if you have more than one PC at home. The Family Pack comes as an upgrade option, not the full version.

Windows 7 system requirements

Nothing too onerous here, and indeed some reviewers have reported that Windows 7 runs faster than Windows Vista on older computers.

- 1GHz processor
- 1GB RAM
- 16GB hard disk space
- DirectX 9-capable graphics card

Key features in Windows 7

Here's a whistle-stop tour of what to expect if you do take the plunge and upgrade to Windows 7.

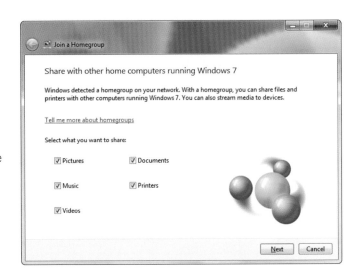

HomeGroup

For the first time, Windows 7 makes it easy to connect PCs in a home network and share files, folders and printers. However, the welcome HomeGroup feature only works with Windows 7 PCs, not with Windows XP or Vista machines – which means it's of very little value at all unless you upgrade every computer you own to Windows 7.

BitLocker To Go

Automatically encrypts data on a USB stick drive. Given that so many of us are prone to store important information on USB drives and lose these drives, this is an excellent innovation. Unfortunately, you only get BitLocker To Go on the Ultimate (and Enterprise) edition of Windows 7.

Aero Peek

A small icon in the Taskbar allows you to make all open windows transparent (as an alternative to minimising them). This is handy if you want to have a quick look at the Desktop without moving or closing your windows.

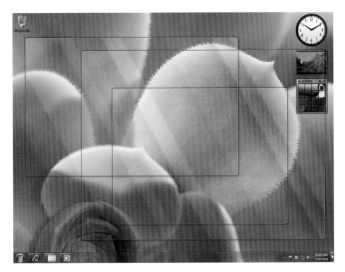

Window snapping

Drag a window to the top of the screen and it automatically maximises. Drag a window to the left and it automatically resizes to fill the left-hand half of the screen. Drag another window to the right and it snaps into place alongside it, offering you a dual display. Small touches, perhaps, but welcome.

Preview Pane

This enhanced version of Windows Explorer makes it easier than ever to see what your files are before opening them.

Windows Taskbar

The new Taskbar features jumbo-sized icons. For the first time, you can drag and drop these around the Taskbar into an order that suits you. When you have multiple versions of the same program open, or multiple browser windows, Taskbar Peek shows you a good-sized preview of each, making it easy to return to the window you want without guesswork.

Jumplists

Jumplists allows you to quickly access, or jump to, recently opened files just by right-clicking a program icon in the Start menu or on the Taskbar. Very useful.

Search

As with Windows Vista, search is everywhere in Windows 7. However, it's grown a little smarter. As you start entering a search term, you'll see results grouped logically by type e.g. program, image, document or song.

And not forgetting... User Account Control

It sounded like a good idea in Windows Vista – Windows would stop with a warning whenever a user tried to make a change that might, just conceivably, go wrong, or when software tried to take an action that you might not want – but in practice it was hugely intrusive and hugely unpopular. In Windows 7, you have full control over this feature rather than just the nuclear option of disabling it completely.

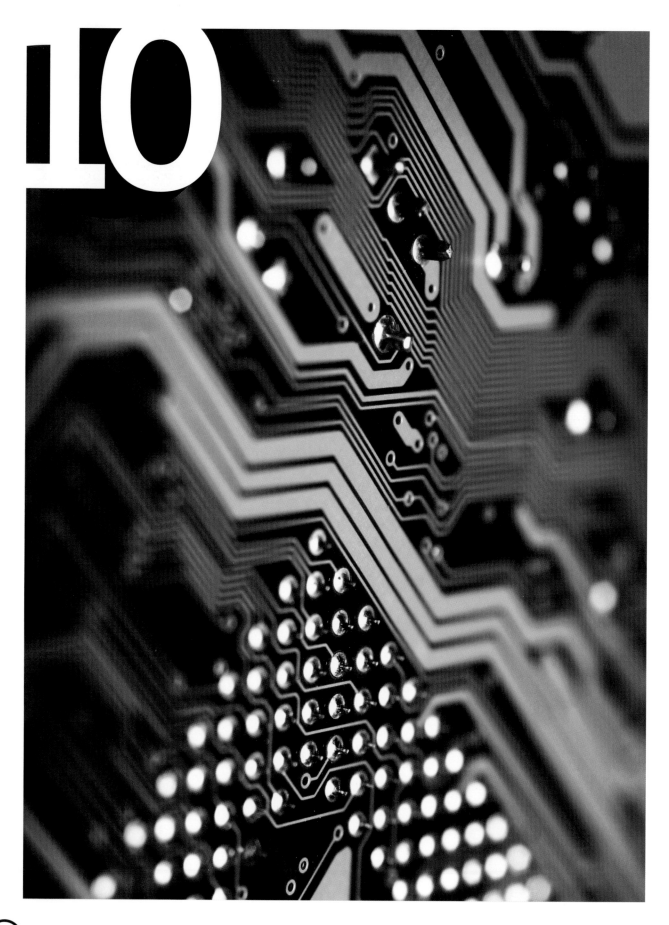

10

PART

New life for old hardware

Although we are all in favour of computer upgrades –
which is handy given the nature of this book – our
enthusiasm is tempered with a concern for avoiding
needless expense and hassle. All too often, people are
persuaded to part with their cash for swanky new
software that they don't really need – and are then forced
to upgrade their hardware because that swanky new
software demands a supercomputer specification. Here
we look at two alternative approaches to keeping older
computers in active service.

NEW LIFE FOR OLD HARDWARE

Installing Linux

Just because a PC can't handle the very latest version of Windows doesn't mean you should send it off for recycling. Installing Linux can make old PCs young again – and it won't cost you a penny.

If you hang on to a PC for long enough, sooner or later you'll discover that it simply doesn't have enough horsepower to run the latest version of Windows. For example, although Windows 7 is designed to be less demanding than Windows Vista, it still asks for a 1GHz processor, 1GB of RAM and 16GB of hard disk space. That's the minimum specification, too, not the recommended one and upgrading an old PC to meet those requirements can be an expensive business. The good news is that there's an alternative and it's free.

Linux is an alternative to Windows, and it needs much more modest hardware than Microsoft's operating system. Where Windows wants a 1GHz processor, Ubuntu Linux will work on a 300MHz one; where Windows wants a gigabyte of memory, Ubuntu will function with just 64MB; and where Windows wants 16GB of disk space, Ubuntu fits into 4GB. Even the recommended system requirements are modest: a 700MHz processor, 384MB of RAM and 8GB of hard disk space. That means that Linux runs much faster than Windows, especially on older or low-powered hardware.

Linux lingo

With Windows, there are only a few versions to worry about. With Linux there are dozens. They all have the same fundamental underpinnings but different websites offer different versions, known as distributions. Different distributions offer slightly different interfaces or software or do some things in very slightly different ways. For the average PC user, however, one particular version of Linux is worth checking out first: Ubuntu. It has been designed specifically for Linux newcomers, it's easy to install and it's a joy to use. It also comes packed with all the software you're likely to need including music and photo software and a full Office suite for word processing, spreadsheets and presentations.

Is Linux for you?

If you're the type of PC user who likes to have printed manuals, fancy packaging and a dedicated technical support number, free versions of Linux aren't for you: even the most painless installation will probably involve a bit of Googling to find the latest drivers for your sound card or other peripherals. However, if you don't mind the odd bit of fiddling and fancy bringing an old PC back to life without spending a penny, we think you'll like Linux a lot. There are huge numbers of websites, magazines and books that will take you through every aspect of Linux if you're technically inclined, but Ubuntu works just as well as an 'install and forget about it' operating system.

In this section, we show you how to test Ubuntu and then

There are lots of versions of Linux available, but Ubuntu is particularly good for people switching from Windows.

install it on your system. Before we start we need three things: access to a fast internet connection, because the installer is massive; a CD burner; and a blank CD with 700MB of storage capacity. If you don't have such things, you can get Ubuntu to send you an installation CD, but it can take a month or two for the disc to turn up.

As with any other operating system upgrade or installation, make sure you have a backup of essential files before making any changes to your PC. That's particularly important when you install a brand new operating system over the top of an ageing copy of Windows, as the installer erases Windows and all its data before putting the new operating system onto your PC.

Testing Ubuntu without installing it

One of the things we really like about Ubuntu is that you can run it from the installation CD without making any changes to your system. If you like it, you can install it and if you don't, you can simply eject the disc, restart your PC and return to Windows. Let's put it through its paces now.

*The first thing we need to do is get hold of a copy of Ubuntu. It's a free download from **Ubuntu.com**, but it's worth noting that the file is nearly 700MB in size – so a fast broadband connection is a must unless you plan to leave the download running overnight. Be careful if you have a monthly data transfer limit on your broadband connection, as some ISPs limit you to 1GB or 2GB of data transfer per month. If you go over the limit – and if you have a few unsuccessful download attempts with Ubuntu, you might – then you may have to pay a surcharge.*

2

Once the download has completed, you need to burn it to a blank CD. Most PCs come with CD-burning software, as do most third-party CD drives, but if you don't have dedicated CD-burning software we'd thoroughly recommend the free and very useful InfraRecorder. You can download it from **www.infrarecorder.org**.

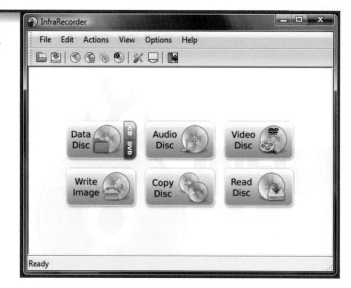

3

In InfraRecorder, click on Data Disc, then click on the Actions menu and select Burn Image. If you have other CD-burning software, the specific options may differ but the process is identical. Burn Image, sometimes described as Burn Disc Image, is the option you're looking for.

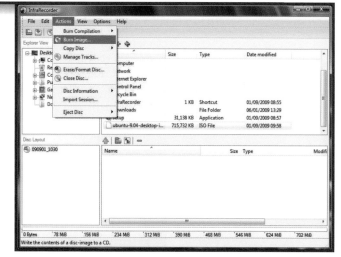

4

Your CD-burning software will now ask you what image file you want to burn. The file you're looking for is the giant Ubuntu download, which should be just under 700MB in size. Keep a careful eye on your download size: it's not unusual for the download to appear complete, but if you right-click on it and choose Properties, you'll see that it's some way short of the full 700-ish MB. If the download isn't complete there's no point burning it to CD, as it simply won't work.

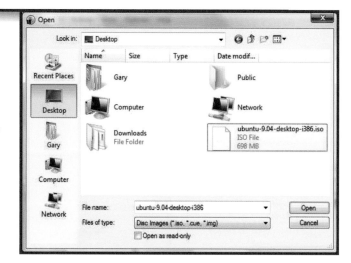

5

Insert a blank CD in the drive. In the case of InfraRecorder, you'll now be asked to choose a few options. By default, the program uses the maximum write speed and the Session At Once write method; you can stick with these options unless you've encountered problems with them in the past. Make sure that Close The Disc After Writing is selected, as this finishes off the disc so that it's ready to use.

6

This would be an excellent time for a cup of tea. Don't worry about warnings such as 'The DMA speed test has been skipped'; what's important is that InfraRecorder has started to create the CD. The process takes a few minutes and shouldn't pop up any warnings unless there's a problem with the disc. It's a very good idea to ensure that nothing else is running on your system while the CD burns: while CD burning is pretty reliable these days, an overloaded PC can still turn a blank CD into a shiny beer mat. Incidentally, when InfraRecorder burns a disc it displays an animation of smoke above the dialog box. Don't worry, your PC isn't on fire!

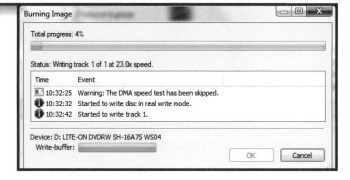

7

When the burning process is finished, you should see something like this. You can now click on OK and close InfraRecorder. Keep the CD in the drive, unless you're going to install Ubuntu on a different computer. The next step is to reboot your PC. In most cases, your computer automatically looks at the CD and runs that when it restarts; if it doesn't, you need to change the boot order in your system BIOS. This typically means pressing DEL or F12 when your PC starts, waiting for the BIOS configuration screen to appear and then navigating to the Boot option. For more details of BIOS configuration please see page 208.

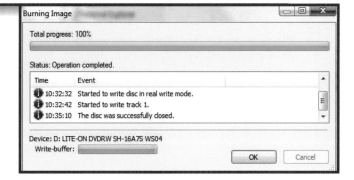

After a bit of whirring and churning, Ubuntu's menu screen loads. The first thing you need to do is to select your language. English is the default, so unless you want to choose a different language simply press Enter to continue. If you choose the wrong language by mistake, just restart your PC to load the installer again.

As you can see, we have a number of options here. The one we're interested in is 'Try Ubuntu without any change to your computer', which enables us to put Ubuntu through its paces without actually installing it. We think this is a superb idea, but it's important to realise that it won't run as quickly as a normal installation: CD drives simply aren't as fast as hard disks. It's fine for a test drive, though.

After a moment or two, Ubuntu starts up but instead of showing the desktop it asks you for a username. The default is 'ubuntu' (without the inverted commas), so enter that here. When you install Ubuntu, you'll be able to create your own usernames.

Once you've entered the username you'll also be asked for a password. You can skip this by pressing Enter. On a normal installation, however, we'd recommend protecting your PC with a username and a password – especially if your PC is going to be used by several different people.

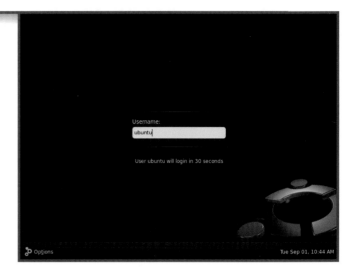

Ladies and gentlemen, welcome to Ubuntu. There are a few crucial differences between the way Ubuntu looks and the way Windows looks, but they're not too dramatic: Ubuntu's interface is essentially Windows interface turned upside down, with all the important stuff at the top.

Kicking the tyres and checking for smoke

We're running Ubuntu here as a test drive, so it's important to check that the things you want to do actually work. You'll find programs in the Applications bit of the menu bar, which is divided into categories so you can find office software, internet software, media software and so on. Have a play with all of them to check that things such as music and video playback work, and click on the little network icon in the top centre of the menu (it looks like two little computers) to ensure that Ubuntu recognises your hardware such as your Ethernet card or your wireless networking card.

Anything that doesn't work properly here won't work properly with a normal installation, so it makes sense to find out now. Google for the necessary drivers and have them downloaded before you actually install Ubuntu on your system.

Once you're happy that Ubuntu works, it's time to install it properly. Remember to back up your important documents, photos, music or anything else you want to keep before you start this next section.

Installing Ubuntu

You can install Ubuntu from the same CD you've just been using. There are two ways to do it: you can double-click on the Install icon from within Ubuntu or you can restart your PC and install from the main menu. We'd recommend the second option, as in our experience, the first option can be a little bit flaky with the installer packing up before it even gets going. If you're installing from within Ubuntu, just skip the first step below.

There's one more thing to think about before we install Ubuntu and that's whether to install it as the only operating system on your PC or to dual boot it. Dual booting means you'll have two operating systems, Windows and Ubuntu, and you can choose which one you want when your PC starts. For older or more modest hardware, we don't think dual-booting is the best approach: it takes up much more hard disk space and the whole point of this exercise is to make our PC leaner and faster. If you want to dual boot, however, the installer makes the necessary changes for you.

Restart your PC with the Ubuntu CD still in the drive. After a little while, you see the main menu as before. This time we're going to use the second option, Install Ubuntu, so use the arrow keys to highlight it and then press Enter.

After a few seconds the installer starts and the first thing it wants you to do is to choose a language. This affects not just the installer but the version of Ubuntu you install. In a nice touch, clicking on any language changes the display immediately. Select your language – English is the default – and then click on Forward.

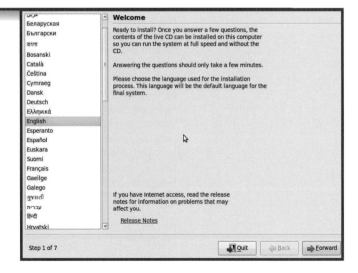

3

Now we need to select the time zone. Using the mouse, move the vertical bar until it's over the UK (or wherever you happen to be) or use the Region and City dropdowns to select the appropriate location. Click on Forward when you've done this.

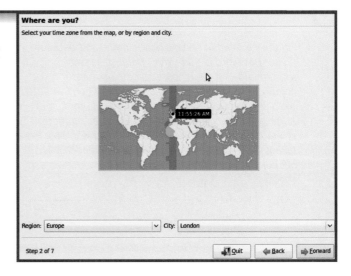

4

The next step is to select the keyboard language – choose the wrong one and you'll get @ when you want ", and so on. Once again, Ubuntu usually guesses correctly, so for example here it's recommending the standard United Kingdom layout. Click on Forward to continue.

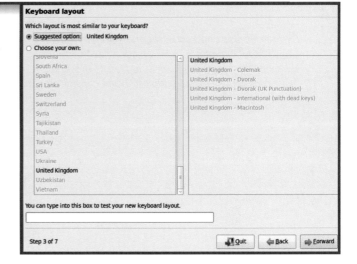

5

Now Ubuntu asks where you want to install it. We've wiped our hard disk, which is why Ubuntu is telling us our PC doesn't have an operating system, but if you've already got Windows installed you'll see it in this screen. Unless you're dual booting, select Use The Entire Disk and then click on Forward.

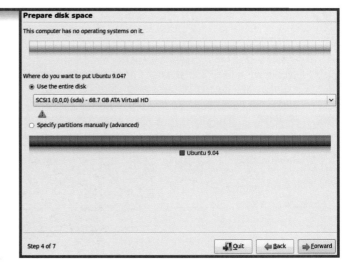

6

Finally, we need to choose a user name and password. If your password is quite short the installer will recommend that you choose something more complicated, but you don't have to if you don't want to. You'll see there are two options at the bottom: Log In Automatically and Require A Password To Log In. If you're the only person using your PC and won't be taking it out and about then Log In Automatically is fine; otherwise, keep the Require A Password box checked.

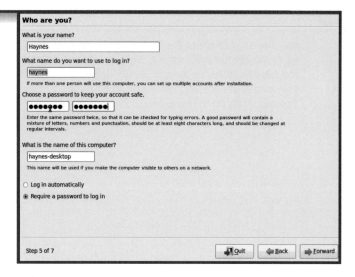

7

Click on Forward and you'll see the summary screen shown here. Time for a quick check – have you selected the correct language and layout? If everything's okay, click on the Install button to begin copying files to your PC.

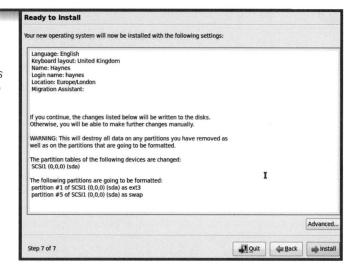

8

Once again this would be a good time to make a cup of tea. Provided the progress bar keeps on moving everything is okay and you don't need to worry, so you might as well go and do something more interesting and come back in half an hour when the installation is finished!

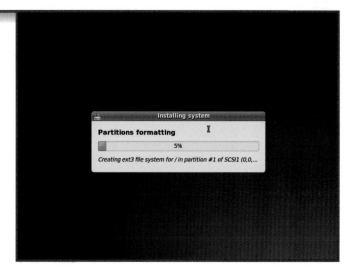

You should see this message when you return from your tea break: it's telling you that everything went smoothly. Eject the installation CD from your PC and press Restart Now to run Ubuntu for the very first time.

When you restart your PC, you'll see the usual BIOS messages, but once they've finished you'll see the loading screen shown here. This tells you that Ubuntu is loading and it won't be on screen for very long.

If you chose the Log In Automatically option during installation, you'll be taken straight to the Ubuntu desktop, but if you selected a username and password you need to enter them before you can continue.

Congratulations: Ubuntu is up and running on your PC. Time for a quick tour: your username is displayed in the top right corner, and clicking on it enables you to log out, shut down or restart your PC; programs and system features are in the top left section of the menu, and there are shortcut icons for the Firefox web browser, the email program and the help system.

When you install Ubuntu you also install its package of applications; for example, if you click on Applications > Office you'll see that Ubuntu has automatically installed the OpenOffice.org software, which includes word processing, spreadsheet and presentations. You also get the excellent Evolution email and calendar program, which is similar to Microsoft Outlook.

As you can see, while Ubuntu is a little different to Windows, it's not that different – so clicking on the Firefox icon or launching it from the Applications menu brings up the Firefox web browser, which looks and works exactly as it does on a Windows PC.

Changing system settings isn't that different from Windows either: to change the desktop colour scheme, theme, screen resolution and other visual effects just right-click on the desktop and bring up the Appearance Preferences dialogue box. As with Windows' Control Panel you can also access system options directly, but in Ubuntu you do it by clicking on the System menu at the top of the screen.

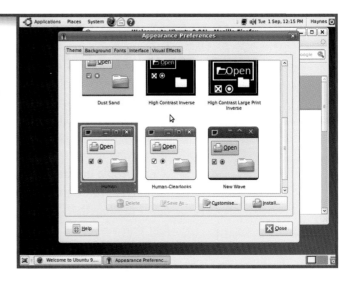

Further reading

While Ubuntu doesn't come with manuals or technical support, there is a great deal of help available online. First port of call should be the Ubuntu website itself at **www.ubuntu.com**, where you'll find extensive documentation (for example the most recent version as we went to press, version 9.04, comes with exhaustive documentation at **https://help.ubuntu.com/9.04**). There's a particularly good guide for people moving to Ubuntu from Windows, which you'll find at **https://help.ubuntu.com/9.04/switching**. It even lists the Linux equivalents to Windows programs such as Outlook, Skype, Windows Messenger and iTunes.

There are lots of Ubuntu-specific discussion forums online too. **Ubuntuforums.org** has a particularly good beginners' section, while the Linux Forums' Ubuntu section (**www.linuxforums.org/forum/ubuntu-help**) is a good place to find technical help.

TECHIE CORNER

PUT LINUX ON A NETBOOK OR SMALL LAPTOP

In this section, we've covered Ubuntu on a typical desktop PC, but what about netbooks – the ultra-portable, fairly low-powered laptops that you can pick up secondhand for pennies? There's a version of Linux for them too and it's extremely impressive – which isn't a surprise, as it's got the backing of chip giant Intel. The software is called Moblin and you'll find it at http://moblin.org. To run it, you need a PC or netbook running an Intel graphics chipset. You need to install it from either a CD or a USB flash drive. Intel reckons it takes around 30 minutes to download, install and start using it. As you can see from the screenshot, it's gorgeous.

Intel is backing Moblin, a version of Linux designed specifically for the small screens and modest processors of netbooks and ultra-portable laptops.

Software as a service

We're all in favour of preserving the useful life of a computer through judicious upgrades, as you will have gathered by now. However, what exactly does 'preserving useful life' mean in this context? All too often, people are persuaded to buy new hardware – memory, hard disk space, perhaps even a processor or a new PC altogether – simply to keep pace with software. And that strikes us as a little back-to-face.

Consider, for instance, the minimum system requirements for the Microsoft Office 97 suite of tools (word processor, spreadsheet etc):

● 500MHz processor
● 256MB RAM
● 1.5GB hard disk space

Now ask yourself what you'll actually do with a suite of programs like Office 97. If the answer is write some letters and compile the odd spreadsheet, that hardly justifies upgrading your PC. So we're going to suggest an altogether different approach – an approach whereby system requirements become all but completely irrelevant.

There's no question that programs like Microsoft Excel are powerful and flexible. But does your computer need an overhaul just to run it?

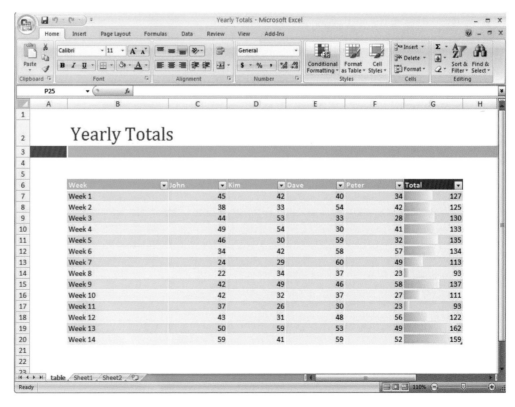

What is SAAS?

Software as a service (SAAS) is a radical model of software licensing. Programs are not installed on your computer at all. Rather, you access software on the internet.

We're going to look at Google Docs here: a suite of office applications that you can access for free with nothing more than a web browser such as Internet Explorer or Firefox. The key advantages are these:

- It is free.
- There is no installation.
- There are no patches or updates.
- There are no system requirements – so long as your computer can access the web, you can use Google Docs.
- You can access your files from any computer, anywhere, at any time.
- You can collaborate on documents with other people very easily.
- You don't need to save copies of your files locally (i.e. on any specific computer).
- Your files are very unlikely to get damaged or lost.
- You can even access your files from a mobile phone (with an internet connection).

As for the downside? Well, there are certain limitations on file sizes and the number of files you can store with Google:

- The maximum size of documents is 500KB.
- Spreadsheets are limited to 256 columns, 200,000 cells, and 99 sheets.
- You can have a total of 5000 documents and presentations and 1000 spreadsheets at any time.

There's certainly nothing there to worry about for most of us.

So how does it work? Here we walk you through the key steps to get up and running with Google Docs. Bear in mind that you can perform these steps on any computer. Once you've completed the steps, you can access all of your files from any computer, anytime, anywhere.

Using Google Docs

Sign up for a Google account. If you already have a Gmail (also called Googlemail) email address, you already have a Google account (though you may not have realised this) so simply log in to your Gmail inbox and take it from there. Otherwise, visit **www.google.co.uk/accounts** *and sign up for a free account.*

2

When you have confirmed your email address, you can sign into Google at **www.google.co.uk**. The search box is doubtless familiar but you're looking for a link to Documents, just one of Google's many free services. You may have to click a More link to find it (Google keeps shifting things around on this page).

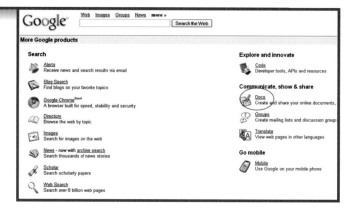

3

Once you're in Google Docs, start as you mean to go on – with efficient folder organisation. Click New > Folder. What you're doing here is creating a folder in which to store new documents as you make them.

4

Google Docs prompts you to give your folder a name and a brief description. Do so and click Save.

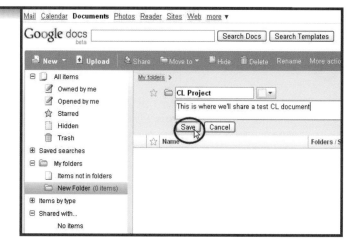

5

You should now see your new folder in the My Folders section of the sidebar on the left. Select the folder with a click and you'll see its contents (empty for now) and description in the main window panel.

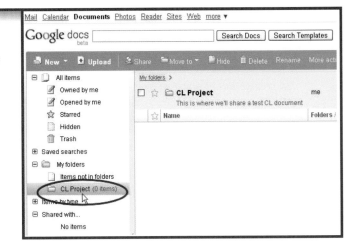

6

Return to the New menu and this time click Document. A document in Google's language is similar to a Word document – essentially, a blank sheet of paper to which you add text.

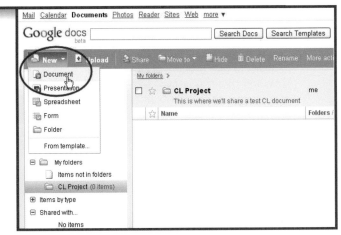

7

This takes you straight to document-editing mode. If you're familiar with word processors, such as Microsoft Word, this works in just the same way. Click in the white page and start typing. You can format your text with the basic toolbar: make text bold or italic, add bullets or numbers, indent or realign your text, etc.

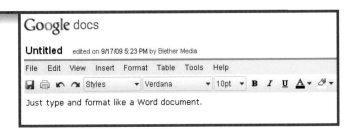

Don't forget to give your document a title. Simply click on the default 'Untitled' title above the toolbar and enter a document name. Click OK to save the title. You can change this at any time by clicking on and editing the title.

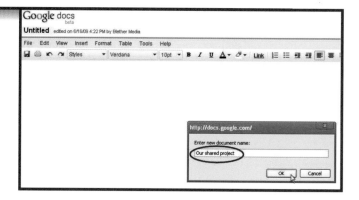

Just as in a 'traditional' word-processing application, Google Docs allows you to create tables and add other elements to your documents. To see this in action, click Table and specify your table settings. We'll use this example to invite people to an event so we need lots of columns and a couple of rows.

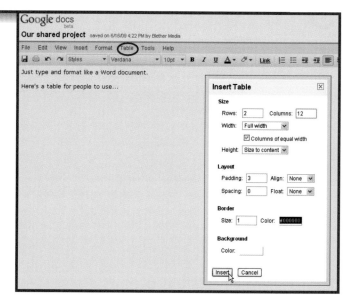

Now add some text to the table fields. Here we're asking people whether or not they can come – a simple question that requires a yes/no response. Incidentally, just as you should do with any program, remember to click Save frequently as you go along.

Now, normally if you want people to respond to a question on a form like this, you'd probably email it to them. That might mean 10 or more emails with you having to collate the data at the end; or you might ask people to forward the document once they are finished with it, but inevitably somebody would forget. Google Docs changes this completely. Click Share and select Invite people.

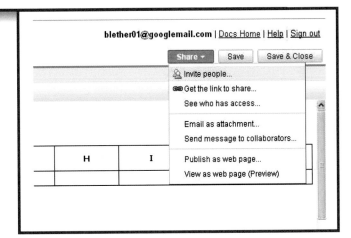

You can either invite people to view your document or you can give them permission to collaborate on the document, that is, to edit it. That's what we want to do here. Enter the email address of everybody you want to share the document with; and, just as you would in an email, write a short explanatory message.

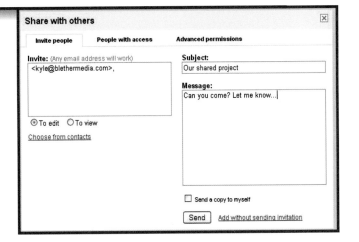

Google now confirms the status of your document. You can change each person's permission from 'can edit' to 'can view' if you decide you need to impose some restrictions. Also note the important note about sign-in being required to edit the document. This means that the people you add as collaborators must all have their own Google accounts before they can see or edit your document. That's probably not what you want.

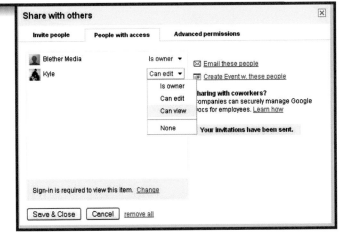

Click Change and select 'People can edit this item without signing in'. Now click Save & Close. Your collaborators will receive an email inviting them to view your document online. They are not sent the document as an attachment; rather, they are sent a link to the document's location within your Google Docs account.

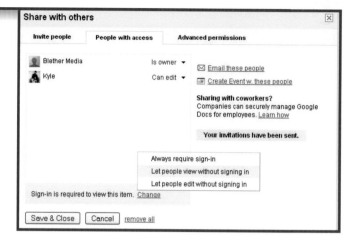

So long as you made the change in Step 14, each of your collaborators can edit the document and save it. Again, all they need is a browser and an internet connection. There is no document to edit, save and pass on – changes are made live on the web.

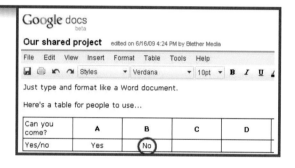

You can, in fact, see your document being edited live if you have it open in Google Docs while others are working on it. Otherwise, you see the changes next time you open the document. You can also click Tools and Revision history to see a summary of all changes.

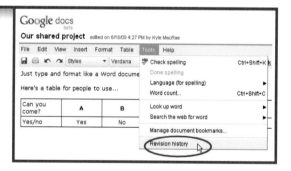

Unless you require people to sign in with their own Google accounts, Google Docs has no means of identifying who has made what changes, so unknown editors are listed as Guests. Where people do sign in, they are names in the revision history. If you're working on a business document, it is good practice to require signing in.

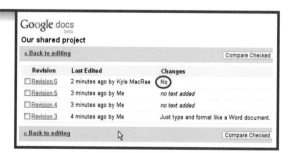

Back in Step 3, you created a folder. Let's say you want to store this document in that folder. There are two ways of doing this. Put a check mark in the box next to your document and click Move to in the toolbar. You can now select your folder and click the Move button.

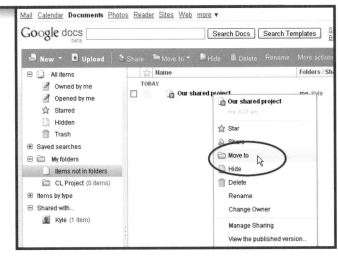

Alternatively, you can drag and drop documents from the central panel right into folders in the My folders section of the sidebar. This is quicker when you get the hang of it. You can also move files from one folder to another in the sidebar in this manner. Document management is easy – in fact, just as easy as managing documents on your own PC.

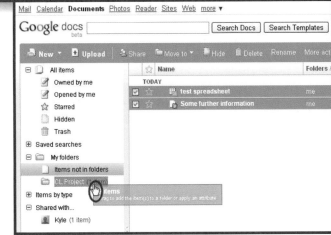

As well as creating documents in Google Docs, you can upload files from your computer, perhaps to make them easier to share with others, perhaps to be able to access them from any location, or simply for safe-keeping. Remember, you can access your files and folders from any computer just by signing in to your Google account at **www.google.co.uk**. Click Upload.

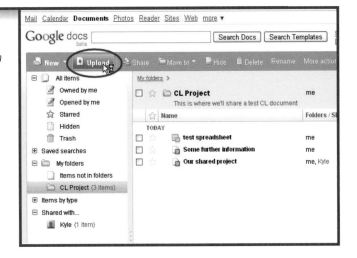

Now select a file from your computer. We'll upload a spreadsheet. Google Docs shows you what kind of files it can accept. Word documents, Excel spreadsheets and PowerPoint presentations are all supported.

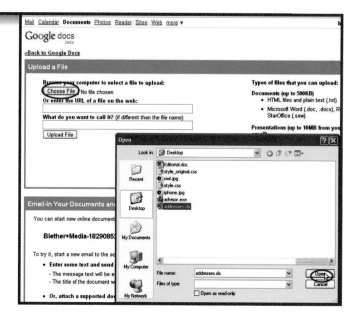

Our spreadsheet now opens in Google Docs. It keeps the same document title by default but you can of course change this. You can also move the file to a folder and, just as with documents you create within Google Docs, you can share with viewers or collaborators.

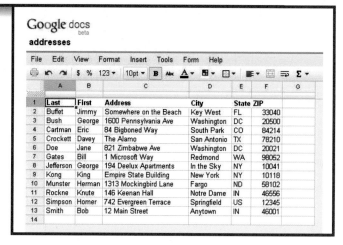

Here's an alternative way of sharing a document. While your file is open, click Share > Get the link to share.

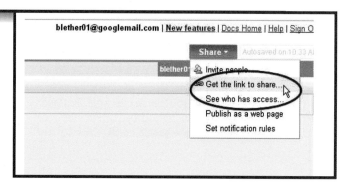

Google Docs now gives you a unique URL (web address) for the file. You can allow people to view the file without signing into Google with their own account, just as previously, and optionally allow them to edit the file as well. Copy the URL and click Save & Close. Email this link to your collaborators. You might even publish the URL on a website or a blog if you want people whose email addresses you don't know to contribute to the document.

At any time, you can download copies of files from Google Docs to whatever computer you happen to be working on. One useful trick is to convert files into PDF format. Just click File > Export and make your choice. The file format options are determined by the type of file you have open e.g. a spreadsheet can be downloaded as an Excel-compatible XLS file, and a document as a Word-compatible DOC file.

Summary

Google Docs uses software-as-a-service functionality to make it easy to use office-style applications on the web, with no software required on your computer. Additional benefits such as collaboration, upload and download options, and even file format conversions, make it a pretty compelling proposition, especially on an older computer that struggles to run full-blown (and bloated) software suites. In fact, you may find that software as a service fundamentally changes the way you use your computer – and if that means fewer upgrades forced upon you by software requirements, we're all for that!

One additional comment. Even if you don't use Google Docs to create or edit files, consider it as a backup option. If you upload files to Google Docs, you know that you can always access and download them in the future no matter what happens to your computers and any backup copies on external disks. Short of Google's global data storage facilities going up in flames – an unlikely occurrence – you'll have safe and secure copies of all your important data online. To get to it, you need only sign in to your Google account.

COMPUTER MANUAL

PART

Appendices

Appendix 1
BIOS and CMOS

Two more dreaded acronyms!

BIOS (Basic Input/Output System)

This is usually found in the shape of a chip on the motherboard. BIOS kicks in when you first start your PC to get the essential parts of the system – keyboard, monitor, hard disk, ports and so on – up and running before (and independently of) the operating system. Modern BIOSs are Plug-and-Play, which means that they can automatically recognise and configure most new expansion cards and hardware devices. They tend also to be flash-upgradeable – i.e. they can be updated via an internet download. The historical trouble with BIOS is that pre-1994 versions couldn't recognise hard disks larger than 528MB; pre-1996 versions managed no more than 2.1GB; and more recent chips gave up at 8.4GB. The good news is that special software (usually supplied with large hard disk drives) can circumvent these infuriating limitations. However, a flash upgrade or even a replacement chip is a better long-term option. If your computer was made by a major manufacturer like Compaq or Dell, you should be able to download a BIOS upgrade from the Support section of the manufacturer's website. With smaller PC brands, however, you'll have to find out who made your PC's BIOS. Look for the name during the start-up process – probably Award, Phoenix or AMI – or follow this procedure:

 Start

 Settings

 Control Panel

 System

 the Device Manager tab.

Now click the Print button, select System Summary, and click OK. At the very top of the first page to be printed you'll find the BIOS details.

A Device Manager report reveals who made your BIOS. Check the manufacturer's website for further details.

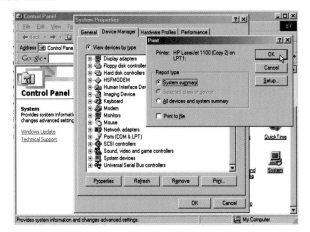

Changing the boot order

You can use the BIOS setup program to determine certain key system settings, including which drive the computer boots from first. Ordinarily, BIOS is set up to check the floppy drive for a bootable disk – i.e., a disk containing a program that can start the computer – and, if it finds nothing, to boot Windows from the hard disk (C: drive). This is exactly the arrangement that you want, as it lets you start the computer with a start-up disk (see pp26-28) in the event that there is a problem with Windows.

However, you may want to start the computer with a bootable CD-ROM instead, particularly if you want to install Windows XP on a new hard disk or work with the XP Recovery Console. To do this, you must configure BIOS to check the CD (or DVD) drive before booting from, or attempting to boot from, the hard disk.

To get to the BIOS setup program, restart the computer and press the F1, F2 or Delete keys while it is running through its self-checking routine. Check the motherboard or PC manual for details of which key is required. One of the opening screens may say 'Press DEL to run Setup', in which case take that as your cue. Otherwise, just keep pressing those keys until the BIOS menu appears.

Once in BIOS setup, you need to find the boot order priority menu and move the CD drive higher in the priority list than the hard disk. All BIOS menus are controlled by the keyboard alone, not the mouse, but you should find an explanatory guide to navigation at the bottom of each screen. Change the boot order to floppy drive first, followed by CD drive, and finally hard drive. You now have the option of booting from a floppy disk or CD at any time.

Once you have reordered the boot list, be sure to save your changes when you exit the setup routine. This usually means pressing the F10 key but, again, help is provided on screen.

CMOS (Complementary Metal-Oxide Semiconductor)

This is essentially a form of permanent memory, powered by a battery, which keeps a record of your system's configuration when the power is off. Here you might change details about, for instance, the drive order in which your PC tries to boot (usually floppy drive followed by the hard disk), power management settings, port configuration and BIOS settings.

Doesn't sound like much fun, does it? Truth to tell, you might never need to go near the CMOS. However, should the motherboard battery fail or something else go seriously awry, a permanent record of your CMOS setup would prove invaluable. Now would be a very good time indeed to make just such a document.

You can access the CMOS records through the BIOS setup routine just described. Go to the CMOS menus and write down everything you see, especially material pertaining to the computer's disk drives, like capacity, cylinders, heads, landing zone (don't ask), sectors and all the rest. When you're through, press the Escape key until you're back at the start page, and confirm that you want to exit without making any changes. Windows will now start as normal.

For more on this stuff, check the excellent BIOS survival guide here: **http://burks.bton.ac.uk/burks/pcinfo/hardware/bios_sg/bios_sg.htm**

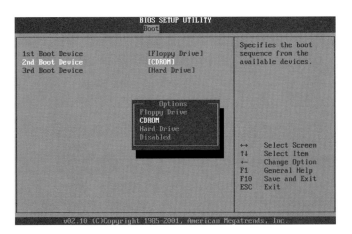

Shuffle the CD drive up the priority list if you need to start the computer from a bootable CD-ROM.

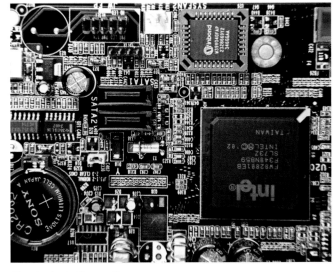

The circular battery on the motherboard (lower left corner) means that CMOS retains its memory when the mains power is off.

Appendix 2
Guide to connectors

PS2 ports and plugs.

Serial port and plug.

Parallel port and plug.

USB ports and plug.

FireWire port and plug.

RJ-45 port and plug.

3.5mm ports and plug.

VGA port and plug.

RJ-11 port and plug.

S-video port and plug.

DVI port and plug.

SPDIF port and plug.

Composite video port and plug (yellow) plus stereo audio (red and white).

UHF/VHF port and plug.

Too many holes and don't know how to fill them?
Here's a quick guide to common computer connectors.

Name	Connects what?
PS/2	Mouse and keyboard
Serial	Mouse (old-style), modem or handheld electronic PDA/organiser
Parallel	Printer and sometimes a scanner
USB (Universal Serial Bus)	Pretty much all new peripherals that once used the slower serial or parallel connectors
FireWire (or IEEE 1394)	External drives. Also ideal for connecting digital camcorders
RJ-45 (Ethernet)	Computer to a network
3.5mm	Speakers and microphone
VGA (Video Graphics Array)	Monitor
RJ-11	Modem to the telephone line
S-video TV-out	Computer to TV set (very high image quality)
DVI (Digital Visual Interface)	Digital monitor
SPDIF (Sony/Philips Digital Interface)	Speakers or external audio decoder. This is an optical interface
Composite audio/video	Computer to TV set (high image quality). A separate stereo audio signal is transferred through the red and white cables
UHF/VHF (Ultra/Very High Frequency) TV-in	A standard rooftop aerial for TV reception on the PC

PART 1

APPENDICES

Appendix 3
Installing a new motherboard

A new motherboard is a fearsome thing to contemplate, right? Actually, wrong. Installing one is easy. The trick is buying the right one.

A new motherboard is the ultimate computer repair, or upgrade, or both. The motherboard lies at the heart of the computer. Indeed, it is the computer. Everything else, from the processor to memory to the hard disk to the monitor, is an accessory, and a replaceable accessory at that.

We've looked already at swapping one sound or video card for another, changing the hard drive and adding an extra slice of memory. Finally, we must consider the business of changing the motherboard itself. Why would you want to do such a thing?

● **You want a faster computer.** The two primary ways to speed up a slow system are with a memory and/or processor upgrade. As we've said, memory matters more. However, there may come a point where an extra memory module just won't suffice, particularly if you're running on an old (and hard to get hold of) format. A processor upgrade will improve performance to a degree but you may find that your motherboard doesn't support a faster chip than the one that's currently installed. It certainly won't support a shift from, say, a Pentium III to a Pentium 4 on account of the different slot and socket designs.

● **You want to play computer games or work with digital video.** The bottleneck here would be the graphics card. If your motherboard lacks an AGP slot, upgrading to a more powerful graphics card will be limited to a PCI model, and that's a severe restriction. Even if you do have AGP, you can't use a fast 8x-speed card in a 2x or 4x-speed slot.

● **The motherboard is broken.** Motherboard failure does happen, although relatively rarely. With the best will in the world, you increase the risk of damage every time you open the case covers or perform minor internal surgery. Indeed, we recently fried a motherboard (that's fried as in rising smoke!) during a routine processor replacement. We never found out what went wrong, but there's the rub: it's far, far easier to replace a dead component, even a motherboard, than attempting to diagnose and repair a serious problem.

In each case, you needn't necessarily buy a new computer to achieve your goal. Remember, PCs are modular. If you want to change or upgrade component A, there's every chance that components B, C and D are still perfectly functional. Even with a new motherboard, you can reuse much of what remains.

Here are the most likely candidates:

Case So long as the new motherboard fits the old case, as it will if you stick with the industry-standard ATX design, you can simply rebuild your new system in the old case.

Sound card You would want to chuck out an old ISA sound card but any PCI version will fit your new motherboard. Besides which, you may prefer the simplicity of a motherboard with integrated multi-channel audio (we certainly would).

Graphics card As indicated above, this really depends whether your old card is an AGP model, whether it's compatible with your new motherboard (see especially the voltage concerns on p90), and whether you're content with its performance. Again though, you may opt for integrated (AGP) graphics, in which case you won't need your old card.

Hard disk Should be no problem. A faster or bigger disk may be desirable but the old one will work just fine. The one exception would be if you buy a motherboard with Serial ATA sockets only. For maximum compatibility, seek out a model with SATA and IDE/ATA sockets.

Network, modem, USB, FireWire and other expansion cards Anything PCI-flavoured will transfer across just fine.

Monitor, keyboard and mouse Plug them in and use them as before.

And those less likely:

● **Processor** For reasons stated, you can only replace like for like. In the best case, your old motherboard might have a Socket 478 interface with an early Celeron or P4 processor installed. Chances are – but check the manual first – that you could reuse this processor in your new Socket 478 motherboard. However, it's more likely that a PC in need of a motherboard upgrade or repair has an earlier Pentium II or III (or AMD Athlon equivalent) chip onboard, in which case you'll certainly need a new processor. This shouldn't prove too onerous: the very latest

processors always cost a fortune but anything just slightly past its peak will be more than capable and surprisingly cheap.

● **Memory** Again, your old memory probably uses an outmoded design or runs at an incompatible speed. We would always advise that you buy new memory modules when installing a new motherboard.

● **Power Supply Unit** An important consideration. There are actually two potential problems here. First, if you have been systematically upgrading your computer or intend to do so now, your old PSU may be a touch underpowered to run the whole show. A 300 watt PSU is really the minimum you should have in a Pentium 4-class computer. Check the old PSU casing for details of its power output.

Secondly, and more importantly, you will certainly need to replace the PSU if your system currently has an AMD Athlon processor and you're moving to an Intel Pentium motherboard. This is because Pentium 4 motherboards have an additional power connector (called ATX 12V) and only a P4-compliant PSU has the requisite cable. In fact, this may also apply if you're moving from a Pentium II or III system. Just to be awkward, AMD stipulates that any PSU designed for use in an Athlon-based system should have its cooling fans arranged in a particular way.

The bottom line is thus that you may well need to replace the PSU at the same time as your motherboard. Not that this is a bad thing, as such, for you should get years of trouble-free service from a fresh device, but it is something to be aware of (and budget for).

On a related note, you should also check whether a potential motherboard requires a third power connection known as ATX Auxiliary. If it does, you need a PSU with the requisite cable.

Main power A standard design compatible with all ATX motherboards.

ATX Auxiliary Uncommon, but you'll need a PSU with this cable if the motherboard has an ATX Auxiliary socket.

ATX 12V Required by all Pentium 4 motherboards. Don't reuse your old PSU with a P4 system unless it has this cable.

5.25-inch drive This plug powers the hard drive and CD/DVD drives.

3.5-inch drive This plug powers the floppy drive (and/or a media card reader).

Input/output panels

The procedure for installing a new motherboard is essentially straightforward. Industry standards like the ATX form factor mean that any compatible motherboard will fit in any compatible case, and your drives and expansion cards can be easily reconnected. The only slightly fiddly part is whipping out the old input/output panel faceplate and installing its replacement. So a word about that now.

All motherboards provide a built-in range of inputs and outputs. How many you get depends on how many features are integrated within the motherboard itself rather than provided by additional expansion cards. The recent trend has been heavily towards integration, with the result that today's motherboards typically have many more inputs and outputs than yesterday's. But in order to ensure compatibility with computer cases, these sockets are all located in the same corner of the motherboard and are arranged in a panel of fixed dimensions. This panel fits a hole in the case, and so the inputs and outputs can be accessed externally.

Because designs vary so widely, all new motherboards are supplied with an input/output panel template. This must be installed in the case first in order that the sockets can poke through – and this in turn means removing the old template first.

One other factor to be aware of are the motherboard standoffs. Rather than attaching directly to the case, motherboards are screwed into little raised pillars called standoffs that attach to pre-drilled holes in the case (and vary significantly in design and method). When you remove the old motherboard, the standoffs should stay in place. However, while the ATX form factor guarantees that the case will have standoff positions to match the holes in your new motherboard, there is no cast-iron guarantee that the existing standoffs will all be in the right position, particularly if you're installing a smaller (but still ATX-compliant) motherboard than the one you're removing (as, in fact, is the case in our worked example). This means that you may need to move a few standoffs around before you can install the new motherboard. A minor hassle, but don't skimp it: the last thing you want is a motherboard that's not properly supported for want of a standoff in the right position.

Three motherboards from different eras but each is compliant with the ATX form factor. This means that their input/output panels will fit the same hole in any ATX case. The wide variations in socket layouts highlights the importance of input/output templates.

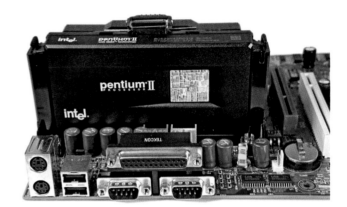

Installing a motherboard

Here, we remove an old slot-based motherboard and replace it with a Socket 478 (Pentium 4) model.

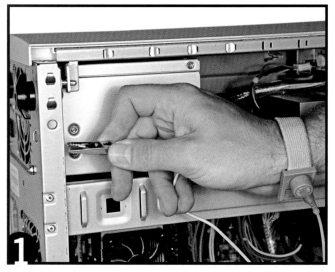

Before commencing any internal work on your PC, re-read the safety precautions on p33.

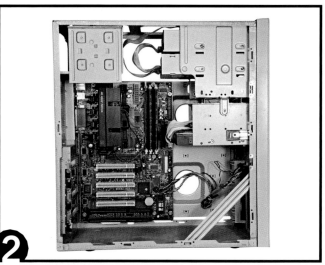

Strip the motherboard clean by unplugging all drive cables and power cables and removing all expansion cards. This is also the time to remove the Power Supply Unit itself if you have to replace it. You should end up with a motherboard that is no longer connected to the computer in any way. However, there is no need to remove the processor or memory modules. If you intend to reuse them, they can be more easily removed when the motherboard is outside the case. Here, we have still to unplug the cables running to the front case buttons (bottom right) but everything else has been stripped.

Unscrew the motherboard from the case (or, more correctly, from the case standoffs). You'll find screws around the edges of the motherboard, in the corners, and also one or two dotted around the middle. Be sure to get them all. Now remove the motherboard from the case. You may have to tug a bit to free it from the input/output panel.

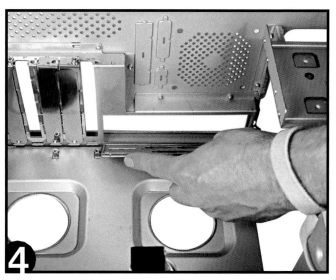

Remove the old input/output panel template. Some clip in and out of place; some slide; some screw. Install the new template panel according to the directions. Be sure to get it the right way round. The side with the two round holes for the PS/2 mouse and keyboard connections will be adjacent to the power supply.

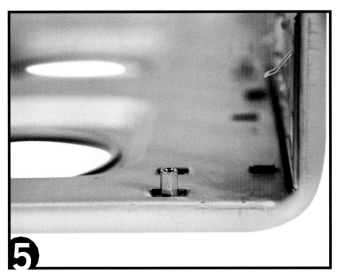

5

Here we can see the motherboard standoffs still in place. Carefully remove your new motherboard from its anti-static bag and, holding it only by the edges, match its drill-holes with the standoff positions. If necessary, move the standoffs around until you have a perfect match. You might prefer to remove them altogether and start afresh with the standoffs supplied with your new motherboard. Either way, you must have a standoff in the correct position for every drill-hole in the motherboard.

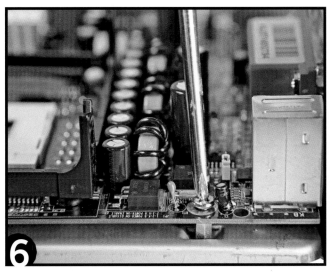

6

Very carefully install the motherboard in the case and screw it to the standoffs. Do not over-tighten the screws as it's possible to distort or even crack the motherboard with excessive force (yes, that's experience talking again).

7

The tricky bit with a motherboard installation, as you'll now have discovered, is matching the inputs and outputs with the template. Sometimes, it seems they just don't want to mesh, but mesh they will in the end. It's a two-handed job, or better still two person. Here we see the end result: lots of lovely sockets perfectly aligned with holes in the template.

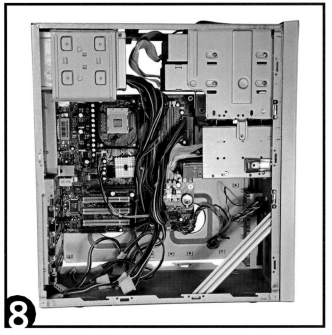

8

Installation of the motherboard itself is complete. If you compare this shot with Step 2, you'll see the difference in motherboard size. This new version is smaller but considerably more adept. We have also installed the replacement P4-compliant PSU and made that all-important ATX 12V cable connection. All that remains is to install a processor and heatsink/fan and a memory module or two, reconnect the drives and plug in all the old expansion cards. Oh, and put the case covers back on.

Appendix 4
Backing up your files to the internet

There are lots of ways to back up your files via the internet, but there tend to be two areas of concern: first, they tend to cost money; and secondly, they often come from firms who could well vanish tomorrow. Unless you've got thousands of files to back up, an excellent alternative is Live Mesh from Microsoft. It doesn't cost anything and the likelihood

of Microsoft going out of business is remote, to say the least.

There's another good reason to use Live Mesh, too: it's designed to share files between different computers, so you can access your backups from anywhere you can get an internet connection. There's also a decent amount of space: 5GB, which is more than enough for your documents, prized photos and top-secret plans for world domination.

The first thing we need to do is to sign up for a Live Mesh account and download the software. To do this, visit **www.mesh.com** *and click on Sign In at the top of the screen. You can now sign in with your Windows Live ID; if you don't have one, you can get one for free here. We'd recommend having such an ID even if you don't fancy Live Mesh, as it gives you access to lots of free Microsoft services.*

Once you've signed in, Live Mesh takes you to the Devices screen. To begin with, you only have the Live Desktop enabled but, as you can see, Live Mesh also supports Your PC, Your Mobile and Your Mac. Let's add your PC. To do this, click on Add Device.

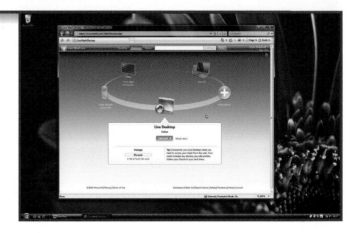

3

Now we need to install the software. Live Mesh automatically guesses the right download for you — in this case, the software for the 64-bit edition of Windows Vista. Click on Install and run the mesh.exe file when it's finished.

4

You'll see a little blue bubble at the bottom right of your screen telling you what's going on. Make sure you're connected to the internet throughout the installation process: Live Mesh needs to be connected in order to work.

5

Live Mesh asks you to sign in with your Windows Live ID. If you wish you can get the program to remember your ID and log you in automatically. Don't do this if you're using a shared computer, though, as it means anybody can access your files.

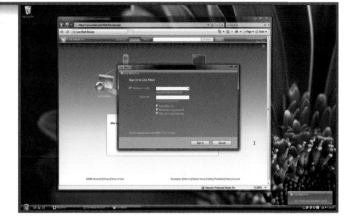

6

Live Mesh now asks you to give your PC a name. If you're running Windows Vista there's a check box marked 'Enable synchronisation attachments…' There's no particular reason why you would need to disable these features, so just keep the box checked. Click Add Device when you're finished.

7

You should now see your PC in the Live Mesh window of your web browser. This means you can sign in to Live Mesh from any PC and even access your own PC if it's switched on and connected to the internet. For now, we'll concentrate on backups.

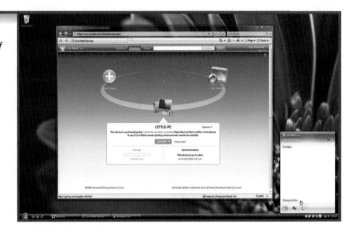

8

Open Windows Explorer and you'll see a new folder, Live Mesh Folders under your username (e.g. Users > Bob > Live Mesh Folders). Open this folder and right-click. Now select Live Mesh Options > Create Folder in Live Mesh.

The folder you create here is your backup folder, so give it a meaningful name. By default this folder lives on your Desktop, which is as good a place as any. Click on OK to continue.

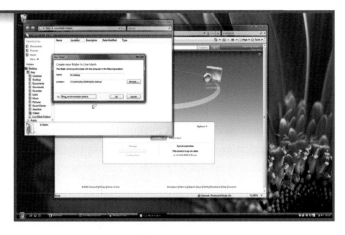

Live Mesh now creates the folder. Adding files is just a matter of dragging them and dropping them into the new folder with your mouse. For example, here we've added a bunch of important documents. Whenever you add files, Live Mesh uploads them to your Live Mesh account.

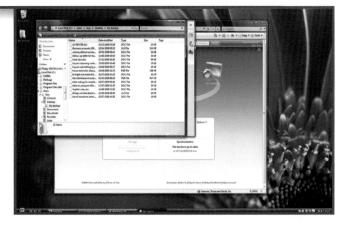

In this screenshot, we've signed into **www.mesh.com** and opened the My Backup folder. As you can see, the files have been added to our Mesh folder. The green orbs mean that the files are currently uploading. Now all you have to do is remember to copy files into your backup folder whenever you want to safeguard them.

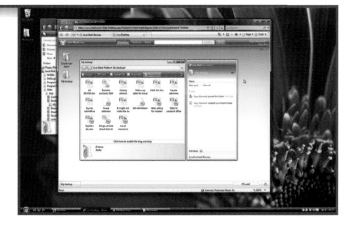

PART Appendix 5
Glossary

Here's an at-a-glance guide to many of the techie terms used throughout this manual, along with several more that you'll doubtless come across on your travels around the mind-numbing world of computer jargon. Always remember this: if in doubt about what something means, just ask (at which point you'll invariably find that the salesperson, who is so keen to take your money, doesn't really have a clue either).

Let's start with a table of the storage units used in computer-speak.

Name	Symbol	Size
Bit	b	A single binary unit (i.e. a 1 or a 0)
Byte	B	8 bits
Kilobit	Kb	1,024 bits (= 128 bytes)
Kilobyte	KB	1,024 bytes
Megabit	Mb	1,048,576 bits (= 131,072 bytes)
Megabyte	MB	1,048,576 bytes (= 1,024 kilobytes)
Gigabyte	GB	1,073,741,824 bytes (= 1,024 megabytes)

286/386/486 Early processors from Intel used to power desktop computers and superseded by the Pentium processor

56,000bps/56Kbps The theoretical top speed of modern modems (i.e. capable of receiving up to 56,000 bits of data per second)

512,000bps/512Kbps The accepted norm for a broadband internet connection, just under ten times faster than a modem connection

ADF Automatic Document Feeder. An attachment for scanners and printers that enables multiple sheets to be processed without manual intervention

ADSL Asymmetric Digital Subscriber Line. A broadband internet service that uses the existing copper wire telephone network

AGP Accelerated Graphics Port. A computer interface (usually a slot on the motherboard) designed for a high-performance graphics display

AMD Advanced Micro Devices. A manufacturer of computer processors and related hardware

Analogue A continuous signal

Anti-virus software A program designed to protect a computer from malicious viruses

ATAPI Advanced Technology Attachment Packet Interface. An interface for connecting disk drives to a computer

Athlon A family of powerful processors developed by AMD

ATX An industry-standard form factor (size and shape) for computer motherboards and cases

Backup A copy of vital computer files made for safekeeping

Bandwidth A measure of how much data can be transferred at any one time

BIOS Basic Input/Output System. Software stored in a chip that controls the operation of a computer at its most fundamental level

Blanking plates Removable covers on a computer case that protect unused expansion slots

Bluetooth A wireless networking technology

Boot To start a computer from a floppy disk, a CD or the hard disk

Broadband A high-speed internet connection service

Bus A path on a motherboard through which data can pass

C

CD-ROM A version of the compact disc that holds computer Data; CD-R (Recordable) and CD-RW (Rewritable) formats are blank discs on which files may be saved with a CD writer drive

Celeron A slower but cheaper version of the Pentium processor

Chipset Integrated circuits on the motherboard that provide support for the microprocessor, memory and expansion slots

Clock speed The rate at which a computer's processor operates, expressed in megaHertz or gigaHertz

CMOS Complementary Metal-Oxide Semiconductor. A chip that remembers basic system settings

Colour depth A measure of how many colours a monitor can display: 1-bit colour is black and white; 24-bit colour is up to 16.7 million distinct hues

COM port Communications port. A connector for devices such as printers and modems

Composite video A method of transferring a video signal from one device to another, commonly used to connect computers to television sets

Control panel An area in Windows where you can configure your PC

CPU Central Processing Unit. The main system processor

Crash When the computer goes wrong and stops working!

CRT Cathode Ray Tube. The glass tube used to produce an image in a television set and computer monitor (uses an electron gun to stimulate a phosphorous coating on the screen)

Cursor An arrow on the screen controlled by the mouse, or an insertion point in a document

Data Binary information

Default An action performed automatically in the absence of any alternative instruction

Defragment To reorganise files that have become split up and are stored piecemeal on the hard disk

Desktop The main screen within Windows before you launch any programs, home to icons such as My Computer and the Recycle Bin

Dial-up Networking The program Windows uses to connect a computer to the internet through a phone line

Digital In contrast to analogue, a digital signal is composed of discrete packets of information (basically, a series of on/off signals)

DOS Disk Operating System. A text-based operating system for PCs developed by Microsoft, the precursor to Windows

Dot pitch The distance between the tiny dots on a monitor screen that together make up a picture

Download The process of acquiring a file on to your PC from the internet

DPI Dots Per Inch. A measure of an image's resolution: the higher the DPI, the greater the clarity

Drive A machine that reads data from and writes data to a disk

Drive bay A space in a computer reserved for a drive

Driver A software program that lets the operating system 'talk' to and control a device

DSL Digital Subscriber Line. A technology that offers high-speed internet connections over standard copper telephone lines. The common UK version is Asymmetric DSL (ADSL), which allows more data to be downloaded than uploaded

Duron A slower but cheaper version of the Athlon processor

DVD Digital Versatile Disc. A type of compact disc capable of storing a huge amount of data, including movies. There are currently three families of recordable DVD drives: DVD-R/RW, DVD+R/RW and DVD-RAM

DVI Digital Visual Interface. An interface used to connect digital monitors to computers

EPP Enhanced Parallel Port. The modern, fast version of the parallel port used to connect a printer (a replacement for the slower Centronics standard)

ESD Electrostatic discharge. Static electricity, potentially fatal for computer components

Ethernet A technology that enables several computers to be connected together in a network

Expansion card A circuit board that can be added to a computer to enhance its capabilities

Expansion slot An interface on a motherboard used to connect an expansion card

FAT File Allocation Table. A cataloguing system that records where every file is stored on a hard disk

Firewall A program that aims to protect a computer against unauthorised access, particularly by hackers

FireWire (also known as IEEE 1394 and i.LINK). A high-speed interface with which devices can be connected to a computer

Flatbed A type of scanner that uses a flat glass plate, much like a photocopier

Floppy disk A non-floppy plastic square that holds up to 1.44MB of data (okay, it's floppy on the inside!)

Format To format a disk is to make it usable in a certain type of drive

Full duplex The ability to send and receive data simultaneously

GPU Graphics Processing Unit. A processor integrated on a graphics card with the purpose of producing 3-D and other video effects

Graphics card (sometimes called a video card). The circuitry in a computer that controls the monitor display, usually in the form of an expansion card

Hard disk A magnetic disk on which may be stored a great deal of data, including a computer's operating system

Hardware The physical components that make up a computer system

Hub A device that sits between other devices and provides a common connection point, typically in a network

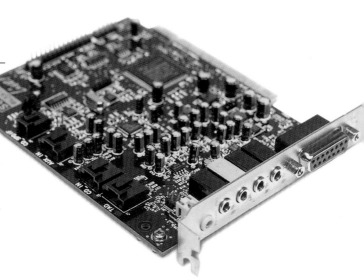

Icon A small clickable image that denotes a file or application within Windows

IDE/ATA Integrated Drive Electronics/Advanced Technology Attachment. The interface used to connect hard disk drives to the computer's motherboard

Inkjet printer A device that squirts wet ink on to paper in order to print text and images

Intel A manufacturer of computer processors and related hardware

Interface The look and feel of a software program; or the means by which computer components communicate

IRQ Interrupt Request. One of the means by which hardware devices gain the processor's attention

ISA Industry Standard Architecture. The oldest type of expansion slot still found in PCs

Jaz drive A high-capacity storage device made by Iomega

Joystick A device for controlling the action in computer games

Jumper Small pins that control the settings on drives and motherboards

Laser printer A device that uses dry toner and laser light to print text and images

LCD Liquid Crystal Display. The technology used in flat-panel monitors whereby liquid crystal is charged with an electric current

Memory card A small, solid-state (no moving parts) chunk of memory used to store photos and/or data in portable devices such as digital cameras and handheld computers

MIDI Musical Instrument Digital Interface. A means of connecting electronic musical instruments to a computer

Modem A device that enables a computer to use the telephone line in order to communicate with other computers in a network, especially the internet

Motherboard The central circuit board in a computer to which all other devices are attached

Multimedia Loosely speaking, a combination of text, sound and video. Most CD-ROMs are multimedia, as are many websites

Network An arrangement of two or more connected computers in which they have shared access to resources like folders, printers and the internet

NIC Network Interface Card. An expansion card that enables a computer to join a network

Notebook A portable computer. Used to be called a laptop. Still is by some

NTFS New Technology File System. The successor to FAT

OEM Original Equipment Manufacturer. This refers to computer components sold directly and exclusively to manufacturers (i.e. not available to the public)

Operating system Software that governs the workings of a computer, both in terms of hardware and applications

Optical disc A storage medium such as a CD or DVD from which data is read by a laser

Partition A sub-division of a hard disk that the computer treats just like a separate hard disk

PCI Peripheral Component Interconnect. An expansion slot standard, faster and more flexible than ISA

Pentium A family of powerful processors developed by Intel

Pin 1 A method of ensuring that computer cables are connected correctly, involving colour-coding on the cable and an identifying mark on the device and connector

Pixel The smallest single point on a display screen. At a screen resolution of 1,024 x 768, the full image is made up of 786,432 pixels

Plug-and-Play A standard that enables a Windows-based PC automatically to recognise and configure any new device

Port An external socket used to connect devices to a computer

Processor A silicon chip that processes data. Effectively, your PC's brain

Program A set of instructions that enables a computer to perform certain tasks. One example is a word processor

PS/2 A round 6-pin interface used to connect mice and keyboards to a computer

PSU Power Supply Unit. A unit that plugs into the mains electricity and supplies a computer's motherboard and drives with the current they require to operate

QWERTY The standard layout of the keys on a computer keyboard, where the first 6 letters on the top row are Q,W,E,R,T and Y

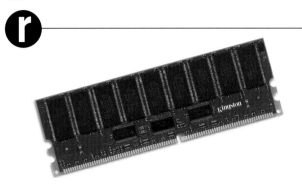

RAM Random Access Memory. Dynamic memory used by a PC as its working space

Registry Windows' database with information on all hardware and software that together comprises the PC system

Resolution A measure of the level of detail in an image on either a monitor screen or printed page

RF Radio Frequency. A wireless technology used to connect peripheral devices such as keyboard and mice without the use of cables

ROM Read Only Memory. As in a BIOS chip or CD-ROM, this is a form of memory used for data storage that can be accessed (read) but not changed (written)

Router A network device that controls the flow of data among connected computers

SATA Serial ATA A new serial (as opposed to parallel) interface for connecting hard disk drives to a computer. Unlike IDE/ATA, each SATA channel supports only one drive. SATA allows for much faster data transfers between the drive and the motherboard

Scanner A device that uses a light sensor to convert printed documents into data which can then be interpreted by software on a computer

SCSI Small Computer System Interface. A fast interface used to connect devices to a computer

Serial port A port on the back of a PC used to connect devices such as mice and modems

Software Computer programs, including application software, such as a spreadsheet program, and operating systems, such as Windows

SPDIF Sony/Philips Digital Interface. A digital audio interface that can be either an electronic plug and socket arrangement (typically using a 1/8-inch jack called phono or RCA) or a fibre-optic cable in which the signal is transmitted optically (i.e. with light)

S-video A method of transferring a video signal from one device to another, commonly used to connect computers to television sets; S-video generally offers better quality than composite video

Swap file An area of the hard disk used by Windows as 'virtual memory', or surrogate RAM

Taskbar A bar running along the bottom of the screen in Windows that shows a button for each program that is running

TFT Thin Film Transistor. A method of controlling an LCD display by means of transistors

TWAIN The software interface standard that enables scanners to work with imaging software

USB Universal Serial Bus. A relatively fast interface with which peripherals can easily connect to a computer

Upgrade To improve, enhance or modify the performance of your computer

Utility A software program designed to offer useful extra features or to automate routine tasks

V.90/V.92 Communications standards that modern modems adhere to

VGA Video Graphics Array. A basic standard governing monitor displays (16 colours at a resolution of 640 x 480)

Video card See graphics card

Virus A malicious computer program, usually spread on disk or over the internet

Virus writer A berk

Webcam A (usually low resolution) video camera that connects to a computer and lets you send live video images over the internet

Wi-Fi Wireless Fidelity. A radio frequency networking technology that works without direct cable connections

WYSIWYG What You See Is What You Get. This means that the image you see on your monitor is exactly what comes out of your printer

Z

Zip drive A high-capacity storage device made by Iomega

Index

ACKNOWLEDGEMENTS
The author would like to thank John Sabine and Jon Sayers
for their invaluable technical expertise. He would
particularly like to thank Harry Sabbers, reformed geek, for
his unwavering practical and moral support.

Author	**Kyle MacRae**
Technical Editors, UK	**John Sabine, Jon Sayers**
Technical consultant	**Jonathan Edgington**
Copy editor	**Shena Deuchars**
Page build	**James Robertson**
Photography	**Paul Tanswell, Tom Bain and Iain McLean**
Illustrations	**Matthew Marke**
Index	**Shena Deuchars**
Project Manager	**Louise McIntyre**